Generis

PUBLISHING

Strategic Retention Framework to Reduce Employee Attrition in Non-profit Organizations

Dr. Adijat Adefila-Aransi

Title: Strategic Retention Framework to Reduce Employee Attrition in Non-profit Organizations

ISBN: 979-8-88676-548-9

Author: Dr. Adijat Adefila-Aransi

Cover image: www.pixabay.com

Publisher: Generis Publishing
Online orders: www.generis-publishing.com
Contact email: info@generis-publishing.com

Acknowledgements

I want to acknowledge and express my profound gratitude to my research supervisor, Professor Eugene Kozlovski, whose expertise was invaluable throughout this research. His insightful feedback and support helped push me to achieve an excellent and relevant piece of research that not only accomplishes its set objectives but also contributes immensely to the body of knowledge on the subject matter.

My sincere appreciation also goes to Dr Edna Ijeoma Stan-Maduka for her encouraging comments and insight regarding my research and her intriguing questions that encouraged me to broaden my research perspective.

I want to thank all my lecturers and member of staff at the University of the West of Scotland that have supported me all through the writing of this dissertation. Without their immense support, this study would not have been achievable.

My heartfelt gratitude also goes to my entire family, husband, son, parents, elder brother, younger siblings, and parent-in-law, who have provided me with words of encouragement, emotional support, and other forms of support throughout this research and all aspects of my life.

Table of Contents

List of Tables

List of Figures

Abbreviations

NPOs: Non-profit Organisations

FPOs: For Profit Organisations

CEO: Chief Executive Officer

ERC: Employee Retention Connection

IACAD: The Islamic Affairs and Charitable Activities Department Dubai

IHC: International Humanitarian City

DIFC: Dubai International Financial Centre

GDP: Gross Domestic Product

US: United State

UK: United Kingdom

GNI: Gross National Income

UAE: United Arab Emirate

UNOCHA: UN Office for the Coordination of Humanitarian Affairs

VoIP: Voice over Internet Protocol

ERC: Employee Retention Connection Model

Abstract

Non-profit organisations are mostly all about making a difference which is essential in today's world. The purpose of this research is to identify the key factors leading to employee attrition in non-profit organisations and recommend effective strategies that will help enhance employee retention in non-profit organisations using a comparative analysis between UK and UAE based organisations. This study is vital because Non-profit organisations have been facing challenges in retaining skilled workers, which has impacted the way they operate. The impact and roles non-profit organisations play in any country cannot be overemphasised. Every country deserves successful non-profit organisations due to the values and economic impact it has on its environment. However, most of the current literature focuses on profit-making organisations, which led to minimal research in the non-profit sectors regarding employee retention and attrition. No comparative analysis has also been carried out in the two case studies adopted, which were some of the gaps this research helped bridge.

This research considered work-life balance, job satisfaction, organisation culture, career progression, training and development, effort acknowledgement and reward, employee engagement, leadership style, job satisfaction, motivation and many other factors.

This study took various theories like Herzberg's two factors theory, Social exchange theory, Vroom expectancy theory, Maslow theory, Equity and Employee Motivation theory, McClelland human motivation theory, Porter and Edward Lawler's Expectancy Theory, Job coupling model, Job embeddedness model, Zinger retention model, ERC Retention Model, Integrated retention model into account for an in-depth analysis and understanding of employee attrition and retention. This study considers various strategies that non-profit organisations can utilise to reduce these challenges by unravelling recommendations and results that would help fill the literature gap on employee attrition and retention in non-profit organisations. This research was carried out using a qualitative research method supported with elements of statistical analysis through interviews and self-completed survey questionnaires from 100 top, middle and low-level employees from UK and UAE based organisations. No comparative studies have been done on the differences and similarities amongst the respective employee opinions in the UK and UAE non-profit organisations, coupled with limited research on employee attrition and retention in non-profit organisations, which is why this research focuses its investigation on this area.

This research uncovered the similarities these two case studies have in common regarding employee attrition: Understaffing, inadequate feedback, too much workload, unrealistic expectations, unstructured Job satisfaction measurement, lack of appreciation, and unstructured employee retention policies, amongst others. In terms of differences, while one case study is facing the issue of work-life balance, rigid working hours, lack of opportunities to transfer to other affiliates, absence of schedule flexibility, inadequate means of transportation, language barriers, management focusing on personal interest, open-ended work format and so on. The other case study is facing attrition issues of bad management, toxic working environment, bad communication, lack of acknowledgement, too much focus on criticism, inadequate involvement in decision-making, and so on. Based on these issues, various retention strategies were recommended, such as encouraging non-profit organisations to implement information technology systems and encouraging more volunteers and employees to work remotely, implementing structured retention policies, etc.

This research utilised various multidisciplinary models to examine the factors contributing to employee attrition in the non-profit sectors. It developed a theoretical framework that will enhance employee retention in this sector. In terms of theory and practice, this research contributed to already developed attrition and retention theories and formulated new ones. Examples of such contributions are retention strategies and their process, cultural differences, leadership, information technology, etc. In practice, contributions were made towards employee's workload, retention policies, work-life balance, employee engagement and relationship, recruitment strategies, and so on.

Chapter One

1. Introduction

Non-profit organisations are solely established to benefit or fulfil a certain cause or purpose. This type of organisation is not profit-based like other organisations (Anheier, 2014). This thesis is about the reduction of employee attrition in non-profit organisations using a comparative analysis of two different non-profit organisations based in two different countries and continents. Non-profit organisations have been facing challenges in retaining skilled workers, and this has impacted so much on the way they operate (Kellner et al., 2017). The ability to retain skilled workers and avoid employee attrition in any organisation is paramount to the success of such an organisation, which was what brought about this research topic. This research was carried out using qualitative research analysis supported by elements of descriptive statistics.

This first chapter introduced what this research is about by analysing the justification for the topic selection, research sector, background of the study, the statement of problem, the aim of this research, research objectives, the scope of research, the significance of study alongside the structure this research follows in other to attain expected results.

1.1.Justification for Research Area

The researcher of this study aspires to kick start a non-profit organisation after the end of this DBA course at the University of the West of Scotland and to be able to achieve a successful non-profit organisation. A study was carried out on how the non-profit organisations sector works, and it was discovered that one of the main challenges that hinder the success rate in most non-profit organisations is employee attrition and the inability to retain skilled workers. This research considers various strategies that can be utilised to reduce these challenges. The experience and results derived from this research will equip the researcher with adequate knowledge and skills needed to achieve this goal. Secondly, after studying various literature, it was realised that the recommendations and results generated from this research would help to fill the literature gap on employee attrition in non-profit organisations. This research aims to also help other non-profit organisations in implementing a successful strategy to retain their skilled employees, thus reducing employee attrition. For these reasons, this topic is very important for businesses and governments interested in non-profit success rates and also potential investors in this sector and shareholders, and it can also be utilised by organisations in other sectors facing employee attrition challenges. Carrying out this research now is very paramount in attaining these set goals.

1.2.Background of the Study

Employee attrition can hinder the successful running of any organisation. Employees are known to be the backbone of any organisation, which makes it paramount for them to be retained. Suppose the right retention strategies are put in place in any organisation. In that case, such an organisation provides satisfactory services that help maintain stakeholders' loyalty in sticking to such organisation, which will help boost the organisational success and the achievement of the corporate goal (Idris, A. 2014). In a situation where the employee attrition rate in an organisation keeps increasing, such an organisation is liable to keep spending on training new employees recurrently due to the frequent intake of new employees (Roberts and Analytics, 2015). This situation might lead to low productivity because employees are mostly on probation or starting phase of their roles in such organisations. When this happens, the quality of services rendered to consumers or those benefitting from the cause of the organisation would be affected (Dhar, 2015). Some organisations do not employ more workers to fill in the roles that have been rendered vacant due to employee attrition but instead split the roles between the available employees, and this approach often not only slows down productivity but also negatively affects the quality of service rendered (Yoo and Arnold, 2016). The ability to provide satisfactory services to stakeholders is the key to the success of any organisation, and this can be achieved if each organisational role can be carried out by an expert in the specific field (Cappelli, 2015). It is vital to tackle the employee attrition challenges to avoid directing funds meant for services provision on recurring training, advertisement of frequent vacant roles and hiring new employees. There is no problem in employing new employees if the reason is to provide efficient services to stakeholders, but if the situation is due to frequent employee attrition, then that makes it a great challenge for such organisations to survive long term in the sector it operates in (Anguzu and Basheka, 2017). Non-profit organisations always serve a cause that benefits the public or people around their environs. It is very important for such organisations to thrive and survive any form of challenges that might hinder their set goals (Anderson and Dees, 2017). The profit-based organisation sector has some retention strategies in place to reduce employee attrition, but since NPO are not profit-based, most of the FPO strategies cannot be implemented;

therefore, strategies that suit the non-profit organisation must be put in place (Maldonado et al., 2015).

Most non-profit organisations have many volunteers who render services without being paid. At the same time, some only get a token at the end of every month, but they get to leave easily if there's no form of appreciation or fulfilment in the voluntary roles assigned to them (Ramdhani et al., 2017). Some also leave the organisation due to a lack of direction or unfocused goals by the non-profit organisation, and in other to avoid all these issues from reoccurring, adequate retention strategies must be developed. Some paid employees also leave the non-profit organisation due to unclear career progression as a result of inadequate transparency on the part of the organisation involved (Huhtala and Feldt, 2016). The non-profit organisation has a lot of issues hindering its retention success rate. These issues must be identified and tackled because that is the only way employee attrition can be reduced or overcome. This research investigated the reason behind the already identified issues and other unidentified issues causing employee attrition in non-profit organisations. These issues were analysed in other to be able to develop an efficient and effective retention framework that will help curb or reduce employee retention in non-profit organisations.

This research aims at providing reliable strategies that will help reduce employee attrition and increase the retention rate of skilled workers in non-profit organisations.

1.3.Problem Statement

Non-profit organisations are facing a major challenge of employee attrition. Employee attrition is a major problem in the non-profit organisation as it affects productivity and services rendered by the non-profit organisation to the public (Anheier, H. K., 2014). Many scholars have carried out research regarding these challenges, but the issue is still on the high side because most scholars focus on the profit-based sector. Since these challenges keep reoccurring, this research addressed both past work and unresolved problems that lead to employee attrition in the non-profit organisation. The rate at which employees leaves an organisation can also be referred to as turnover rate as it explains the rate an organisation's workforce keeps leaving and replaced with new or existing employees (Hom et al., 2017). According to Part Streets People article UK, the average total turnover rate in industries that are based in the United Kingdom has increased to 16.7% as of 2015. Meanwhile, the non-profit sector alone accounts for 15.7%. The article analysed further that non-profit voluntary turnover was at 11.6% in 2015.

Crain's Chicago Business article also mentioned that the employee attrition rate in the United States has increased from 16% to 19% between the years 2013 to 2015. The understanding behind retention is to keep the loyal organisation employees (Deery and Jago, 2015). For profit-based organisations, if the employee turnover is on the high side, this will adversely influence the company's revenue and profitability. (Demirtas and Akdogan, 2015). But for non-profit organisations on which this research is based, attrition will affect the quality of services the non-profit organisation will render to stakeholders. Shareholders will not be impressed either. The adverse result of a high employee attrition rate tends to be many. It leads to incurring high hiring costs, training expenses, low-quality services, low productivity, the inability to achieve organisational goals, and many more (Holtom and Burch, 2016).

The investigation of past studies for factors causing employee attrition shows that some employees find it challenging to cope with their role due to inadequate training and unavailability of skills resources in the organisation (Huhtala and Feldt, 2016). Environmental factors can also be the determinant of employee attrition. Situations like work overload or overworking the labour force can impact employee attrition because any organisation known for overburdening its employees with work will find it challenging to attract key talents. If they attract key talents, such skilled employees tend to leave for less stressful roles in other organisations (Wong and Laschinger, 2015). If all of these keep happening in any non-profit organisation, customers or shareholders or stakeholder loyalty will be affected, which is detrimental to the organisation's growth. Loyalty will be lost if unsatisfactory services keep reoccurring. Therefore, organisations must maintain a low attrition rate, and this can be achieved if good retention strategies are adopted to prevent the employees from quitting.

1.4.Overview of Research Environment and Sector

This research was carried out between a non-profit organisation in the UK and a non-profit organisation in the UAE as a comparative analysis.

1.4.1. United Kingdom

United Kingdom is known for its high practice in non-profit (Anheier, H. K.,2014). Based on the data provided by the Charity Register on the 31st of December 2016, England and Wales have over 167,100 Charity organisations. According to the National Council of Voluntary Organisations (NCVO), non-profit organisations are usually known for providing social, religious, cultural and recreational services and activities. The Charity Commission explains that in the year 2016, £73.1 billion was estimated as the total income generated in the United Kingdom from the non-profit sector.

Regarding government support in 2014/2015, for the first time in 10 years, the local government income was lower than the central government income. The government had total revenue of £15.3 billion. 48% of this income was from the central government, 47% from the local government, and the rest from foreign sources (NCVO, 2015).

In 2015/2016, community life survey data indicates that approximately £7.6 billion was acquired through gifts, donations, and legacies in the non-profit sector. 73% of adults contributed towards charitable organisations for four weeks prior to when the research was carried out. 17.4% gave less than 4 pounds, while 13.5% contributed over 50 pounds (Community life survey, 2016). Under the survey regarding volunteering in 2015/2016, the age range between 16-25 years, which is seen as the most active age group, volunteered in charitable organisations. 44% volunteered in the formal roles, while 32% volunteered in informal roles at least once a year. Formal volunteering was not common among the 26-34 age group. Around just 29% of the 50-65 age group volunteered informally.

In the year 2016 United Kingdom had a population of 65,595,565 and a life expectancy at birth of 80.96 years. The GNI per capita shows that the United Kingdom had 42,370 GNI in 2016. Annual GDP is forecasted at 1.54% in 2019 (The World Bank Data, 2017).

Charity name	Average Spending On Charitable Activities As % Income Last Three Financial Years	Last Financial Year Income	Last Financial Year Spending On Charitable Activities
Lloyd's Register Foundation	1%	£1,062,537,000	£14,490,000
The Racing Foundation	3%	£50,932,901	£1,146,153
The Motability Tenth Anniversary Trust	8%	£54,376,000	£4,093,000
Consumers' Association	24%	£102,831,000	£22,796,000
Sheffield City Trust	25%	£48,186,000	£17,021,000
The Grace Trust	33%	£91,678,745	£29,874,716
British Heart Foundation	46%	£288,200,000	£113,700,000
Sue Ryder	46%	£95,431,000	£42,585,000
Age UK	48%	£174,575,000	£83,956,000
Oasis Charitable Trust	57%	£271,709,000	£151,935,000
The Royal Horticultural Society	60%	£73,157,000	£47,641,000
Dogs Trust	63%	£84,743,000	£57,185,000
Cancer Research UK	64%	£634,900,000	£422,700,000
The Guide Dogs For The Blind Association	64%	£101,100,000	£56,400,000
Shelter, National Campaign For Homeless People	64%	£69,565,000	£39,541,000
The Royal National Lifeboat Institution	64%	£190,100,000	£122,200,000
Marie Curie	65%	£154,805,000	£105,585,000
	Average 43% *	£3,548,826,646	£1,332,848,869

(Source: True and Fair Foundation, 2015)

Figure 1: UK Charities Average Spending and Incomes

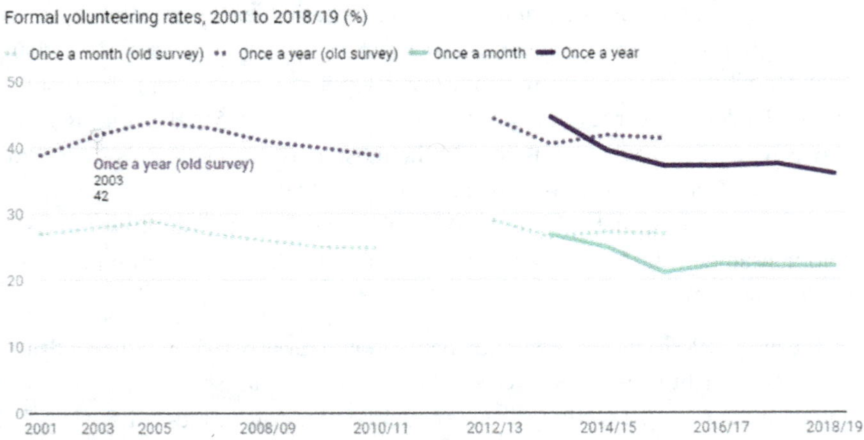

Figure 2: UK Formal Volunteering Rate

(Source: Community Life Survey, Citizen Survey)

Figure 3: Activities of Recent Volunteers (UK)

1.4.2. United Arab Emirate (UAE)

UAE consists of seven emirates: Dubai, Ras al-Khaimah, Abu Dhabi, Sharjah, Fujairah, Umm al-Quwain, and Ajman. Due to natural disasters and war occurring in the Arab part of the world, the UAE has been very active in supporting and donating towards charitable causes around the world. In 2014 the United Arab Emirates donated more than 506.2 million Dirham, as said by the UNOCHA (UN Office for the Coordination of Humanitarian Affairs, 2014). During an interview with the minister for international and development Sheikh Lubna Al-Qasimi by National News Middle East, the minister explained that UAE was the largest foreign aid donor in 2013 based on gross national income percentage. Syria is at the top list of the countries that benefitted from this opportunity, including the refugee relief houses in Lebanon and Jordan. This Aid activity covers areas like feeding provision, shelter, and medication.

According to the UNOCHA, 2014 the UAE has four (4) main philanthropic organisations, which are named Public Welfare Associations (PWAs), Charitable Societies, Non-profit Organisations (NPOs), and Non-profit Incorporate Organisations (NPIOS). The various regulatory body uses these different terms to be conscious of which registration authority established organisations fall under. The Ministry of social affairs carries out its activities at the federal level, while the philanthropic organisations that operate within Dubai are under the regulatory framework of IACAD, which deals with charitable organisations' activities. The IHC and DIFC regulatory bodies are for the regulatory of non-profit organisations' activities. Sharjah operates in terms of alms and grants regulations for the benefit of the public. For any philanthropic organisation to operate in UAE, it must be under one of these regulatory bodies.

Non-profit organisations which are under the guidance of the ministry of social affairs are only permitted to carry out tasks that align with their set goals which must have already been reviewed by its regulatory body. Any deviation from the purpose it set to serve might lead to termination of services for such organisations. UAE non-profit is also exempted from paying tax and customs duties on products that might be needed for the successful running of such an organisation (The UAE Philanthropy Law report, 2016).

United Arab Emirate GDP was 348.743 billion dollars with a population of 9,269,612 and a life expectancy at birth of 77.256 years in 2016. The GNI per capita using the atlas method shows that the UAE had 40,480 GNI in 2016, with an annual forecast GDP of 3.3% in 2020 (The World Bank Data Report, 2017).

UAE Humanitarian Agencies		
S.N	Agency	Mandate
1	Human Appeal International UAE	International aid organization established in the United Arab Emirates operating in the field of development and socio-economic relief
2	Zayed Foundation	Charitable and humanitarian foundation, involved in supporting mosques and cultural centers, schools and education institutes, hospitals and clinics in UAE and the world
3	Khalifa Bin Zayed Humanitarian Foundation	Charitable and humanitarian foundation, aims to help victims of different disasters all around the world
4	Dubai Cares	Social organization aims to help and educate children in poor countries
5	Make Poverty History	Non-governmental organization in UAE aiming to raise awareness about poverty, aids and other problems in the Middle East
6	Beit Al Khair Society UAE	Social organization in UAE aims to provide financial aids to the needy people including the poor and the hormones.
7	International Humanitarian City (IHC), UAE	Non political and nonprofit organization provides international humanitarian aid and development efforts in Dubai, UAE.
8	Start UAE	Aims to give art education for children living in disadvantaged areas in the Middle East.
9	Humaid Bin Rashid Al-Nuaimi Foundation for Human Development	Non-profit foundation in Ajman, serves the community and provides ideal employment of human resources and more.
10	Mohammed bin Rashid Al-Maktoum Foundation	Dubai-based foundation launched by H.H. Sheikh Mohammed bin Rashid Al-Maktoum, with the aim of empowering future generations to devise sustainable home-grown solutions to challenges faced by the Arab World.
11	All As One (AAO)	Aims to help orphans of Sierra Leone who have a need for food, housing, education and medical support in Dubai, UAE.
12	Al-Maktoum Foundation, UAE	A multicultural foundation in UK aims to promote and present an understanding of Islam and Muslims in all over the world.
13	Blood Bank - UAE	Charity website aims to build a database of names of blood donors, their blood groups and mobile numbers in UAE.
14	Vote for Beautiful People	Organization works in UAE and abroad on behalf of artists with special needs. Financially supports many projects and provides training to develop artistic skills through the forty seven art studios associated with the organization.
15	The Red Crescent	A member in the international federation for red cross and red crescent societies

Source: www.uaeinteract.ae

Figure 4: UAE Humanitarian Agencies

1.5. Aim of Research

This research aims to identify the key factors leading to employee attrition in non-profit organisations and recommend effective strategies that will help enhance employee retention in non-profit organisations.

1.6. Research Question and Research Objectives

Question 1: What are the policies governing non-profit organisations?

The findings of this research question helped identify the policies and guidelines surrounding both the establishment of non-profit organisations and the activities that can occur within the limits of these policies. Identifying the non-profit policies helped clarify the best solutions that can be recommended to reduce the challenges of employee attrition facing the Non-profit organisation. Some of the policies governing the non-profit organisation are why most of the strategic framework used in the for-profit organisations cannot be utilised in the non-profit section. An example is that most NPO does not pay tax, and they cannot earn profit as their name implies.

Question 2: What are the factors that lead to employee attrition in such organisations?

The findings of this second research question play a strong role in determining the causes of employee attrition in non-profit organisations. Before finding solutions to any problem, it is necessary to understand the factors underpinning it. The factors leading to employee attrition in non-profit organisations were identified as they will help apply practical retention strategies and recommendations to reduce the challenges of employee attrition.

Question 3: What are the successful employee retention strategies for non-profit organisations?

This research question aids this research in considering detailed retention strategies that are already in place to curb employee attrition in non-profit organisations. This question helped to avoid repetition of such strategies as new solutions were provided except for the solutions that were not well analysed or broad enough; in such a scenario, it was properly analysed for it to be implemented effectively. After identifying these strategies, it becomes more feasible to identify other effective strategies that have not been considered towards the reduction of employee attrition in non-profit organisations.

Question 4: What strategic framework can be recommended in this context to enhance Retention?

After considering the first three questions, the answer to this research question was considered. The most effective strategic framework that will be recommended to reduce employee attrition in non-profit organisations. The recommendation of these strategies will thereby help in enhancing employee retention. This fourth research question is a vital part of the research because it helped provide recommendations that help reduce employee attrition challenges facing the non-profit organisation after different policies have been considered and understood and key factors causing employee attrition have been identified.

1.6.1. Research Objectives

The research objectives are generated from the research questions. This is very important as it creates a pointer towards the research aim. Employee attrition high rate in the non-profit organisation will be well looked into. These questions will be answered in a broad and detailed format in other to achieve the aim of this research.

Objective 1: To clearly state policies governing non-profit organisation.

Objective 2: To identify key factors that lead to employee's attrition in such organisation.

Objective 3: To identify successful retention strategies for non-profit organisation.

Objective 4: To create a suitable strategic framework to enhance retention of non-profit organisation employees.

1.7.Scope of the Research

This research was carried out in two different organisations based in two different countries in two different continents. The first organisation is a non-profit organisation based in the UK, while the other organisation is based in the United Arab Emirates for comparative analysis. This research did not cover the whole country because it is only applicable to non-profit organisations, and the two organisations that were picked for this research majored in non-profit activities in a very Broad way. The NPO in the United Arab Emirate is in Ras al-Khaimah, with over 30 employees. Ras al-Khaimah is one of the seven Emirates in the UAE. This NPO is one of the major leaders in non-profits in the United Arab Emirate, which makes it a great choice for this research. The other NPO in the UK is in Peterborough, with more than 200 employees, which include main employees, contract staff and volunteers. This non-profit organisation dominates every non-profit activity in Peterborough; thus, it's a great organisation for this research. With these two organisations, it was straightforward to achieve the set objectives and aim of this research as they implement every aspect of the non-profit guidelines and activities daily. These two organisations follow the laid down rules and policies governing non-profits in their individual country. Both organisations share some similarities, and they also have a lot of differences in their respective operations and activities.

1.8.Significance of Study

This research is worth undertaking because non-profit organisations have been facing challenges in retaining skilled workers, which has impacted so much on the way they operate. The impact and roles non-profit organisations play in any country cannot be overemphasized. Every country deserves successful non-profit organisations due to the values and economic impact on their environments. The ability to retain skilled workers and avoid employee attrition in any organisation is paramount to the success of such an organisation, which was what brought about this research topic. In a situation where the employee attrition rate in an organisation keeps increasing, such an organisation is liable to keep spending on training new employees recurrently due to the frequent intake of new employees (Demirtas and Akdongon,2015). This situation might lead to low productivity because employees are mostly starting a new phase of their roles in such an organisation. When this happens, the quality of services rendered to consumers or those benefitting from the cause of the organisation would be affected (Deery and Jago, 2015).

This study is significant because it contributes to the body of knowledge by providing effective strategies to minimise the turnover rate in non-profit organisations. This study is also important because it helps identify the factors underpinning attrition which serves as a directory for finding efficient strategies to reduce it. This study expanded existing knowledge on employee attrition and introduced new aspects to this existing knowledge. This study was able to develop a strategic framework that will enhance employee retention in non-profit organisations.

1.9.Research Methodology

In other to carry out a study, it is required to understand which research methodology will best suit the research. Saunder's research onion was used as a benchmark in explaining the analysis of the best methodology for this research (Saunders et al., 2016). These entail research philosophy, research strategy, research approach, research procedure and design. This study is mainly based on a qualitative approach with elements of descriptive statistics. The purposive sampling method was utilized in this research in other to obtain the required information for this study (Etikan et al., 2016). The primary data for this research was derived from two different organisations, one from the UK and the second in the United Arab Emirates. One hundred top, middle and low-level management participants participated in this research through interviews and self-completed questionnaires.

1.10. Structure and Presentation of the Study

This section summarises what other chapters entail to achieve adequate and concise results for this study.

1.10.1. Literature Review

This chapter reviews past studies on employee attrition and retention in non-profit organisations. It explains in detail the effect of employee attrition in non-profits and why it is very important to consider this research. It can also be referred to as the secondary source of information for this research. Various academic articles and journals were considered and critically analysed. In this chapter, the findings of the articles, journals and other secondary data were analysed and compared by their effectiveness as the chapter gives a broad understanding of what has been done so far to reduce the non-profit attrition challenges. This aspect of the research also helped in determining the successful retention strategies that are already in place and the in-active strategies that should be reconsidered for the success of this research.

1.10.2. Conceptual Framework

The conceptual framework is an integral aspect of this research. This chapter guide the process this research followed. All the conceptual pointers in this research were represented in a pictorial form with descriptive directional links showing both the dependent, moderating and independent variables that were used in this research. This aspect was also explained in detail in a textual format. This chapter describes the relationship between the frameworks used in this research, as it is very important to explain the relationships in other to have a clear analysis of the effect of each of the pointers in this research. This chapter also explains and helps distinguish different levels of theories and their application to study.

1.10.3. Research Methodology

This chapter explains the actions that were undertaken in other to achieve a concise and practical investigation regarding the factors surrounding employee attrition in a non-profit organisation. This chapter also explains the application of the techniques that were used in identifying, selecting, and analysing the employee attrition issue at hand. Furthermore, it helps to prove the reliability and validity of this research. This research focused on qualitative analysis supported by a few elements of descriptive statistical analysis. In this research, both surveys and interviews were conducted in the two organisations to achieve substantial findings and achieve the purpose of this research. This chapter also explains the justification for choosing the qualitative method and descriptive statistical analysis for this study.

In this chapter, the data collection methodology for this research was explained in detail. The primary data for this research was gathered from both the surveys and interviews conducted in the United Kingdom and United Arab Emirates non-profit organisations to capture quality evidence that will provide reliable answers to the research questions. The interviews for this study were conducted one-on-one and through voice over internet protocol (VoIP), encouraging open-ended responses. Response from this interview was well written and recorded when permitted by participants. The survey questions were designed using numeric values printed on hard copies for participants' easy access and sent through an online method using the Zoho survey software, which has been tested to be very effective for survey data collection.

1.10.4. Result, Analysis and Discussion

This chapter helped analyse the information gathered through the data collection phase. In other to analyse the data collected for this study, the qualitative aspect was well described. Data collected were transcribed using the NVivo tool, and the data was organised using the research objectives as pointers, after which data collected was coded in other to make the analysis more logical because the result must be consistent and reliable. This section is very important because it helps the researcher draw a conclusion from the data collected. All the findings from the data collection phase were interpreted, and the link between the findings and the research objective was established. The research questions were answered at this phase of the data analysis. The descriptive statistic aspect of the data was also analysed using mean and a few statistical data analysis tools.

1.10.5. Conclusion and Recommendation

This section helped draw conclusions from the findings made from the data collection and data analysis. This chapter also delineates the recommendation of effective retention strategic framework that will help reduce employee attrition in non-profit organisations. It further explains the process and method of this research, including the pros and cons of this research. This concluding part of the write up also points out the limitations and the area of the study that requires future studies. Furthermore, it provided answers to the last research question and fourth research objective, which are paramount to this research and a vital contribution to knowledge and the business world at large.

Chapter Two

2. Literature Review

This chapter considered past studies on employee attrition in non-profit organisations (NPOs). The first part of this section explains what employee attrition is about and the relationship it has with non-profit organisations. Next, the retention strategies that have already been in place and their impact was also considered. These then lead to the analyses of the issues facing retention in a non-profit organisation. These analyses helped in determining the research gap between employee attrition and retention in non-profit organisations.

Figure 5: Retention Model (Friedman and Schnorr, 2015)

2.1. About Non-Profit Organisations (NPO)

Non-profit Organisations (NPOs) are a form of organisation that is not profit dependent because they are created solely to improve the welfare of people in other to achieve a specific set of goals (Butler and Wilson, 2015). NPOs are usually referred to as charitable or philanthropic organisations because they are regulated under the federal tax code, which exempts them from paying taxes. The sole reason for its establishment is to serve the public through policy advancement, social services, educational empowerment, and so on. NPOs usually get their financial strength from donations or through various forms of fundraising programmes (Butler and Wilson, 2015). It was discovered that NPOs started growing in the 19th century, and since then, there has been an improvement in the growth of NPOs to date (Hammack, 2001). Non-profit organisations in 1940 were said to be about 12,500 and 50,000 in the year 1950, as at 1967 it increased to about 309,000 and just a bit under a million in 1989 (Dart, 2004). Currently, the number has risen to over 1.8 million NPO organisations. The number keeps growing substantially. The more growth in the establishment of this sector, the more it influences the nation's economy. The educational and health systems tend to be more involved in NPOs, but currently, rapid growth in the social services area of the sector is increasing. In the UK, more than 760,000 employees are being paid in the charity sector, and their combined income is about 39 billion pounds per year. At the same time, donations are derived from over 44 million on a regular basis which is an average of 16 pounds per month (Liu et al., 2015).

2.2. Benefits and Issues with NPO

Another employer that needs to retain its staff members is the non-Profit organisation (NPO). NPO is defined by Drucker (2012) as a sector that provides services that private and public sectors are unable to offer. They offer services that contribute to the building of community needs by providing help unavailable to the occupants of such communities. They exist for different causes and concerns, and they put together their goals and mission through their staff or volunteers to fulfil the different goals set in line with already stated rules and codes of conduct (DiMaggio and Anheier, 1990).

NPOs exist for different reasons that range from helping bridge the gaps that exist in various sectors of the economy like Agriculture, and health, to providing emotional support to struggling citizens in different places. Their services are not limited to their state or country of origin. Some NPOs extend their services to developing or developed countries, providing help where and when needed.

2.3. Retention and Attrition Theories

The role of human resources management and leadership was put into consideration in other to understand how it impacts retention; thus, the Herzberg two factors theory (satisfier/motivator & dissatisfier/hygiene) in addition to the social exchange theory were considered. These two theories made it clear that if there is a great leadership style in practice coupled with a very functional human resources management, employee attrition will reduce immensely, which will, in turn, encourage employee retention. These proactive measures will not only stop employees from leaving their job but also promote productivity and quality of service provided. In this case, achieving organisational set goals is reliant on its human resources management practice (Dei Mensah, 2014).

Armstrong (2010) emphasises that the ability, skills and knowledge of people is a huge determinant of their value; thus, employing people with high values will help an organisation maintain its competitive position in its various industry. It is the role of every organisation to recruit skilled and knowledgeable workforce to achieve its required success to remain valuable in their sector because attrition plays an enormous role in productivity and the kind of services provided (Tanwar and Prasad,2016).

It is quite challenging getting skilled employees recurrently, coupled with the financial constraint it will have on any organisation that keeps hiring new and efficient workforce (Kwenin, 2013). In other to avoid this, if a suitable human resources management practice is in place, the rate of attrition will be reduced (Slattery and Rajan, 2005).

Employees tend to stay longer in an organisation with excellent human resources practice because such an organisation doesn't overburden its employees (Steward and brown, 2009). A good human resources practice has a unique leadership style in place. In such a scenario, the retention of skilled employees won't be far reached. Great leadership makes it easier for employees to achieve career fulfilment and development, which encourages retention because an organisation's leadership style can either make an organisation prosper or ruin its progress (Trush, 2012).

For non-profit organisations to run their cause effectively, tremendous human resources practice and leadership style must be in order. For example, every employee wants to work in an organisation where comfort and progress are ascertained. Though the reason behind employee attrition is vast, some of the reasons are lack of reward, job dissatisfaction, lack of work/life balance, and insecurity.

According to the social exchange theory, human connections utilise a subjective cost-benefit ideology which entails economics, psychology and sociology (Homan 1958; Blau 1964).

Social exchange gives the parties involved in the exchange to depend on and influence one another's actions or decisions. The psychological aspect is said to be based on individual behaviour through interactions suggesting that authority, position, conformity, justice and leadership within the social behaviour are vital aspects of the theory (Emerson, 1976). The kind of social exchange relationship that exists in an organisation will determine if retention will be encouraged or discouraged by either party (Cropanzano and Mitchell, 2005). In situations where either party, for example, organisation, employees, customers and so on, realises that the cost of the service they render or receive is higher than the benefit gained, such a relationship won't last. But in the case of NPOs which this research is about, retention can be difficult to achieve if employees don't find their time and contributions worthwhile.

A study by Zin et al. (2012) suggested that intrinsic and extrinsic motivational factors like career development, rewards, training, organisation interpersonal relations, and organisation policies put in place will influence retention. The study further explains that organisational culture strategy can be used as a form of intrinsic and extrinsic factor to achieve retention.

Most employees want to work in organisations that exhibit great leadership style practice. Transformational leaders are unique leaders due to their zeal for helping their followers, in this case, employees, to achieve their potential and goals by prioritising their needs (Fitzgerald and Schutte, 2010). Organisations that operate a transformational form of leadership style mostly end up with motivated employees who, in turn, impact the growth of such an organisation.

According to Gilbert and Kelloway (2016), transformational leadership includes: (a) Attributed charisma- which explains how a leader is perceived by his followers based on his confidence and use of power (b) Behavioural Charisma- Specific behaviour of a leader as regards his beliefs, ethics, purpose, and so on is put into consideration. (c) Inspirational Motivator- This type of leader encourages their followers to achieve their career ambition and pushes them to do better (d) Intellectual stimulator- These types of leaders intellectually stimulate their followers and supports them in solving problems creatively. (e) Individualised consideration- This kind of leader exhibits different leadership traits because the trait they showcase depends on who they are dealing with. That is, everyone has a customised form of expectations. With this clarity, it can be concluded that transformational leadership entails selflessness because they prioritise employees' interests. This type of leadership influences positivity in an organisation because it boosts the confidence of its employees, which in turn improves productivity and quality of services delivered to stakeholders (Ramachandran and Krishnan, 2009).

Herzberg's two-factor theory explains how job satisfaction can encourage retention and job dissatisfaction can lead to attrition. In contrast, the social exchange theory emphasises positive behaviour amongst employees and their organisations. The social exchange theory also compliments Herzberg two factor theory on job satisfaction, as this can be achieved if excellent leadership style and fair human resources management practice are in place because this would be beneficial to both the organisation and its employees. An example of such human resources practice is making sure employees' work-life balance is up to the required standard because this will encourage retention and positively impact organisational productivity and achieving organisational set goals.

Whenever employees leave an organisation, such organisation will incur many unavoidable costs such as the hiring of temporary employees, overtime pay for current employees, training costs and hiring process-related costs. Raja and Kumar (2015) also support the point mentioned above by stating that employee attrition will lead to the recruitment of new employees in other to fill in the positions that were rendered vacant, and this might also affect productivity and elements like hiring, vacancy, training, deployment and exit cost. In other to fill in the vacant positions, a recruitment process must be in place. In situations where the role is sensitive and can't be handled by a new employee, one of the current employees might have to be deployed to take the place of the vacant position. This process will incur moving costs, which would be on the higher side if the redeployment is from a remote location, for example, travelling fares, hotel fees, feeding and so on.

Theories	Author's Opinion	Advantages	Limitations	References
Herzberg Two Factors Theory	Herzberg's two-factor theory explains how job satisfaction can encourage retention and job dissatisfaction can lead to attrition.	This theory focuses on the internal motivation factors of employees and urges organisations to improve their working environment. Money is not treated as a primary factor, but factors like promotion, recognition and the likes are	The satisfied employee might not necessarily increase organisational output. Also, different people have different factors that make them feel happy, and some might prefer more money over a promotion. Age range can also impact this in the process whereby	(Dei Mensah, 2014)

		prioritised regarding employee motivation.	younger people's needs vary from the much older employees. This theory did not consider external factors, thus might limit an organisation's competitive edge.	
Social Exchange Theory	Social exchange theory emphasises positive behaviour between an organisation and its employees.	This theory is focused on increasing benefits while minimising costs.	This theory follows a linear method in measuring relationships, some relationships cannot be analysed based on a cost and benefit factor alone. Some employees do not mind working in an organisation that pays less if they are comfortable. In contrast, some organisations pay more regardless of the level of benefit because they prioritise their employee's loyalty instead.	(Cropanzano and Mitchell, 2005)

Table 1: Herzberg's two factors theory and Social exchange theory

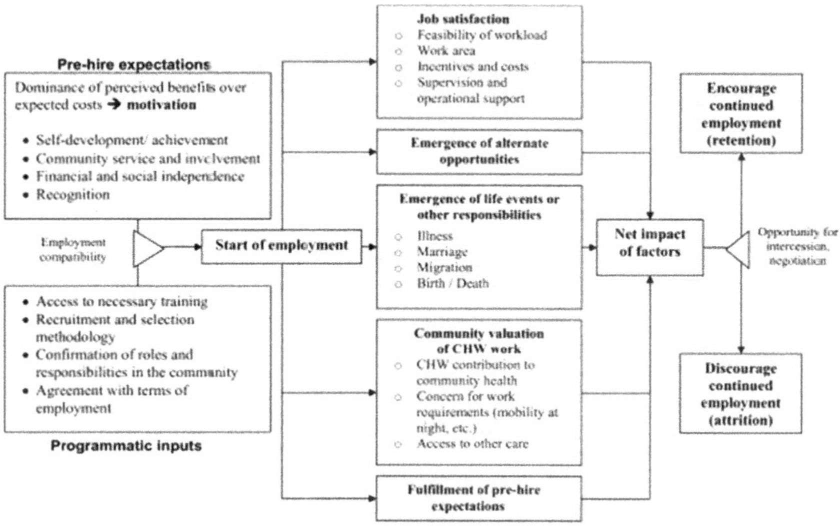

Figure 6: Retention and Attrition Framework (Rahman et al., 2010)

2.4. Theories Related to Employee Attrition

Expectancy theory is the process of selecting or showcasing a certain behavior or attribute out of various options in other to achieve a specific expected result (Chiang and Jang, 2008).

Vroom Expectancy Theory

While Maslow and Herzberg focus on achieving internal needs, Vroom's expectancy theory explains that people's motivation is what motivates their level of productivity. He further explains that a person makes an individual decision out of numerous options for comfort based on their skills, knowledge, experiences and personal motivation (Parijat and Bagga, 2014). Vroom explains this using expectancy, Valence and Instrumentality variables.

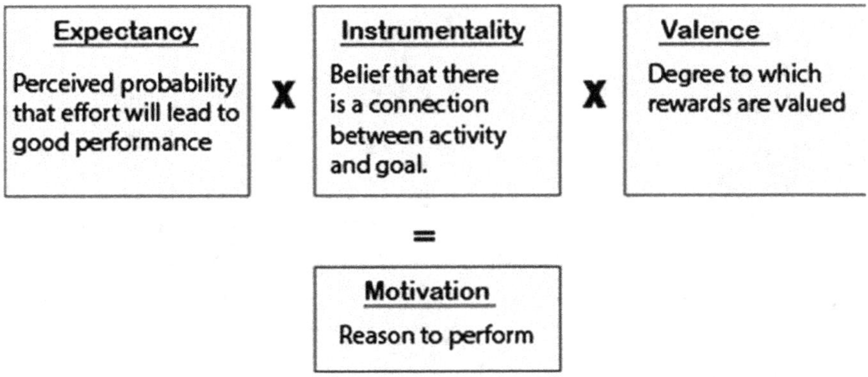

Figure 7: Vroom Expectancy Theory (Palistha Maharjan, 2018)

Expectancy: This has to do with the mindset that the amount of effort put into a certain task will determine the result to be achieved, meaning the expectation of energy equates to performance. But this mindset can be affected by the availability of resources needed to achieve the set goals, the essential training required to possess the necessary skill and the required set of leadership or support to get the task done.

Instrumentality: This has to do with the belief that excellent performance will be well rewarded. Which means there will always be a form of gain for a job well done, but this notion can be affected if an unclear relationship exists between performances and results. Transparency and trust in the people who decide who to be rewarded for a job well done will also determine if the instrumentality variable will be feasible.

Valence: This has to do with the value placed on the outcome expected. For example, People who are only motivated to get a job done because of the pay they will receive afterwards might not place any importance on factors like holidays and so on.

These three variables give a direct pointer which is effort equals performance which in turn equals reward and the importance of the reward. The most critical factor in the Vroom theory is "individual perception". In the case of an organisation, if an organisation puts different measures in place to motivate its employees, a group of employees will not be driven due to their perception of what can personally motivate them.

Porter and Edward Lawler's Expectancy Theory

Porter and Edward Lawler's Expectancy Theory (1969) is an extension of Vroom's Expectancy Theory which also supports the idea that an individual's desire to achieve a particular result is motivated based on the expected reward. Porter and Edward Lawler introduced intrinsic and extrinsic factors in addition to the already developed Vroom's Expectancy theory. Intrinsic reward is the internal fulfilment an individual feels after completing a task. In contrast, the extrinsic reward is the external expectation an individual feels he deserves after the successful completion of a job; this can be in the form of a promotion or bonus. Thus, the fulfilment and expected reward will determine if an individual will be motivated or not. This theory explains further that motivation is also affected by the capacity of executing and understanding a task, and such individual motivation will reduce if they don't achieve both their intrinsic and extrinsic expectation after the completion of a task (Vroom et al., 2005). The theory idealises the fact that rewards lead to satisfaction and that performance leads to reward. The four factors of this approach are the value of the reward, effort, performance, understating the probability of an effort-reward, reward and satisfaction.

Porter and Lawler clarify that motivation is not as simple as it seems. Organisations should not just assume that a specific means of motivation will work for all their employees. Instead, they should employ the right person for a job based on their skills and attribute. Organisations should explain job roles and how to obtain rewards in detail and analyse the expected level of performance. They should also describe the appropriate level of performance that will yield rewards for motivation and make sure that individual employees will value the rewards put in place. This theory emphasises the relationship that exists between job performance and satisfaction to yield motivation (Miner, 2015).

Abraham Maslow Theory

Abraham Maslow's theory explains in a hierarchical order that five different types of needs motivate people, and what is needed by an individual is determined by their current situation at a point in time (Mcleod, 2007). Therefore, if employers strategize employees' needs effectively, it will drastically reduce the rate of employee attrition. These needs start with self-actualisation, esteem, love-belonging, safety and physiological need. Employee needs could be at any of these levels at a point in time (Mcleod, 2007).

Self-actualisation - This is a process where self-development is encouraged by an employer. Employees can go through some form of career or personal progression, and this will, in turn, motivate employees and bring more value to the organisation.

Esteem- If an employee's sense of belonging is met, it will drastically improve their self-esteem. This factor can be achieved if a great leadership style is in practice and organisations continue to instil confidence in their employees through their supervisors or direct management. Employees with high self-esteem are usually inclined to do better because they are motivated by the organisation's belief and trust in them.

Love/Belonging- This third level motivates employees and encourages retention. Recognition programs and performance rewards should be in place to make employees feel appreciated, thus enabling them to remain in the organisation.

Safety- Job security is a significant example here. If employees feel that their job security is certain, it will motivate them to put in their best and make them plan to stay longer in the organisation. Safety can also mean good organisational policy or how superiors treat lower-level employees.

Physiological need- This level is usually applicable to lower-level employees because most of them are on the job for survival. Money is often a critical motivation here. A pay increase will motivate such employees.

Giving employees the same priority as customers

Cardy and Lengnick-Hall (2011) analysed a model focused on employee attrition and Job satisfaction. This model explains that organisations should give the same priorities they give to their customers to employees. Because this will make them pay attention to employee satisfaction, and they will be able to earn the same loyalty portrayed by their customers in their employees. For example, customer equity is more focused on long term patronise from its customer other than profit; this can also apply to employees; their values should not only be about what they are bringing to the table but their loyalty towards the organisation. Employee equity embodies three factors (Cardy and Lengnick-Hall, 2011). The first factor is employee equity, which entails how an employee analyses his service in relation to the benefits the organisation offers, just like the cost to value ratio analysis from customers (Lai, 2011). In this scenario, an employee might want to render their service elsewhere if they perceive that their return of service benefits is not considerable enough.

The second factor is brand equity. This second factor entails the emotional connection an employee has towards their organisation based on organisational branding (Altaf et al., 2017). This emotional connection helps employees maintain their loyalty towards an organisation regardless of the benefits provided by the organisation because of the employee's strong will to continue working in the organisation due to the way its branded to keep employees connected (Ibrahim and Al Falasi, 2014).

The third factor is retention equity, and this is about the value an organisation instils in its employees that keeps them loyal to the organisation. This third factor also has to do with the way employee perceives how they are prioritised by the organisation (Cardy and Lengnick-Hall, 2011).

Equity Theory and Employee Motivation

Equity theory is one of the significant factors towards motivation because this gives employees the understanding that they are treated fairly by receiving the same benefits as fellow employees who provide similar input towards the progress of an organisation (Muogbo, 2013). Most employees compare their efforts and how they are seen and appreciated by employers to their colleagues, they most times strive to meet up with their colleague's output in other to receive similar recognition (Hassan, 2013). If employees realise that an organisation is being biased, or the recognition accorded to them was below expectation in comparison to a colleague with a similar task outcome, this might make them quit their job and go in search of opportunities that would not make them feel less of themselves. This reality was backed up by research carried out by Taylor and Westover (2011), which explains the importance of maintaining equity in workplaces, especially in public service. Their write up analysed that most individuals are motivated by increased wages or pay.

Theories	Author's Opinion	Advantages	Limitation	References
Vroom Expectancy Theory	Vroom's expectancy theory explains that people's motivation is what motivates their level of productivity.	This theory lays emphasis on self-interest. This theory is about self-satisfaction from results, rewards and recognition with minimum discomfort.	This theory does not encourage teamwork because most employees will individually target results that would lead to personal rewards. Also, there is no guarantee for fair rewards because some employees will expect more based on their position.	(Parijat and Bagga, 2014)

Porter and Edward Lawler's Expectancy Theory	This theory introduced intrinsic and extrinsic factors in addition to the already developed Vroom's Expectancy theory. Intrinsic reward is the internal fulfilment an individual feels after completing a task. In contrast, the extrinsic reward is the external expectation an individual feels he deserves after the successful completion of a job which can be in the form of a bonus or promotion	The theory idealises the fact that rewards lead to satisfaction and that performance leads to reward.	Employee's zeal to perform better drops if they do not get the expected reward or recognition	(Vroom et al., 2005) (Miner, 2015)
Maslow Theory	Explains in a hierarchical order that five different types of needs motivate people, and what is needed by an individual is determined by their current situation at a point in time	This theory summarises human needs, which helps employers focus on what's essential in retaining their employees.	The level of satisfaction cannot be measured to determine the best time to move to another factor in the hierarchy. Therefore, the theory is not applicable in all situations, and the hierarchy arrangement varies because it might not be all needed to achieve satisfaction.	(Mcleod, 2007)
Equity Theory and Employee Motivation	Equity theory is one of the significant factors towards motivation because this gives employees the understanding that they are treated fair by receiving the same benefits as fellow	It reduces imbalance and any form of discrimination in treating employees, whereby employees who do the same set of work get the same kind of pay or	Perception might vary in a situation where some group of employees feels they are treated unequally compared to others without having the detailed information that other employees yield more output for the organisation.	(Muogbo, 2013)

employees who provide similar input towards the progress of an organisation	rewards. This theory encourages teamwork and works relationship because employees are motivated to work together since they will all receive an equal and fair form of appreciation.	This practice increases the need to compare among employees, and other factors are not considered; this might increase employee attrition because some employees might feel they deserve better than others due to their efforts

Table 2: Employee Attrition Theory

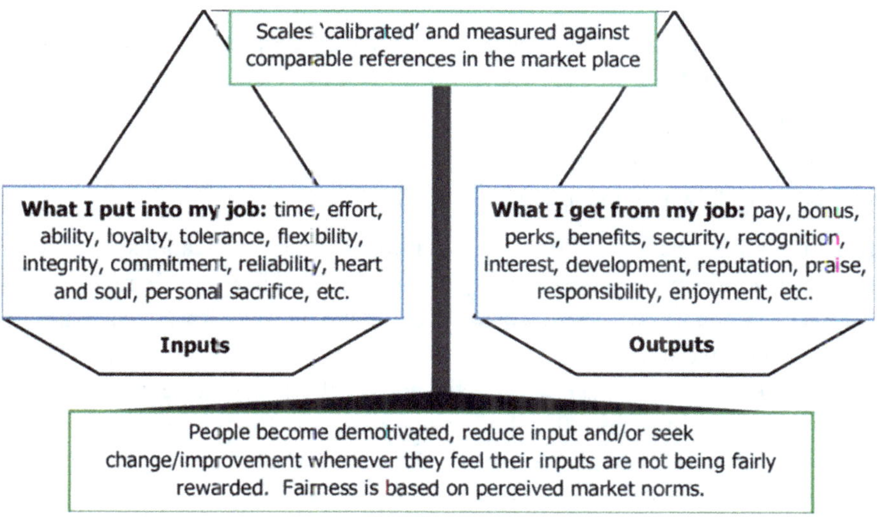

Figure 8: Adam's Equity Theory (Hoat, 2008)

2.5. Retention Theories

Employee retention strategies are a must for any organisation that wishes to continue to thrive in its industry of operation and maintain its competitive edge. Below are some of the retention theories that have been created to aid employee retention.

McClelland Human Motivation Theory

This theory mention that all human exhibits three motivators' traits; the need for power, achievement and affiliation, and explains further that one of the characteristics is more dominance than the other in all individuals. Any organisation that finds a means to understand which one is attributed to its employees will find a more straightforward process in motivating their employees (McClelland, 1987).

Power Dominance- These types of leaders like to be in charge of situations and have the trait of influencing their colleagues. They value recognition, and they are very competitive.

Achievement Dominance- These employees value independent tasks and priorities to achieve their set goals regardless of how tedious, and they would not appreciate anything that will undermine their effort. Employees with this trait like to get regular feedback because it will assure their progress (Mclelland, 2005).

Affiliation Dominance- These types of employees are great followers or team players. They prefer to work in conjunction with others and rarely take a risk.

Once all these traits are identified and put into consideration, it will help organisations to strategize the best method of a motivational process that will be well perceived by individuals (Mclelland, 2005).

Employees with the power dominance trait thrive better in situations where they are given a task that requires their input and decisions by their employers. In contrast, the employees with achievement dominance traits thrive better in challenging conditions because they value positive results. Employers won't have problems when giving day to day individual feedback to employees with this trait due to their zeal for always getting better. Employees with affiliate dominance traits are good team players and rarely handle the task given to them independently. Employers should always try to pair employees with affiliate traits up with other employees in other to achieve great results, and feedback should be provided in the form of a group (Moore et al., 2010).

This model encourages employers to treat and reward their employees based on their identified traits and personality because this will help yield excellent organisation performance. Employees will also be happy and most likely stay, knowing they are treated well (Deci and Ryan, 2014).

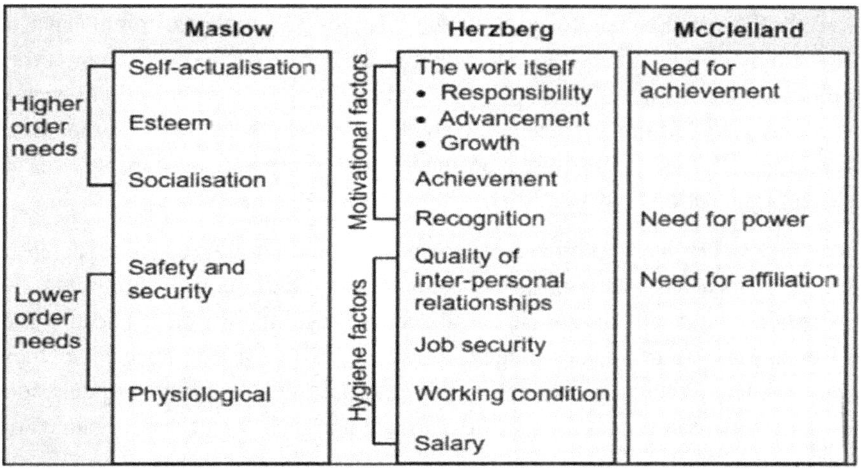

Figure 9: Needs Theories of Motivation (McClelland's Need Theory, 2020)

Job Coupling

According to a 2010 publication by the African Journal of business management, job coupling is explained as a means of retention strategies. The model focuses on two approaches which are the on-the-job and off-the-job coupling, which have three factors. The factors are linkage, fitness and sacrifice (WeiBo et al., 2010).

Linkage analysis of both the official and non-official relationships employees have with their colleagues and employers. This connection has so much to do with the effect working in an organisation has on employees, which could be financially or mentally. The stronger the linkage, the more likely employees are bound to not leaving. For example, suppose a family is happy as a result of the family-related programs an organisation keeps putting in place for their comfort. In that case, the main employee will be drawn to the organisation on a long-term basis and not want to leave such organisation for the sake of their family's comfort.

Fitness- Employees who discover that their career goals align with their organisation's goal would prioritise staying in such an establishment. For example, an employee who aims at attaining a certain level of skill will most likely remain in an organisation with career advancement opportunities (Zheng et al., 2012).

Employees who find their skills in alignment with the employer's requirements will be more comfortable staying in the organisation.

Sacrifice- This factor has to do with the changes an employee might have to make if they decide to leave an organisation. If the best decision is staying other than going, such employees will be inclined to stay in the organisation because they won't get what the organisation provides somewhere else. For example, if a promotion is in view, an employee tends to stay other than starting over in another organisation (WeiBo, 2010).

These factors can be used by employers to keep their employees more rooted in their organisations. Organisations should try and create programs or opportunities that will give their employees a sense of fulfilment because this will encourage them to stay longer. When employees feel connected to their organisation and their personal and career goals align well with the organisation, they will make the necessary sacrifices in staying back in such an organisation (Long et al., 2012).

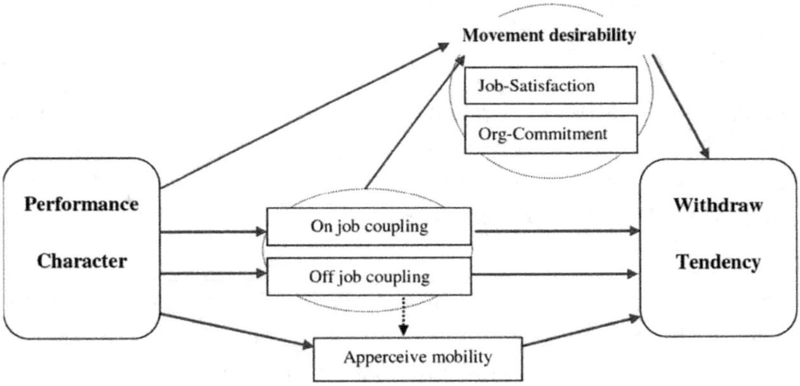

Figure 10: Job Coupling (WeiBo et al., 2010)

Theories	Author's Opinion	Advantages	Limitations	References
Mcclelland Human Motivation Theory	This theory mention that all human exhibits three motivator traits: The need for power, achievement and affiliation. This theory explains further that one of the characteristics	One of the significant advantages of this past study is that it was noted that employees are motivated through handling tasks that match their needs, and this helps eliminate blaming	This theory did not consider basic needs, which usually seem to be more critical, for example, shelter. It might be difficult for organisations to get satisfactory roles needed for	(McClelland, 1987)

	is more dominance than the other in all individuals.	employers for the job left undone. Organisations that practise this theory have motivated employees because their interest is a priority.	all their employees, and this can lead to chaos, especially if more people are yarning for a particular position. Also, some employees might get stuck in one specific role for a long time.	
Job Coupling	This theory focuses on two approaches which are the off the job and on the job coupling, which exhibit three factors. The factors are linkage, fitness and sacrifice	This theory emphasises the comfort of employees, which makes them commit fully to their jobs. This theory is grand because it prioritises employees' Compatibility with the organisation they work with. If employees' goals and careers are compatible with organisation culture, then retention can be ascertained.	An employee can appear compatible with an organisation at the onset, but with time things might still go downhill since human needs are insatiable	(WeiBo et al. et al., 2010)

Table 3: Retention Theories

2.6.Retention Models

Below are some of the retention models this research studied and reviewed.

Job Embeddedness

Job embeddedness is one of the models that exhibit factors supporting employee retention. This model exhibit three factors which are job fits, relationships and sacrifice (Reitz and Anderson, 2011). These factors are both internal and external.

Fit- This explains the alignments that exist between an employee and the organisation they work with, such as the same end goals, having the required skill and a conducive work environment (Van et al., 2013).

Relationships- This has to do with the effects a job has on the relationship of an employee, most especially external relationships (Robinson et al., 2014).

Sacrifice- Sacrifice has to do with the Effect attrition will have on an employee; it is usually easier for employees to withdraw from an organisation if they have not created a long-lasting relationship with their colleagues (Young et al., 2013).

These three factors can be internally or externally influenced. The Internal has a lot to do with the workplace, while the external is environmentally influenced.

Many studies have been carried out on job embeddedness as regards retention. Reitz et al., 2010 explained that it could be difficult at times to understand if an employee left the job willingly or not. Due to the challenges attached to getting accurate information from the employee after they have left because an organisation might not be a hundred per cent truthful about the reason why their employees are leaving. The research carried out by Mallol et al., 2007 across multiple cultures shows that the link factor that exists in the Job embeddedness has a lot to do with external family commitment. This study explains that family commitment largely influences the ability of an employee to stay long-term in an organisation. Hezarvand, 2013 argued that various elements influence retention; as there is no one reason why attrition occurs, they further explained that job satisfaction alone could not establish if employees would stick to their organisations.

Zinger Retention Model

Zinger Retention Model emphasises the benefit of connection and engagement amongst organisations, employees and customers in achieving any form of organisational goal In order for any organisation to maintain a certain level of a retention strategy. Such an organisation will have to learn the process of making sure its employees are all engaged in the decision-making process because the relationship that exists between teams at various levels will determine the level of productivity, as well as achieving organisational goals (Kaur, 2017).

This model also mentions the importance of recognising and rewarding the efforts of skilled and competent employees while making sure employees are not overburdened with workload because this will encourage retention. Retention plays a considerable role in organisation performance and will help maintain critical employees. Furthermore, for employees to serve customers well, there will be a level of commitment registered in the mind of the employees, and this can only be possible if there is a secure connection between an organisation and its employees. The model also analysis and explains that organisations should give their employees room for career and personal development. This development will help the employees improve on their strengths and weaknesses because these values will benefit the organisation through the service rendered by the employees to their customers or stakeholders (Ibrahim, 2019).

Organisations should make their employee's well-being a priority because the well-being of each key employee will have a drastic effect on organisational productivity and will affect organisational goals with time if not handled well. Happy employees lead to happy customer service and a successful organisation (Choudhary, 2016).

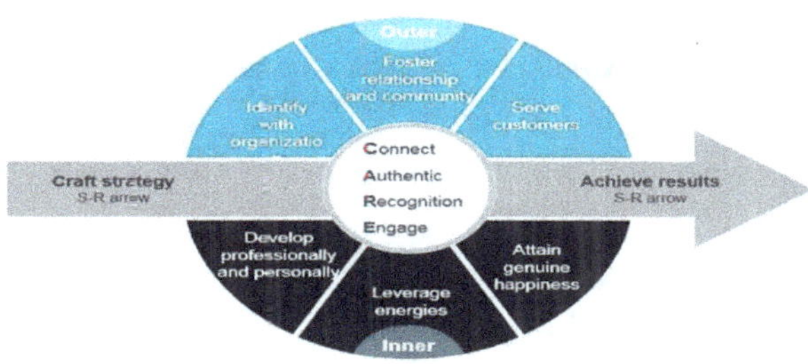

Figure 11: David Zinger's Employee Engagement Model

Employee Retention Connection (ERC) Retention Model

ERC model uses stimulating work, leadership and recognition/award as the three key factors in achieving retention.

This model explains that organisations can stimulate their employees by giving them varieties of work to do while providing the required resources needed to achieve the task alongside enough support. Employees' decisions should also matter while giving them feedback on work done with necessary acknowledgement and appreciation for a job well done (Shahin, 2014).

Leaders with a motivational style of operating also encourage employees due to their ability to open to new ideas. In addition, such leaders usually lead by example and share insights with others in other to have a shared end goal, and this will help to instil a sense of belonging in others because shared values will aid positive outcomes on any task handled.

Organisations should prioritise the benefit and importance of recognising employees' efforts. For example, suppose an employee excellently executes a task. In that case, the organisation should acknowledge the employee's effort because this will boost the employee's self-esteem and ability to do better on other tasks. Moreover, this act of appreciation and acknowledgement will also encourage other employees to do better in their various job to be appreciated (Khan and Ahmad, 2019).

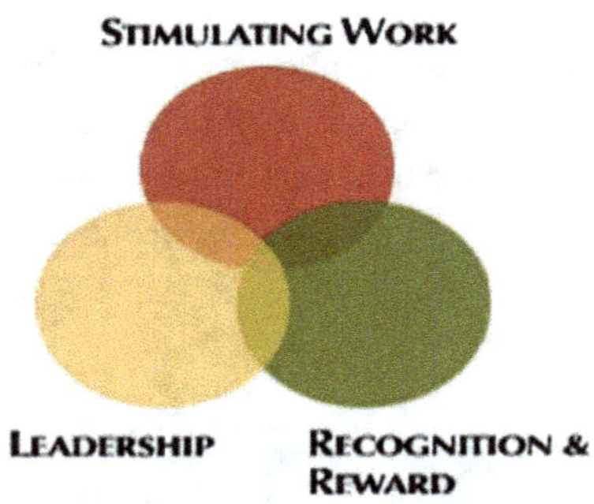

Figure 12: ERC Retention Model (Kaur, 2017)

Integrated System for Retaining Employees

The integrated retention model uses five different approaches in explaining the system used to retain key employees. Employee retention connection will help an organisation maintain a competitive position and maintain a tremendous cultural balance.

The first approach is to understand the form of motivational processes used in an organisation coupled with its retention culture. These can be achieved through surveys or focus groups to help analyse organisational driving forces and what needs improvement (Hughes and Rog, 2008).

The second approach involves designing exciting role opportunities. If employees have the opportunity to work with variety in their role with the required resources, it will excite them to go to work every because they know every day won't be the same. They will get to learn and develop their values continuously. Allowing employees to make decisions and giving feedback will make them feel involved, and this factor will encourage retention (Kaur, 2017).

The third approach is to equip leaders, for example, managers and supervisors with motivational skills so they can practice the motivational style of leadership towards employees. This skill will give them the ability to have a shared vision with others and focus on improving employees' capabilities. Superiors who display a motivational form of leadership will help promote organisational change because they know the value of acknowledging and rewarding employees' contributions. These superiors are perceived as role models and imitated by their followers (Ibrahim, 2019).

The fourth approach has to do with encouraging employees' career development. Organisations should continue to train their employees with skills that will be beneficial to them and the organisation. Organisations should give mentorship opportunities to employees, and this will help employees get better in their role and feel elated, knowing they can deliver their role better (Kaur, 2017).

The fifth and last approach of employee retention connections emphasises on the building of an award and recognition scheme that will suit each organisation's cultural belief. Organisations should let employee performance be a determinant of the kind of recognition or award that will be presented. This process will stand as a motivational channel to encourage employees toward retention in an organisation (Chen and Hsieh, 2006).

Figure 13: Integrated Retention Model (Kaur, 2017)

Theories	Author's Opinion	Advantages	Limitations	References
Job Embeddedness	This model exhibit three factors which are job fits, relationships and sacrifice	Job fit can encourage employee retention	Compatibility alone is not enough to guarantee retention, and other external factors can lead to employee attrition	(Reitz and Anderson, 2011)
Zinger Retention Model	The model explains the benefit of connection and engagement amongst organisations, employees and customers in achieving any form of organisational goal	Employees feel involved thus, inclined to stay in the organisation.	If the same form of engagement is used for all employees, some of the employees might still feel left out, while trying varieties might be costly for the organisation	(Kaur, 2017)

ERC Retention Model	This model explains that organisations can stimulate their employees by giving them a variety of work while providing the required resources needed to achieve the task alongside enough support.	Employees will be eager to go to work every day and encourage them to stay long term in an organisation because they would not be bored as they are mentally stimulated regularly.	Varieties can lead to a loss of direction and reduce the ability to become an expert in a specific role.	(Shahin, 2014)
Integrated Retention Model	ERC encourages designing a job in such a way where employees are fully involved alongside training organisation leaders to maintain a motivating form of leadership	Employee retention connection will help an organisation maintain a competitive position and maintain a tremendous cultural balance	ERC focuses on internal means of retaining employees; external factors like family can also impact employee attrition.	(Hughes and Rog, 2008)

Table 4: Retention Models

2.7. Underlying Factors of Attrition and Retention

Aside from job satisfaction and motivation, other factors explain and analyse what attrition and retention are all about, although most theories focus on job satisfaction as the main factor influencing retention.

Economic Condition: Economic and labour market conditions are one of the factors underpinning job retention because this can affect an employment decision in regards to what job is worth maintaining (Kelchtermans, 2017). In a study carried out by Cotton and Tuttle (1986), it was explained that if the economic condition is favourable, it is more likely for an employee to quit their job due to numerous options available. Another study also shows that if an employee stays in a job for a long time, it is likely for them not to leave due to age constraints (Hom and Xiao, 2011).

Environmental Factors: The environmental factor is another determinant of why employees might leave their place of work because the policies and rules practised in a workplace can determine if an employee will be comfortable staying in an organisation long-term (Alhassan et al., 2016). Policies like career advancement and promotion opportunities and policies practices in an organisation would encourage retention (Yang et al., 2012). Though some studies argue that the more training opportunities an employee has, the more equipped they are to leave. But some member of staff also quit their jobs due to a non-conducive environment, social harassment, gender discrimination and emotional-related stress (Mackusick and Minick, 2010).

Organisational Relationships: The kind of relationship an employee has with an organisation can also determine if retention will be on the high side or not (Aguenza and Som, 2012). Most employees always have social networking outside the organisation they work with, and this gives them the opportunity to compare their benefits and salary to employees in other organisations (Cloutier et al., 2015). However, due to the relationship they have with their current organisation and co-workers, it will make it a bit difficult for them to decide to leave for another organisation also because they are unsure if the new organisation is going to have the same friendly attributes and benefits their current place of work possess. Thus, maintaining a strong relationship with employees is beneficial (Moynihan and Pandey, 2008).

Employees Relationship: Most employees like to work in an organisation where teamwork improves their knowledge because this has a natural way of boosting their self-esteem, which in turn makes them perform better (Vasquez, 2014). This relationship is mostly extended outside the organisation, and due to the long-term friendship, they might have established, employees will find it a bit challenging to leave (Nwokocha and Iheriohanma, 2012).

Employee Compatibility with the Organisation: If an employee feels that their goals and value align with the organisation they work with, they tend to stay longer in such organisation because it makes them feel fulfilled. This factor is mostly referred to as person-organisation fits (Monynihan and Pandey, 2008). For example, if an employee is interested in medical research and they are opportune to work in an organisation with similar goals, such an employee will most likely stay longer in the organisation. That is why organisations need to employ people who are in sync and ready to work towards the same end goal as the organisation due to their likelihood of staying longer (Starks, 2007).

2.8.Effect of Attrition in NPO

Employee attrition is a significant challenge for management in today's workplace. One of the reasons why some organisations' human resources management pay detailed attention to its employees is because they perceive employees as assets, thus making a significant investment in their employees' development through recurrent training plans and reward systems that will, in return, encourage the achievement of the organisational set goals. In most organisations, human resources try to balance up the rate of organisation employee attrition by putting the effect on employee's income. However, this might appear as a temporary solution in the short run; in the long run, the organisational growth will be affected negatively (Kazi et al., 2012). The rate at which employee attrition is occurring everywhere has triggered both the managerial and academic interest, and so much interest has been placed into unravelling the cause. Understanding the cause of the increasing rate of employee attrition will assist the various organisation in channelling the right strategies to curb it. As alarming as the attrition issue is, it is expected to catch the interest of various researchers. Still, less than the expected research rate was found (Amankwaa and Anku-Tsede, 2015), especially in the non-profit sector. Sageer et al. (2012) made it known that employee satisfaction and retention aid the success of any organisation. Şahin (2011) Also explains that for retention to occur in an organisation, it will mean that its employees exhibit job satisfaction traits.

Other research has also shown that any establishment's success is based on its capability to maintain its skilled workers. This fact was deduced from a social circle basis regarding people's role in an organisation, organisational role towards its employee career development and the training available to improve employee's skills in the organisations (Sahin, 2011). These factors could be both internally and externally influenced by an organisation. If the working environment of an organisation is motivating and flexible in terms of task allocation, it encourages employees to use their skills and knowledge through dedicated participation to help drive such an organisation to success (Das and Baruah, 2013). WeiBo et al. (2010) explain that the reoccurrence of attrition in an organisation discourages new entrants of talented employees. Skilled employees prefer to work in an organisation that has a promising job security standard for retaining its staff. Mbah and Ikemefuna (2012) throw in more light by explaining that a positive form of turnover occurs when new entrants are accepted as a replacement for employees who had to leave regardless of the organisational ways of operating, but if the employees resigned due to lack of job satisfaction, then that is detrimental to such organisation. Medina (2012) explains employee turnover as a controlled ending of a relationship with an organisation by the employees. Several kinds of research have been carried out on the issue of attrition, but only a few studies analyse the cause because the reasons for attrition in various organisations vary. Thus, different strategies will work for different organisations and sectors. For example (Awan and Anjam, 2014) pinpoint that if employees receive more benefits from their organisation instead of conditional compensations, it will curb the rate of attrition. This idea is right except for the fact that different strategies work will work for different organisations because the cause of attrition in various organisations is not uniform. Sometimes attrition issues occur as a result of personal or domestic problems, which affect work-related tasks negatively, thus putting frustration on the job (Chang et al., 2010). The longer employees stay in an organisation, the less the level of attrition or turnover.

Turnover and attrition have some similarities; attrition always has an adverse effect on organisations because it denotes the reoccurring exit of employees, but turnover can be positive if the rate at which employees are leaving an organisation is low, especially in an involuntary process (Woon et al., 2017). One major disadvantage of employee attrition is the increase in workload for the remaining employees, which will impact their work performance drastically and impede the organisation's effectiveness. (Bacha, 2016) Also, mention that current staff in an organisation known for attrition will most likely work more hours as a result of the extra workload that would have been carried out by the workers who left. Such a situation will increase work stress levels, leading to low performance and frequent leave-permit requests by employees and encouraging more employees to resign if they cannot cope with the workload.

2.8.1. Causes of Employees Attrition

There will always be an increase in employee attrition if organisations employees keep complaining about job satisfaction or if such employees are having issues with the cultural way of doing things in an organisation. Being unhappy is not the only reason for attrition; skilled employees always see the need for promotion, recognition and, most likely, reward. If these are not forthcoming in an organisation after putting in so much work effort, the skilled employees will be discouraged and most likely leave for a better organisation with considerable work benefits, recognition and career prospect. It is paramount for organisations to acknowledge their employee's skills and efforts as this will improve their satisfaction level with the organisation (Omonijo et al., 2015). Some of the issues that lead to employee attrition are organisational stability, employee pay level, and the organisation's industry.

Organisational Stability

Organisations that report a high level of instability are prone to record more reoccurrence of employee attrition (Hausknecht and Trevor, 2011).

Organisational instability is one of the primary reasons for attrition. If an organisation's aims and objectives do not align well with their activities and changes keep occurring, the employees of such organisation will be left frustrated, thus leading to attrition. Most employees will prefer to work in an organisation with a clear direction of its objective (Khan, 2014).

Pay Structure

A strong connection exists between employers and employees when it comes to pay structures because this helps the organisations to brainstorm decisions that will aid the achievement of their set objectives and plans (Al-Zawahreh and Al-Madi, 2012). This connection includes inter and external equity. External equity is the means by which various top management earns closely related wages even though they work in different organisations. For any organisation to remain competitive and not lose its skilled employees, it has to understand the deserving pay for such employees, and this can be derived by understanding the pay structure of other organisations. Internal equity means the level of pay structure amongst employees working in the same organisation. When employees know that an organisational internal and external equity level is biased and not just, they tend to leave such an organisation for a more fulfilling one (Al-Zawahreh and Al-Madi, 2012).

Industry

Another primary reason for attrition is the industry in which an organisation operates. Working in an industry that does not have many prospects for development discourages employees from staying (Taplin, Winterton, & Winterton, 2003). For example, when the blackberry business was going down, most of its employees started looking for employment in other technology manufacturing companies. The information technology industry is growing very fast, and any IT organisation that cannot provide its employees with the needed and adequate infrastructure will lose them to other organisations with good infrastructures in place because employees want to grow in their careers and area of expertise.

2.9. Employee Retention

Bisht et al., 2016 described retention as the entirety of activities targeted at encouraging employees to stick to an organisation, coupled with different opportunities for growth. Employee retention is identified as the opposite of voluntary and involuntary turnover (Hom et al., 2017). According to Bisht et al.,

2016 having dedicated employees is crucial for the survival of an organisation, which was also supported by Chandio et al., 2013, having a strong team of a devoted and creative group of workers is indispensable to preserve their brand uniqueness which will place the organisation in a more competitive position. Therefore, organisations must design apt methods to keep hold of their quality employees.

Studies by some authors like Priyasad and Weerasinghe, 2017 identified that employees often mentioned factors like salary above the market rate, warm working environment, good work interaction and job security as reasons for them to remain in an organisation.

Based on Herzberg's motivator-hygiene theory, several factors lead to employee happiness; these are hygiene and motivator factors. Hygiene factors are transient. They do not give long-term contentment but are still essential for employee contentment; they describe the system of the workplace and signify the inherent needs that are to be met (Sanjeev and Surya, 2016). Hygiene factors include but are not limited to a competitive salary, health care plans, safe working environment, modern work equipment, good relationship with other employees and overall job security. While motivator factors are directly related to work, they inspire workers to do more and become high achievers. These factors are called satisfiers, and they include receiving well deserved praise and accolades for a job well done; this serves as an additional reward as the employee feels valued and appreciated (Sanjeev and Surya, 2016). The role and workspace should be challenging yet encouraging with a manager or boss that leaves room for employee growth and creativity, amongst others are viewed as additional benefits. The cost associated with losing capable employees is high, and as such, companies identify retention as a critical component of achieving their all-encompassing plan to maintain and better their service delivery (Khoele and Daya, 2014).

According to Zopiatis et al., 2014, employee retention has gained more significance than before because the cost associated with losing valuable members of staff and hiring an equally good replacement is high. They went further to state that this cost is also borne by companies that do have skilled employees present because a good retention plan affects the image, public perception and overall profit of the company.

Research has shown that having and keeping a loyal and dedicated staff is essential for the achievement of set goals by firms. Therefore, companies need to devise and develop tactics to retain their staff as much as they can (Islam et al., 2018). These range from complimentary care packages (like lunch) to maintaining a good work-life balance. Organisations that cannot retain and preserve the quality of their staff will appear as under-productive, which will, in turn, affect their market placement, brand perception and consequently their profit generation (Kossek et al., 2018).

Ahsan et al. (2016) stated that employees change work very often, as often as six years. As a result, it is crucial for firms to minimise the rate at which staff members resign (Tatlah et al., 2017). Idris (2014) argues that the aim of retention policies should be to discover and hold on to steadfast employees for as long as the partnership is lucrative for parties involved, it is classed into functional; a case where the high achieving employees remain in the firm's employ while the non-performers go, this is good for the overall performance of the firm and dysfunctional; which is the opposite and has an adverse effect on the ability of the firm (Harhara et al., 2015).

Likewise, Al Mamun and Hasan (2017) cited that firms attempt to create a good work environment with proper remuneration that makes leaving unnecessary for their employees. Wong et al., 2015 mentioned that leaving and staying with a firm are on the opposite sides of the retention coin. According to Johara et al. (2018), there are different ways to ensure staff retention. Although different people stay for various reasons, it is up to the firm to find common ground to accommodate and ensure the retention of staff members. Mehta et al. (2014) stated that every company has to develop retention policies to suit its needs and fulfil the desired purpose. Sandhya and Kumar (2011) cited a significantly positive relationship between a less rigid work environment and organisational responsibility, hence a good chance of employee retention.

Klijn and Tomic (2010) stated that employers have to be innovative in creating a growth-enabling, work-friendly environment and also have to devise a reward system aside from the already agreed upon salary; for instance, recognition award paid vacation for a job well done, amongst others to incentivise and stimulate the need to do more.

Although it was argued that employees leave for various reasons, some reasons are controlled or determined by the employee (for example, going for higher pay), and others might be beyond control (long-term sickness, family-related issues, amongst others). Organisations should have a plan in place to find out the reasons that might be work-related and prevent reoccurrence in the future (Branham, 2012).

Ghosh et al. (2013) opined that the departure of staff members could be functional or dysfunctional. It is functional when underachieving or underperforming staff resigns and dysfunctional when the active team leaves. The functional exit of staff is good for business as it creates room for welcoming better replacements and encourages improvement. The dysfunctional leaving aspect is bad for organisations as it affects operations negatively. The dysfunctional exit of employees may sometimes be caused by reasons that can be avoided on the part of the employers; for example, increasing pay, improving the work environment, among others, while other times it is unavoidable, that is, perhaps death.

A high level of retention is suitable for any business and is one of the ways by which organisations get to achieve results. A low retention level leads to poor performance and increases costs; it generally has an adverse effect on organizational success (Ahammad et al., 2016). Other researchers argue that low retention rates affect the profit-making abilities of firms. Also, retention affects the quality of service provided (Davis, 2013; Khan et al., 2011). Furthermore, low retention prevents business development, and the cost associated makes the firm lose its competitive edge and possibly its customer base. To avoid this, employers should pay attention to prevent losing valuable staff (Hancock et al., 2013).

Voluntary turnover of staff, according to some authors, is a reflection of the level of managerial competence or otherwise because it usually occurs when staff members are not satisfied with their work environment and opts for an available alternative (Nica, 2016). Hence, Griffith et al. (2000) developed a model that explains work satisfaction and external factors that eventually lead to retention or attrition. External factors like demographics (quantifiable characteristics of the people or population around, like their way of life, societal views on issues and reception of outsiders or strangers) or factors that depend on the environment (like weather or atmospheric conditions-people tend to migrate to places that have more conducive environment), these factors combined affect the retention rate of firms.

According to research reported by CIPD in 2015, one primary reason for leaving an organisation is mostly because of an opportunity to grow provided by a new firm in terms of being employed in a higher position than their previous employment. Improving employee involvement and communication is a lucrative means of retaining employees by employers, followed by increased learning and development; enhancing HR skills was the least reported method employed by firms to preserve and maintain their staff strength. Deloitte, in

2004, explained three means for retaining staff; develop, deploy, and connect. The employers refine the skills of their employees by organising skill advancement workshops and training; deployment involves helping the employees develop and harness their skills with different job requirements, while connection means making available the different assistance needed for building cordial relationships both in and outside the firm.

Organisations can increase retention rates by practising good recruitments and selection processes, by recruiting based on competence, conducting staff surveys and making use of resulting data to manage staff and know why staff leave or stay, being clear on what staff should expect at the point of employment, also employers should first advertise vacant positions internally (Chan and Kuok, 2011).

Retention rate, as stated earlier, is a direct reflection of the level of competence and the extent of managers' knowledge in an organisation. A low retention rate might result from low satisfaction of staff members, which leads to high cost of selection and training, leading to poor customer satisfaction and generally low organisational performance (Anzazi, 2017).

The level of retention is also the result of an experience with a firm, which can imply that a high rate of employee retention means that the staff members are satisfied with their firm. In contrast, the opposite is said to be true in the case of low retention (James and Mather, 2012). Consequently, there have been a lot of studies using retention as a means of identifying the success of some organisational procedures and understanding these processes and retention factors like selection, training, mentoring, amongst others, help firms develop the optimum combination of the elements to reduce cost while increasing morale, on the job satisfaction and all-round productivity (Sandhya and Kumae, 2011). Although, over time, there have been various theories and models developed to understand retention better, the majority of them are based on the hypothesis that an unhappy staff member will look for and accept another job (Mowday et al., 2013). Therefore, most retention models focus on job productivity and dedication.

Human resource is crucial to the success of an organisation, coupled with having staff members who have similar ideas with values and share in the company's vision propels the company for the overall success (Boxall and Purcell, 2011). This means employing qualified and seasonal experts is only a part and a step toward the right direction; however, creating and supporting a dedicated and loyal staff base is likely to be achieved by implementing a good human resource network (Lin et al., 2012).

Though expensive when implemented correctly, good human resource strategies and facilities aid favourable outcomes. If there is a good connection between the employees and their employers, such firms would have employees that are able and willing to do more for the firm. Although the cost incurred by firms with low retention is high, firms now embrace practices and strategies that lead to good retention (Chiboiwa et al., 2010).

According to some research (For example, "Boxall et al., 2003; Iverson and Buttigieg, 1999; Malhotra et al., 2007; Meyer and Allen, 1991; Meyer and Smith, 2000; Mowday et al., 1982; Mueller and Price, 1990"), it has been established that some significant work factors determine job fulfilment, organisation's obligations and retention among employees.

When high achieving staff members are underpaid in an organisation, they seek validation outside the firm and end up leaving the firm (Singh and Loncar, 2010). Iqbal (2010) explains some of the factors that encourage an increase in employees' will to remain in an establishment, for example, restrictions in terms of age, job content, and overall satisfaction. From the summary of various research done on retention, job satisfaction, intention to remain or leave, and organisational obligations are amongst the most stated reasons for leaving or staying with a firm and the most researched. Job satisfaction is described as a combination of the components that make an employee content with a career or job (Aziri, 2011). Kwenin et al. (2013) stated job satisfaction as the primary reason for leaving an organisation and a significant cause or determinant of retention because job satisfaction is what translates to a smooth work experience, that is, satisfaction with colleagues and managers. When considered further, a content employee who is well paid will be loyal to the job process and the organisation (Mahal 2012).

Conversely, researchers like Liu et al. (2010) argued that there exists an indirect connection between job satisfaction and retention. The study explained that if workers are not pleased with their jobs, the fault rests on the company's managers, which will lower staff dedication to work and lead to the loss of qualified hands and staff members. This argument was supported by authors like ("Kim and Jogaratham, 2010; Aydogdu and Asikgil, 2011"), all of whom stated that job fulfilment strongly affects retention.

High job satisfaction equals high retention; generally, unhappy employees are more likely to quit when compared to satisfied employees. Voon et al. (2011)

reported that giving the employees a chance to skate freely without fear of reprimand or consequence by handing out and conducting surveys is a good way of appraising job satisfaction and providing room for improvement. The organisational obligation is another factor that has been linked with retention asides from job satisfaction. That is, the sense of duty from the staff to the organisation (Perryer et al. 2010). Lack of obligation or commitment to an organisation has an indirect and significant relationship with retention; this was supported by some authors (Newman et al., 2011; Lumley et al., 2011).

The organisational obligation has a more substantial effect on retention intention than fulfilment from the job (Shen and Jiuhua, 2011). Karatepe (2012) also stated that workers who are loyal and dedicated to their employers would be more intrigued to stay in their firm compared to those who are uncommitted. Other factors that affect retention include restriction policies, workspace environment, work-life balance; in a study carried out by (Chimote and Srivastava, 2013), most of the respondents mentioned that the lack of stability between their personal life and work-life has a significantly high adverse effect on their decision towards staying with an organisation.

Nawab and Bhatti (2011) studied and realised that an effective compensation strategy is a significant factor in ensuring retention. Other factors stated by Yang et al. (2012) include lack of career growth opportunities, unmet expectations, harassment, discrimination, inadequate managerial personnel (poor supervision), job insecurity, the divergence of ideas and vision, no extra benefits for a job done, better opportunities, amongst others.

According to Deery and Jago (2015), retention directly relates to productivity; the more hands-on deck in a firm, the more work will be done and achieved. Kabungaidze et al. (2013) studied retention using the following factors: age, gender, education, contract, and income level (demographic factors), availability of another job opportunity (external and uncontrollable factors), nature of job, remuneration, duty to the organisation, and managerial expertise in terms of supervision (controllable elements).

Laureani and Antony (2010) listed a couple of reasons behind voluntary staff exit from firms; some of which include but are not limited to – conflict of interest, under-appreciation, lack of supervision, low pay, lack of benefits, lack of fulfilment, absence of growth opportunities, no work-life-family balance, underutilisation of staff, impracticable expectations, absence of job security, amongst others.

2.10. Employee Retention in Non-Profit Organisations

NPOs, like private and public sectors, face the dilemma of employee retention; the rate of attrition is one of the factors that hinder the achievement of its set goals and objectives (Hafiza et al., 2011).

Different employee retention methods employed by firms in the public and private sectors may have little or no effect on retaining employees in NPOs. Also, the reasons for applying to work in a non-profit organisation differ from that of applying to a private or public firm. So, creating an environment that can be likened to that of a profit-oriented firm may have no effect on retaining employees. Training and appreciating employees plus a creative approach to solving problems and providing services are some of the ways that ensure retention (Goulet and Frank, 2002).

The sense of contributing to the achievement of a laudable cause is one of the reasons for working with an NPO, not the financial remuneration, as most NPOs offer less than the profit-oriented companies can offer (Bang et al., 2012), so the success of a non-profit organisation is dependent on its human resources and their expertise coupled with their dedication to the cause (Drucker, 2012). According to Vinokur-Kaplan (1994), employees of NPOs usually stay employed in an organisation that is achieving its set goals and objectives, and if the results achieved are in line with what was intended.

Employees in non-leadership positions leave at a faster or quicker rate than those employed in a leadership capacity, and according to (Watson and Abzug, 2005), this requires extra attention as the cost associated with replacing these staff members is high because they need training and an adjustment period which can lower self-esteem and consequently cost the NPO more than expected.

(Christenen and Rog, 2008) opined that NPOs should not be out to employ the highly referred hands but rather to establish harmony between the employees and employers so that workers will be willing to stay. Watson and Abzug (2005) termed this creating ‘fit and embeddedness’. Compatibility between organisational goal and value has a productive influence on organisational retention capabilities. The career success for the staff in cases where such consonance does not exist leads to the loss of employees, and it gives the organisation an image of less significance which may lead to problems with donors and sponsors. To avoid such from happening, employers must make conscious efforts to develop a harmonious environment (Borzaga and Tortia, 2006).

The synergy between the ideas and values of employers and their employees is the motivation behind staff staying with an organisation, as stated by Brown and Yoshioka (2003). Employees that enjoy what they do and buy into the vision of the NPOs require little supervision and go the extra mile in service delivery. Moreover, excellent service delivery attracts more donors who will help fulfil the organisation's objectives.

2.11. Employee Retention Strategies

According to Akingbola (2006), NPOs can better retain staff if the following strategies are implemented and practised; taking time to introduce new recruits into the system and develop a sense of belonging, clear outline of the duties of members of staff, creating a career advancement plans and opportunities, avoid rigidity in the work environment and introduce the concept of mentoring/mentorship.

Most employers become worried if one of their best employees leaves for no just cause. Attrition of key employees always creates challenging situations for employers (Goswami and Jha, 2012).

In addition to the fact that they must discover a substitute for such a gifted employee, it might be challenging to accomplish this due to the high demand for skilled workers. However, such an employer needs to put into consideration the effect this situation might have on fellow employees (Goswami and Jha, 2012).

In most cases, when an employee leaves an organisation, their colleagues try to analyse why such employee leaves (Thwala et al., 2012). Some of the employees might even start to nurse the idea of searching for a new job. Due to this fact, all employers need to prioritise retention and job satisfaction strategies (Li et al.,2016).

Research demonstrates that many fresh recruits quit their jobs after a few months of joining (Mishra, 2007). However, human resources and most organisation management steps in whenever this keeps reoccurring.

If potential workers do not expect to remain with the organisation, it will be a difficult task to maintain an active business. Most organisations spend at least 20 per cent of an employee's salary on recruiting a new employee to fill in vacant roles left by skilled workers (Tracy and Hinkin, 2006). In any case, the disadvantage of losing a skilled workforce will have a considerable impact on an organisation compared to the money spent (Ongori, 2007). Aside from the financial constraints attached to losing an employee, the organisation will also feel the impact of the attrition due to experience gathered from the old employee's usual contribution and, in some cases, the clients he attracted to such organisation (Mohr et al., 2012).

Listed below are some of the strategies that aids retention in most organisations

In other to have a successful retention strategies technique in place, it is crucial to consider situations from the employee's point of view. Individual employees are unique in their ways and have different needs. In any case, every one of them feels the need to be valued by their employees.

They need to be tested and energised by their work, coupled with great pay as a form of appreciation. To retain and connect with employees, organisations should genuinely care about their employees. No strategies will defeat an absence of compassion or appreciation toward employees.

Great start with informed direction: All fresh recruits should be aimed up for progress from the beginning (James and Mathew, 2012). The recruitment method should clarify what an employee's aim should be and shed light on the organisation's practice and ways of doing things, coupled with how they can contribute and flourish in the organisation (Chan and Kuok,2011). This process should be put into consideration from the onset because it will be a form of guidance for all employees (Sandhya and Kumar, 2011). Employee retention strategy should be considered during the recruitment process by explaining clearly in the job application what is expected from an individual and what the organisation has to offer (Nicholson et al., 2011). This strategy will help narrow down the number of qualified employees in the selection process while influencing the formal interview, where the expectations and offer will be reinforced again for in-depth understanding. Utilising psychometric evaluation devices during the employment process will assist selection representatives in ensuring that the applicant's conduct and competency will align well with the organisation's goals and expectations (Sangeetha, 2010). It is effortless for any organisation to strive in its industry if suitable candidates are selected. Organisation goals will be met, and employees will also be satisfied, thus encouraging them to stay long-term (Sangeetha, 2010).

Pointers to choose the right employees: A brief but in-depth introduction about the job requirement, development plans, pay scale, and the organisation culture before starting the recruiting procedure would help kickstart attracting the right candidate for a role (Craig, 2015). Some of these pointers will help in determining the right candidates that will stay long term in an organisation One of these pointers is paying attention to how long these candidates remain in their previous place of work. Pay attention to their loyalty, determination and commitment to their past organisation (Cloutier et al., 2015). The recruitment process should also analyse their experience and understanding of teamwork both at their previous place of work and personal life. That can help disclose that they dedicate their efforts and resources to whatever interests them. Hiring candidates that keep changing jobs might not be a wise decision because such candidates might be challenging to please, let alone retained long term (Lehmann et al., 2012)

Professional Guidance: Assigning a knowledgeable member of staff to mentor a new intake will give an excellent start for new employees (Waterman et al., 2011). This strategy will provide a warm gesture to new employees and make new employees feel welcomed. New employees will learn from their senior colleagues while sharing their fresh perspectives to help grow the organisation (Latham et al., 2011). An excellent mentorship program should be in place, and this will guide employees on how things work in the establishment and get to understand the organisation's vision (Hallam et al., 2012). Considering these, they will be able to consistently absorb the current work culture. Some research explains that it takes a while for a new employee to be ultimately profitable in their new job (Baron and Morin, 2010). On a more extensive scale, a great job onboarding plan connects recruits to their colleagues from day one, which might be the beginning of a substantial learning curve (Allen and Shanock, 2013).

Worker's Pay: For any organisation to maintain its competitive edge in retaining key employees, it is a necessity to not only pay their staff well but also give them generous bonuses (Osibanjo et al., 2014). That incorporates pay rates, rewards, medical insurance and pension packages. These packages should be explained to all new employees from the get-go (Michael et al., 2016). Employers can also be helpful to their employees by providing services that will make them feel more comfortable in the organisation, for example, availability of lunches, discounted gym membership and the like. Employees feel elated when given access to different benefits at their place of work (Ahmad et al , 2013). To maintain retention status in an organisation, employers can think outside the box by offering unique benefits like stock options, monetary awards and many more to encourage their employees (Ahmad et al., 2013).

Regarding employee retention, money is not all that matters, considering competitive pay can make employees feel that their efforts and time are being appreciated (Msengeti and Obwogi, 2015). Employees need to realise their remuneration is realistic enough with what other people who perform comparative work are getting. Paying low pay rates implies that most skilled workers are less likely to stay in the organisation (Scott et al., 2012). Every organisation should implement things that can fulfil the needs of their employees. Investment opportunities, Adaptable planning and other financial benefits, childcare, gym membership, wellness coaching and sabbaticals are apparent advantages (Yamamoto, 2011). Employers should request employees' feedback in other to learn more about the benefits that would genuinely improve their quality of life. Alternatively, organisations should also focus on what will motivate different employees; for example, the younger employees might want a different form of benefits compared to the older generation (Sandhya and Kumar, 2011).

Employee's Health: Making sure employees are keeping fit both physically and intellectually is a great strategy; this process will also help employees perform excellently in their role, which is excellent for any organisation (Sears et al., 2013).

Correspondence and criticism: Maintaining an open correspondence is a conventional method for depicting a training that is fundamental to employee retention (Cloutier et al., 2015). Employees should find it easy to share their thoughts and concerns and be able to ask questions in return for a clear and concise response (Cloutier et al.,2015). If clarifying issues as soon as possible is prioritised, it will make it easy to achieve organisational goals.

Employees feel safe if they are heard in an organisation (Olckers et al., 2012). This sense of belonging makes them more committed to their job and organisation. Laying the foundation of employee involvement from day one also helps attracts the right candidates. For example, IBM sets a genuine model here as they get the recruits acquainted with their leaders on their first day and allow the recruits to have a feel of the organisational culture (Dabirian et al.,2017). Employers should initiate policies that will enable employees to lodge their complaints freely regardless of the position of the complainant and the person causing the issue (Sandhya and Kumar, 2011).

Twitter's onboarding custom is also exceptional, which incorporates an advanced engaging procedure for the fresh recruit. They give the new employees fundamentals like email ID, shirts, refreshments, and breakfast with the CEO alongside a tour through the workplace before they get down to their jobs' principal activities.

Employers should understand the benefit of constructive criticism because if employees receive destructive criticism, it demoralises them and affects their future efforts in the organisation (Singh et al., 2013). Issues that are not in any way serious can also be ignored by employers to give the employees a sense of importance towards issues that are crucial to the organisation. Constructive criticism encourages employees to do better at their work, and it also allows them to perceive criticism as a means to grow (Thompson, 2011). Constructive criticism can be used as a strategic tool in retaining employees if used right. Employees need adequate feedbacks in other to improve and accomplish their possible best especially positive and valuable criticism (Tran et al., 2012). Positive feedback ought to be offered often to encourage employees with the required assurance that will help them accomplish their best work. In any case, corrective and constructive feedback is essential as well, especially when there is a need to address an issue or concern (Whitaker et al., 2012).

Employers should become more mindful of the number of negative remarks they are pointing out to employees in comparison to positive remarks (Van and Kluger, 2011). Move the ratio towards at least six times more positive remarks to each negative remark. Staff members' morale does improve significantly when they find it safe to speak their minds, address misunderstandings, share their ideas and other issues, and engage in organisation development (Hartmann et al., 2010). Employers should make sure all their leaders are always open, transparent, and maintain a respectful means of communication, and encourage this behaviour in everyone involved (Fernandez, 2011). One of the advantages of such practices is that it aids the establishment of trust in the top management, which is a crucial component to maintain employees' satisfaction.

Yearly Audits: Organisations should not overlook yearly auditing as this will help analyse employee performance and examine the organisation's long- and short-term goals (Cascio, 2014). The auditing process also allows employers to discuss future progress with their employees. Organisations should learn not to make unrealistic promises to their staff because failure to fulfil such promises might affect the trust employees have for the organisation (James and Mathew, 2012). At times employees lack a clear understanding of their role requirements, organization form of assessment, and company policies. This creates an immense unsettling drive in them and crushes their morale to the point that employees feel encouraged to search for employment somewhere else (Arora, 2012).

This issue can be solved by communicating with employees, ensuring they understand their job roles, how their performance is being assessed, transparent company policies, and regular feedback (Nagabhaskar, 2014).

Career Advancement: Giving employees the required training in other to help them advance in their various fields should be a necessity for organisations (Alias et al., 2014). Most organisations do this by paying for seminars and short courses for their employees. Further studies paid for by employees are also a strategic means of achieving this. Every employer should make investing in their employees a priority (Foday, 2014). For any organisation to compete effectively in its industry, it has to give its employees the required skills and chances to learn new things and explore their range of abilities.

Organisations should learn to align employees' career advancement needs with organisational requirements (Chen, 2014). From that point forward, recognise the essential abilities and skills that will help achieve business goals by connecting employees' abilities and the additional skill needed for progress. It would be great if organisations could have an in-depth conversation with their employers in other to understand their plan for career progression and see if it can be achieved (Foday, 2014). In the process of career advancement, if an employee feels reluctant to accept a new role, they have capabilities for, the organisation should try to understand such employee situations and let them maintain their current role if that will make them more comfortable. Numerous companies help people outside of their organisation and do not provide continuous training or proper training for their staff members. As a result, employees who cannot see progression in view become less motivated and more inclined to leave (Cascio, 2014). Continuous training keeps employees anticipated, thus making them feel valued. Due to a clear and existing path for growth, employees would feel accepted and a part of the organisation's success (Chen, 2014). Leaders are in a place of authority. They should demonstrate the willpower to encourage employees out of their comfort zone, give them challenging but exciting tasks while providing the necessary support and resources to help achieve them, and acknowledge and appreciate their efforts.

Although many organisations state they appreciate creativity, they usually lack the required policies and platform to showcase it.

For example, Google has a program whereby employees are allowed the chance to take a self-dedicated project to show their creativity. Creativity can also be achieved if organisations can practice diversity in their hiring process (Bryd, 2014). Having employees with different beliefs and knowledge will have a positive impact on the organisation's goals. Employers who invest in their workers will give their employees the chance to broaden their knowledge and acquire new skills, which is an excellent form of investment for both the organisation and its employee (Dabalr et al., 2014). In addition, most employees attached their job fulfilment to the platform organisations gives for career progression (Kibui et al., 2014). One of the ways of investing in employees is by paying for them to attend educative seminars or conferences, offering educational cost-free or flexible repayment schemes, encouraging an in-house mentoring program and so on (Nagabhaskar, 2014).

Effort Acknowledgement and Reward: All individuals feel the need to be acknowledged and appreciated for their efforts (Tarera and Ngirande, 2014). Acknowledgement encourages people to do more and better; making this a culture in an organisation encourages employees' zeal to work harder. Extensive and little efforts should be appreciated (Alfandi and Alkahsawneh, 2014). Organisations should ensure that when demonstrating any form of gratitude towards an employee, they should clarify how the employee's role impacts the organisation positively (Abstein and Spieth, 2014). Various methods of reward programs can be put in place to encourage employees' efforts.

Promoting deserving employees plays a substantial role in making them feel appreciated and the need to put in more effort in their role with a longevity plan (Osibanjo et al., 2014). Every promotion is always supported with more training and career advancement, which is another form of strategy to make employees stay long term. Employers should ensure their employees are treated decently while ensuring they acknowledge their employee's contribution and the effort they put into the organisation's growth (Saleem and Affandi, 2014).

Work-life Balance: Work-life balance usually has a strong influence on individual mental health. A great work-life balance would be an effective strategy for retention (Maphanga, 2014). Employees will be happy to know that their jobs will not hurt their lives outside of work. Anticipating that staff should consistently work for an extended period and be available even outside work hours will deter their passion for working efficiently (Balakrishnan, 2014). A stable work-life balance is essential, and individuals need to realise that their employers comprehend they have lives outside of work. Organisations should Urge their employees to take some time off when necessary and offer opportunities for vacations (Sorensen and Mckim, 2014). Organisations should always take note of exhausted staff members and give significant breaks when necessary. Alternatively, practice getting everyone out of the office for a walk. Assess how organisation schedules affect employees' work-life balance (Idris,

2014). Employees will not have the desire to stay longer if they are continually overworked. In other to achieve this, organisations should try and make sure their employees are not overburdened with workloads (Kar and Misra, 2013). Employers should urge their team members to prioritise reasonable workloads and work-life balance and ensure leaders demonstrates these practices as well, so employees feel comfortable following by example (Coetzee and Stoltz, 2015). Most organisations fear a profitability down plunge if employees do not work twice as hard on their workloads. Research suggests that working less can result in considerably more significant results and profitability (Sushil, 2013).

Flexible Working Hours and Conducive working Environment: Organisations can encourage retention by giving their employees the opportunity of flexible working hours (Idris, 2014). Doing so makes employees feel in charge of their schedule, which helps reduce stress and improve productivity. In addition, if employees are given enough time to recharge their energy, it gives them more energy and zeal to do better at their work, and this can be achieved through enough in between breaks while at work (Grobler and De Bruyn, 2012). Some organisations do so by offering working from home opportunities for a few days of the week to their employees (Idris, 2014).

Employees strive better in a pleasant working environment. If the work environment is not conducive, most employees will be discouraged and opt for better organisations with a better working environment; this can be a result of toxic leaders and relationships or the physical environment itself, i.e., the infrastructure (Kossivi et al., 2016). Dirtiness and clutter are diverting. Furthermore, if people sense danger, they might find it difficult to concentrate on their job (Bibi et al., 2018).

Employees will be spending most of their weekdays or more in the office. As a result, a conducive working environment should be a priority.

Risk appraisal can be carried out in other to navigate through this and unravel possible problems while prioritising health and safety. Even though this study is about employee retention and attrition, it is essential for employers to relinquish employees that are harassing their colleagues or lack cooperation while disrupting the organizational progress (Serbin, 2013).

Lately, employees have now prioritised the need for respect at their respective places of work, and they do not want to be put down or treated badly in their organisations (Sandhya and Kumar, 2011).

According to the CEB's Quarterly Global Labour Market research, people search for the factors below in their organisation-

Stability, remuneration, respect, benefits towards well-being, and work_life balance are some of the major factors job seekers look forward to in their new roles (Garavan et al., 2012).

Organisation Transformation: Organisation requires some changes or transformation at a point in time. Organisations should learn the importance of carrying their employees alongside whenever any form of transformation occurs. For example, if a merger occurs, the organisation should inform its employees as soon as possible to avoid getting wrong information from an external source (Mendes and Stander, 2011) Crucial information can be passed through group meetings, if not individually. Change might be unavoidable, even though it might be challenging. Organisations might see the need to present new ideologies and processes in their organisations to stay afloat in regard to development or to reinforce quality (Knight, 2014).

Employees' mentality can be affected negatively by companies going through many changes at a time (Hussein and Rehman, 2013).

Most employers see their employees as tough individuals who has the ability to adjust when necessary. However, without preceding communication, particularly concerning the state of their roles, employees can start to lose confidence in the organisation (Hussein and Rehman,2013).

Numerous establishments have discovered that it's better to introduce changes one after the other instead of implementing too many changes at a time.

Cultivating Cooperation: In situations where employees work in a group, employers should ensure that every member of the group contributes their ideas without making any one of the members feel irrelevant (Brunetto et al., 2013). Individual work should also be encouraged by the organisation. This form of strategy will increase the feeling of relevance in employees, thus intriguing them to stay (Hussein and Rehman, 2013). Employee engagement is setting aside time to connect with employees. Employee engagement can dramatically affect the viability of any organisation (Bhat and Bharel, 2018).

At the point when an organisation's workforce feels connected, it gives them a reason to help. Moreover, it assists the employees to cut out a niche in their area of expertise, which encourages them to perceive the way they add value to the organisation (Balakrishnan et al., 2013).

Organisations can draw the best out of their workforce by permitting employees to communicate and give suggestions, recognising their input, empowering them with necessary opportunities to grow and so on (Singh et al., 2016).

In an organisation where teamwork is encouraged and practised, organisational goals will be easily achievable. Encouraging teamwork in the working environment will assist organisations in accomplishing more than what individual employees would have accomplished separately. Team works give opportunities for shared thought and more different results (Nelsey and Brownie, 2012).

Recognising Employee's Achievements: Another essential retention strategy is recognising and celebrating employee achievements (Alnaqbi, 2011). For example, celebrating employees' anniversaries in the organisation or executed projects makes employees feel like an essential part of any organisation. Organisations can practice a culture whereby employees will be celebrated yearly for their efforts and contribution to the organisation (Schwartz et al.,2011).

Initiating Innovation: One other method of encouraging retention is by innovating information technology devices for collating data regarding employee satisfaction and needs anonymously (Lichtenthaler, 2011). Surveys will be sent out to employees to fill in anonymously. Acting on the employees' feedback from these data will not only make the company better but also make the employees feel valued (Cloutier et al., 2015). In situations where complaints or worries cannot be rectified, Organisations should try to communicate about them and not just ignore them (Sandhya and Kumar, 2011).

Pulling Results from Data Collated: Information gathered from the data collated can help give organisations an accurate idea of the willingness of attrition from its employees (Cascio, 2014). These results will help in taking precautionary measures early enough. The gathered information will also help organisations understand the factors leading to attrition and how they can be corrected.

For example, suppose most of the employees complain about commuting stress to their place of work. In that case, it might be wise for such an organisation to help with a more straightforward means of transportation (Hong et al., 2012). Alternatively, in a situation where most of the employees live far away from their families, a yearly package of all-expense-paid family travel can be the solution to making employees happy (Chege, 2016).

Have Backup Plan Towards Attrition: Sometimes, it is unavoidable to lose skilled workers. Due to this fact, it is always good for organisations to be ready for it, thus having a backup plan (Yang et al., 2012). An example of such a plan is making sure more than one primary employee is handling a significant role; just in case the primary employee leaves, there will be someone to take their place and keep it running (Oladapo, 2014). Organisations can also do this by including some protective measure clauses in their employment contract and giving enough time to find a replacement if the key employee must leave (Chen, 2019). Organisations that have these kinds of plans do not usually lose their shareholders and stakeholders because the business will continue to run as usual, and their efforts will not go unnoticed (Steingold, 2017).

Keep employees Inspired: Most employees value varieties. That is why it is so essential for employers to give their employee's varied tasks that would stimulate the employees intellectually with a platform for them to thrive in the organisation and their personal lives (Zaniboni et al., 2013). Social projects to encourage bonding between co-workers and a mutual vision for the company would give employees a sense of significance at work (Hutto, 2017). The degree of organisational relationship with its workforce directly corresponds to the organisation's potential for progress (Haider et al., 2015). Inspiration is a crucial segment that drives a specialist to perform sufficiently in any event (James and Mathew, 2012). To understand a candidate's inspiration, Mettl (2020) gives a thorough list that estimates motivation under three essential prerequisites:

Sustainability Needs: One of the critical approaches to persuade the workforce is by tending to their supportability needs. Fiscal sparks, such as wages and pay rates, rewards, retirement benefits, and more, fall under this class. According to a study, 89% of the organisations utilising monetary motivating forces achieve a certain motivation level.

Relatability Needs: It is the most evident method for inspiration if done at the ideal time with exceptional follow up. Acknowledging employees' contributions brings out the best in them, especially if a healthy competition culture is in order.

Growth Needs: The potential for development has a natural way of encouraging employees. When people are inspired, they tend to stay longer and work harder in an organisation. Making employees feel valued is a powerful means of encouraging retention.

Relationship Between Business Owners and Employees: Employers should maintain a certain level of relationship with their employees because this is one of the strategies for retention (Anis et al., 2011). Establishing such relationships would make it easy for employees to be open and articulate their needs and also helps employers in figuring out issues early enough (Das and Baruah, 2013). Excellent relationships with employees can be achieved without really crossing professional boundaries.

Employees tend to perform better in their roles if the management and their supervisors have earned their trust (Chitsaz-Isfahani and Boustani, 2014); this is because they are bound to accomplish the organizational set goals because of their confidence in the organisation and their superiors.

The absence of transparency in leadership communication usually leads to a high attrition rate in most organisations (Tillott et al., 2013).

Suppose an establishment does not have a program for employee engagement. In that case, there is a high chance that employees of such organisations might not trust the organisation as much as organisations might suspect they do (Adi, 2012). For any organisation hoping to earn their employee's trust, it is crucial to develop personal connections and trustworthiness and motivate the employees, give credit and give constructive criticism, and avoid being biased (Abraham, 2012). Nobody wants to feel excluded in their place of work. Employees want to feel they are being employed to fulfil a particular purpose and provide their services to help accomplish the organisational goals (Bhattacharya, 2015).

Employers should practice having conversations with all their employees independently or maintain an open-ended strategic meeting while soliciting each of their team members on their ideas and intake regarding their job in the organisation (Yoerger et al., 2015). Then, listen and take adequate notes of what they say.

Most organisations make a habit of conducting attrition related interviews only. However, not many of them set the same effort towards analysing why some employees choose to stay (Aruna and Anitha, 2015). Requesting from employees the reasons that compelled them to stay in an organisation is vital towards identifying strategies or policies that genuinely encourage employee retention and understanding if there are opportunities or ways to improve it. The main point is to prioritise this feedback, thus letting it influence internal organisation approaches.

2.12. The Identified Research Gap

The analysis of past studies helped in understanding the research gap. The literature review section gives detailed information on the effect employee attrition has on various organisation sectors and some of the ways it has been reduced, different models and theories were considered. Each of these theories and models focuses on its unique way of tackling employee attrition. Various theories and models must be implemented because one strategy might not solve all the employee attrition problems in an organisation. The research literature analysis aids this study to focus on the right questions to be answered to achieve enhanced employee retention and what research gap needs to be closed to achieve a positive result. The Herzberg and social exchange theory gives a depth understanding of the benefit of work-life balance on retention, and this can be achieved if the right leadership style is practised and employees enjoy job satisfaction (Dei Mensah, 2014). While Maslow and Herzberg focus on achieving internal needs, expectancy theory explains that people's motivation is what motivates their level of productivity (Parijat and Bagga, 2014). Equity theory focuses on the fact that employees are motivated if treated fairly (Muogbo, 2013).

The job embeddedness model also explains the importance of employing those whose goals and skills are in sync with what an organisation needs (Reitz et al., 2010). While the Job coupling model has the same stance as it emphasises the importance of having the right person with the right attitude for a job (Zheng et al., 2012).

Zinger's retention model explains the benefit of encouraging members of staff to be involved in decision-making and embrace them by making them feel like a massive part of the organisation (Kaur, 2017). This model also focuses on appreciating employees' efforts while rewarding them as required. The employee retention connection model explains the importance of good leadership, a reward system and the effect of introducing employees to varieties and not doing the same thing every day (Shahin, 2014). These theories and many more were considered in analysing the effect employee attrition has on organisations, especially the non-profit sector. Various organisations face employee attrition due to different reasons.

The role of human resources in retention was also emphasised because employees tend to stay in a working environment where excellent human resources practice is in vogue. After all, such organisations do not overburden their employees (Steward and brown, 2009).

The literature review helped discover that understanding the policies governing an organisation's sector is critical even though most researcher rarely discusses it. The researcher discovered that understanding the sector policy would help guide the implementation of the right retention strategies, and as a result, it became one of the research questions. Past studies also showcase the importance of knowing the root causes of employee attrition. It helps uncover the problem the organisations are facing and what retention strategies other organisations and the case studies have successfully implemented. This depth of knowledge made it easier for this study to focus on various research gaps and create a suitable strategic framework for employee retention in non-profits.

The literature review helped to unfold that there is limited research carried out on employee attrition regarding the non-profit organisation sector because most of the past literature focused on profit-oriented organisations. From the literature review, most of the theories and models focus on keeping employees happy to keep an organisation in a competitive state and increase the generation of profits and revenue. However, in the situation of NPO, which are not driven by profit earning, it is still essential for them to keep their employees to fulfil their aims and social responsibility. One of the factors all the theories and models have in common is the understanding that any organisation with high employee turnover would lose their valued employees and keep spending on recruitment and onboarding of new employees, which would affect the progress of such an organisation. As a result, bridging these research gaps for the non-profit organisation is very important.

Interestingly, models like Zinger's theory that focus on leadership are impactful in the NPOs. For any organisation to run successfully, it needs to be directed by a good leader or set of good leaders.

This study also focuses on two non-profit organisations in two different countries that have not been investigated before regarding employee attrition and retention through a comparative analysis.

2.13. Conclusion

This study literature review gave an in-depth insight into employee attrition and retention and their effect on organisations. Various theories and models were considered, which led to the analysis of various factors that causes employee attrition. It also helps identify the research gap by uncovering that there is limited research regarding employee attrition in the non-profit sector. It also helps discover that no employee attrition research or comparative analysis of the case studies used for this research has been attempted in the past. The required questions to be asked to get the proper responses for bridging the research gap become apparent in this chapter.

Chapter Three

3. Conceptual Framework

A conceptual framework helps provide an analytical process using various variations and contexts to organise ideas more compactly; a researcher can utilise a conceptual framework in a varied way (Leshem and Trafford, 2007). This study considered independent, moderating and dependent variables. This research section also established how career development and organisation culture influenced job satisfaction, economic environment and demographic factors leading to employee attrition or retention.

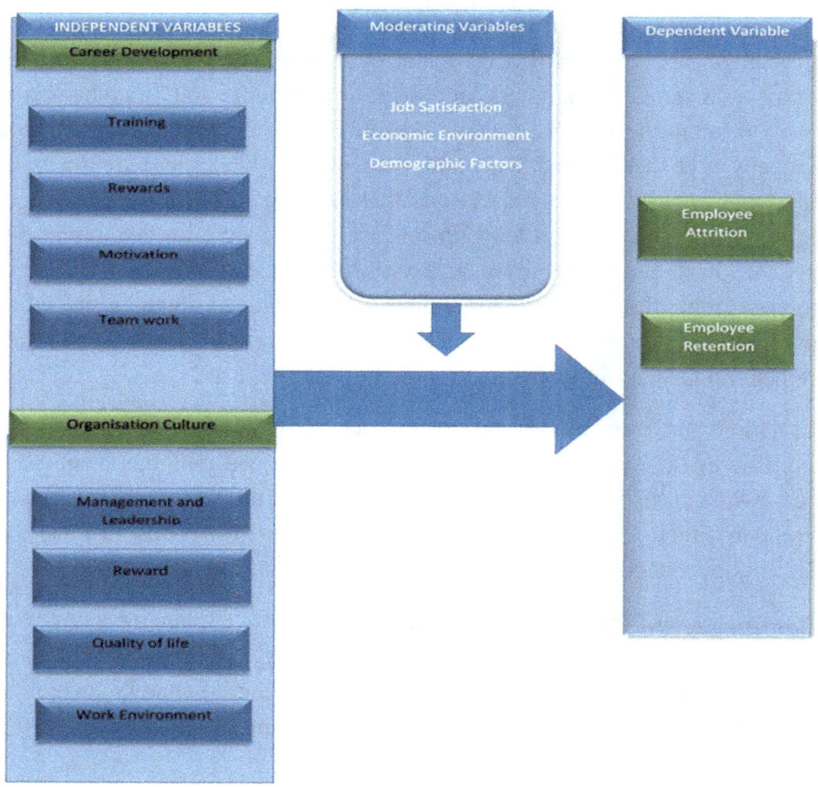

Figure 14: Conceptual Framework

3.1.Career Development

Direnzo et al. (2015) defined a career as the chain of job-related experience concerning evolution in the field chosen or profession, stability, and level of competence one has acquired over a period, usually a lifetime or most of it.

The modern economy has stressed the need for firms to be aggressive or competitive (Lyons et al., 2015); the ability to forecast improvement and advancement in technology enables firms to develop their workforce through education and vital activities. In addition, hiring and sustaining the staff members' skills is essential to the growth and profitability of firms (Mohan et al., 2015).

Opportunities should be given for the work base to grow, for establishments to develop, and it is essential to hire and retain skilled and experienced workers (Albrecht et al., 2015; Froehlich et al., 2014; George, 2015). Human capital development in terms of seminars and workshops for the staff members is a good way to retain the staff base and build self-esteem and confidence. It helps the company withstand difficult economic times; this is because a firm with dedicated and loyal staff members is one that can and would have employees willing to stay with it through hard times. Firms that invest in developing the capacity of their employees have more staff members remaining in their employment regardless of the opportunities available to them from other organisations. Employees who feel confident in their capabilities perform better and are better adjusted irrespective of the circumstance at hand.

A progressive firm in modern times is one that views human capacity development as an asset, not a liability; such firms use enlightenment as a resource, as the composition of its employees dictates the public perception of such company, including the overall competence of such firm, this is good for both the employers and employees (Kooji and Boon, 2018).

Akkermans et al. (2015) explain that having a well-laid plan for employee development, that is, hiring and developing staff on the job, reduces the cost of hiring new hands. Continually changing staff affects the company's image, as such is viewed as having a deficient administration and uncertainty about the direction the firm is heading.

Armstrong (2016) noted that career development is crucial for both employees and employers. The employer benefits from his investment in its employee in terms of better service rendered while the employee gets rewarded in terms of promotion or more money. Armstrong's suggestion was disagreed with by explaining that sometimes as employees advance in their careers, they may be required to possess more than just the basic knowledge as they move from one position to another or from one firm to another (Ahmed et al., 2016). The growth of businesses needs staff members that have information or knowledge that can help carve and hold onto the niche created; this will influence the profitability of the business positively (Ahmed et al., 2016).

Armstrong (2016) stated further that there is a need for employees to consistently and continuously seek ways to improve, particularly those holding managerial positions. Also, company heads should make sure they have an arrangement of some sort that tells what they expect their staff members to possess in terms of training, certificates and general progress as individuals.

Career development should be seen as an advantage that the progress accrued to a firm due to having people ready to work and grow to become good, focused and prepared managers. Career development is expected to occur throughout a person's life and mainly involves a comprehensive course throughout the business levels (Tirtha, 2017). It is based on individual worth, void of any bias. It was understood that when people know they have an equal chance of development at work, they do their best to advance in their chosen field (Ahmed et al., 2016). The combination of effort from the managers and the human resources helps assist in the aspect of employee career progression. These two groups of people are required to develop – the top managers; to make sure the office environment is one set to assist worker's development and such requirements are met, and the human resource manager; to provide career advancement information and opportunities (Mwanje, 2010). An organisation usually gets results based on the amount of work put into the process in terms of the company mission, projection and reward system. The map drawn for the advancement of the staff by the firm would not be practical if management consists of people who do not believe or see the need to advance in their careers (McDonnel, 2018). Giving a job out to be executed rather than have it done by staff members is no longer in style; it makes the development of workers difficult.

Stages of Career Development

Stage one of career development is the preparation for work; at this stage, individuals are hopeful of the work or career in a chosen field based on their educational background. The job chosen could also be based on information acquired about such a profession, not experience (Direnzo et al., 2015). There is a likelihood that the choice of the profession will change in the future. Here, firms are responsible for training their employees, equipping them with an education that makes them valuable in the business world (Patton and McMahon, 2014).

The next stage is entering the organization; Here, work-life has started, the character/individual knows what they want to do, and he has an idea of what his work life and career path would be like. The professional path to follow was chosen based on information gotten and experience. The ever-changing work environment disallows the use of knowledge attained from schools and books; instead, advice from senior members of the firm will be of more value.

Thirdly, the establishment as a young professional; there is a focus on the capabilities of the individual here, based on his familiarity with the work environment. Combining his values and knowledge gives confidence, while the career requirement poses a challenge that cannot be overlooked.

The fourth stages include the aspect of mid-career whereby the individual knows the extent of his knowledge and is more aware of his skills. He takes on more roles and is more involved in the decision-making activities at work. Despite doing so well at work, there is an apprehension of melancholy for ditching personal life for work. As a result, he does an evaluation of his choices which, according to Daniel Levinson (1977), affects the work, and the review has a minor effect on the concern felt by the individual. There tends to be more control over work and personal life.

The last stage of career development focuses on the late career. According to Levinson 1977, the individual has to plan for his retirement and has two main tasks despite maintaining his worth within the firm. He must prepare for another career after retirement. However, there may be situations where the organisation would require the services of an experienced person, except the person has health or personal issues (Low et al., 2016). If such an agreement exists, then it is suitable for both parties.

The stages of career development guide young professionals to plan their careers on their own as it contributes to their objectives and well-being even though the steps and sequence apply differently for people (Bailey et al., 2016).

The Significance of Career Development for the Organisation

To ensure employees stay with them, an organisation must strategise plans to develop its employees. To motivate employees, it is essential to invest in them; that way, the firm will have skilled and content employees. Working towards fulfilling a common goal is good for both the firm and its employees. While the organisation has the final say on how work should be carried out, it also needs to ensure that the work-life balance is in place. Because only a happy worker whose personal life is not threatened would go to any length for an organisation to attain success, in other to ensure adequate diversity in a firm, the firm has to ensure that opportunities are open to both the male and female gender and also that opportunities are given to the less competent staff members to prove their worth and improve on their skills, in doing that, every one of the staff or workforce would be committed to fulfilling the vision of the firm.

The Significance of Career Development to the Individual

One of the primary responsibilities of a person towards his career is to develop it successfully. A successful career results from setting individual goals and plans; the effect of achieving these individual goals is perceived as internal fulfilment. External fulfilment includes promotion, stable monetary rewards and remuneration. In developing a career, the path chosen is a significant factor, and conflicting values of the employee and employer may affect the parties involved. A good plan and clear career path are determined by the individuals since such individuals are liable to take charge of the direction of their work-life, as the external factors are also dependent on these decisions.

Employee and Employer Combined Effort Towards Career Development

A couple of factors contribute to the development of an employee's career, and there are some external factors over which the individual has no control. Company heads or human resource directors have to make career development a nonstop process that is not the sole responsibility of the individual alone but also that of the organisation, and in some cases, the organization has to bear some degree of responsibility towards developing its staff because the firm benefits from the advanced skills of the workforce (McDonald, 2005). Some forms of counselling and workbook are encouraged to be in place in organisations, and these serve as employee assistance programs. Investments in these activities reflect the quality of services they render.

The government also benefits from career development plans regarding increased tax; this is because a worker that is promoted due to his improved skill would be paid more and eventually pay more tax fees.

Employee Retention

For any Organisation to create and maintain its business, it relies on the retention of its employees. The failure of firms is mostly caused by the exit of many workers, which reduces the firm's output. Retaining quality staff members is essential for fulfilling the firm's purpose and providing value for investments (Kwenin et al., 2013). The decision to remain with a firm based on the value an organisation assigns to its employee's skill set makes such employees consider staying long term. Such a situation is usually an indication of the relationship between the employees and their employers, and this decision signifies the power the employee possesses. This power can make or mar the company since the company depends on the workforce to ensure that its customers get the most out of the services they offer. According to Sutherland and Jordan (2004), companies that develop strategic and effective ways of keeping their staff tend to lead the market. Employing and keeping skilled workers is very important to firms in low-income countries; by retaining their workforce, they avoid dealing with the scarcity that comes with the absence of such skills in years to come. In recent times, employers are considering competency while employing rather than loyalty. By doing this, employees were optimistic about gaining and applying such skills to the development of both themselves and the firm and also showed loyalty by remaining with the firm.

Firms or organisations that put the right strategies in place to aid the career advancement of their employees, firms are ensuring that there is no dearth in the skill required at a later point in time (George, 2015). Also, work owners need to change their requirements as time changes. The prospects of advancing in the chosen profession, in addition to the perks that come with it, are one of the primary reasons why employees choose to remain with a firm (Hossain et al., 2017).

Organisational and Individual Perspectives of Employee Retention

Generally, an increase in the level of interest in the makeup of the managerial positions of firms has been noticed. However, firms are also more interested in maintaining their place in the market and sustaining their customer base if not increasing it (Lyons et al., 2014); this can only be achieved by ensuring their staffs remain with them as well as keeping up with the change in technology.

In keeping up with changes in technology, companies have to expand on ensuring the advancement of their staff to ensure that they can keep up with the change. In addition, such a platform given to employees to build their careers provides them with a reason to work at remaining employable and relevant (Albrecht et al., 2015).

Demographically, there is a change in the competence and relevant composition of the population available for employment, the ones viewed as competent are a part of retirement age. In contrast, the young ones are inexperienced and need a lot of work before being considered experienced.

Lyons et al., 2014 also mentioned that losing competent staff through retirement makes it hard for firms to remain competitive because firms that find a way to keep their qualified staff remain competitive and are seen as maintaining their competitive edge in their industry (Mohan et al., 2015).

Top managers are the ones that practically direct the affairs of the company and are viewed as instrumental to the growth of the firm. Given that they are in short supply, companies need to be tactical in ensuring that the exit of these sets of people does not affect the running of the organisation. This is done through the efficient hiring of new hands and new staff that can understudy the managers and take over when they retire; by doing so, the firms can retain their consumer base and eventually make new clients (Gelens et al., 2015). The inability to remain competitive for some firms gave way to a reduction in their breaking new grounds in terms of market or customer base. However, some employees want their career to advance with different firms and, as such, their level of dedication to the job and the firm (Lyons et al., 2015; Mohan et al., 2015). This statement was supported by the studies carried out by SDWorx on a Belgian company; the overall turnover was 17.46 per cent, the turnover of the workforce below 25 years was 39% which indicated that they want their careers to develop with different firms, as against those employees above the 25 years (Demeulenaere et al., 2016) as a result of this, young employees want a wide range of options and choices; for this, firms have to be creative in retaining their employees. Many who have left their place of work did so with their expertise and skills leaving the firm inadequate to compete. Employees actively sought advancement in their careers for future gains, while top managers sought advancement in their careers due to the absence of such in their present employment (Rodgriguez et al., 2014).

The Influence of Career Development on Employee Retention

A good working environment is a major reason when it comes to retention, and staff members tend to stay when the work environment is encouraging and advantageous to the advancement of their careers (Sutherland, 2004). That kind of environment is created when the desires of the future and present staff are met, coupled with good relations between the staff members and the employers.

For career advancement to take place and have desired effect, an enabling environment has to be created by the firm for employees to put such skills, both old and newly acquired, to use (Mayes et al., 2017). Such employees are ever in demand by other firms, but because of the excellent relationship that exists, such staff members remain loyal and dedicated to the firm, and this has a good effect on the production and quality of service rendered by such firms.

The inability of firms to incorporate career development training for their staff into their budget is what causes most employees to leave in search of something better Kwenin et al., 2013). Such exit increases the turnover of the firms, which is not suitable for the firm and as such retaining and maintaining a healthy attitude to work is something that the HR has to manage. Because there is no clear set of rules that can be applied to such situations, methods of staff retention can be somewhat trying; Staff retention methods require creativity and ingenuity on the part of the human resource administration (Sahoo et al., 2017). Employees have to be viewed as an asset to the growth of the firm for retention plans to manifest (Sahoo et al., 2017), who cited the research of the Gallup Organization. Otherwise, a company has to choose between retaining their staff, ensuring development opportunities exist and letting them go. Turnover rates are reduced when the organisations pay attention to the career development of their teams. Sahoo et al. (2017) provided supportive evidence to this statement by citing a 40% to 50% reduction in employee turnover for firms that offer opportunities for growth.

A study was carried out by Newman et al. (2011) on the companies in the service sector of China, this researcher conducted a poll across five multinational companies, and a total of 437 employees revealed there is a direct relationship between the training an organisation provides and retention. The workers stressed that the opportunity to learn given to them informed their commitment. Jehanzeb and Bashir (2013) carried out similar research and stated that contributing to the development of employees is one of the essential assets of a firm, and this encourages its employees to stay in the job of such firms for a long time, long enough for the firm to get returns on their investments.

According to previous research, career advancement opportunities is not the only factor that determines employee retention; work-life balance, job satisfaction, and a good work environment are also essential. Human resource managers should look for an easy way to ensure that all these factors come to play, to lead to an enthusiastic attitude towards work from the staff members, which would be suitable for the development of the organisation. A sound reward system is ideal for both parties. Employees that get promoted on their excellent work tend to stay longer with firms that appreciate their efforts than firms that don't. In other be in a competitive position, an organisation must also train their staff in modern technology; such training should be carried out after a careful evaluation of its relevance to workers' performance and the overall performance of the firm (Zeghal and Maaloul). Hassan et al. (2013) also supported the notion of a direct relationship between training and retention. They explained further that counselling, coaching and supportive management reduce turnover rates.

Importance of Employee Retention

The cost of turnover ranges from losing a competent staff to hiring a new hand. However, having to let go of a skilled and experienced employee and get a new one does not usually measure up in terms of competency, which is disadvantageous to the firm's progress (Memon et al., 2014). Therefore, there is a need to increase firms' attempts to ensure that their staff members remain with them by trying to provide and meet up with one or more of the retention factors. Otherwise, such firms will record a high turnover rate (Shipp et al., 2014).

3.2. Organisational Culture

Culture is a set of customs or social behaviour practised collectively by a group of people (Taslim, 2011). Workplace culture is the behaviour seen as a norm in running an organisation (Edward et al., 2013). Every organisation has a unique way of getting things done and achieving its goals. The type of culture an organisation operates with can determine the success of such an organisation (Singh, 2011). Utilising constructive culture at the workplace will help employees achieve job satisfaction and give the organisation a reputable image in its community (Wanjiku, 2014).

Organisation culture will direct how employees handle issues, communicate, and perform their day-to-day activities (Wanjiku, 2014). That is why organisation management must set their culture from the beginning. Organisational culture should also be reviewed from time to time to fit into the organisation's aspirations (Wong et al., 2014).

It has also been proven that workplace culture impacts retention. Most employees will not mind leaving a great job if the workplace culture is not good (Carter and Baghurst, 2014). An example of a bad culture is a lack of employee engagement. Some organisations do not carry their employees along on decisions made, which makes employees feel left out and less important. Employers and leaders should lead by example (Ghafoor et al., 2011).

Though essential in some instances, rules and regulations can also create a stifling environment if excessive; employees will live fearfully because of small mistakes and be unable to unwind in the workplace (Wambugu, 2014). All of these will prompt a more oppressive atmosphere in the organisation.

Good workplace culture also cultivates effort and commitment; while bad workplace culture emphasises discipline, good workplace culture emphasises reward (Abraham, 2012). Employees who are productive and assist other staff members should be recognised and awarded. Conversely, nothing deteriorates a company's culture faster than underappreciation (Sundaray, 2011).

The Four Types of Organisational Cultures

Every organisation differs, and they have a unique culture they practice. However, some organisations blend different types of cultures in other to function accurately (Suppiah and Sandhu, 2011).

There are four types of organisational culture. The first is the Clan Culture. The second is Adhocracy Culture, then Market Culture, and the Hierarchy Culture (Senarathna et al., 2014). It is an excellent thing if an organisation can be flexible when selecting a culture that will work best for them (Whittaker, 2011).

The Clan Culture: This culture was initiated in a cooperative form. Members of the organisation share traits and see themselves in the form of a family who works and make decisions together (Suppiah and Sandhu, 2011). Leadership appears as mentorship, and the organisation functions on all members' core commitments and traditions (Ogbeibu et al.,2018). The fundamental qualities are rooted in cooperation and communication. Most organisations that practice the clan culture build enviable relationships with their employees, customers, and everyone directly or indirectly connected to the organisation (Ramachandran et al., 2011).

The Adhocracy Culture: This culture depends on creativity (Goa, 2017). In this situation, employers urge their employees to try new things and take risks (Iriana et al., 2013). The leaders are most entrepreneurs. Such organisations usually operate on a trial-and-error basis, focusing on the ideas that work (Ramachandran et al., 2011). Change is a constant factor in organisations that practice this type of culture (Tuan, 2011).

The Market Culture: This culture is determined by the changes that come with rivalry from other organisations, and accomplishing tangible results is vital

(Omerzel et al., 2011). This culture is based on achieving end goals, and the leaders are usually rigorous and always make sure employees are on their best performance (Anitha, 2016). Such organisations have a common goal of leading in their industry, and they are driven by market share and profitability (Yesil and Kaya, 2012).

The Hierarchy Culture: This type of culture is built on specific rules and regulations that must be rigorously adhered to by everyone in the organisation (Suppiah and Sandhu, 2012). Leadership depends on organised coordination and observation, and consistency has to be a priority (Gao, 2017). An example of such an organisation or body is the military force, where members cannot just do what they like but adhere to the military rules.

Different cultural practice is what makes different organisations unique; organisations that operate in more than one of these cultures have one that dominates the others. For example, the UAE organization used in this research operates a blend of the clan and hierarchy culture. In contrast, the UK organization follows a hierarchical culture, impacting how the two organisations operate.

Chapter Four

4. Research Methodology

This chapter explores the significant aspect of the methodology adopted for this study. It is essential to analyse how the research will be carried out to achieve a credible result of good standard and validity. This research study utilised the Saunders research onion (Saunders et al., 2016) in explaining and analysing the process of its methodology. The Saunders research onions comprise six different layers that will help understand the research problems and the accurate means of data collection. The first layer of the research onion explains the necessity of following the philosophy of the research, while the second layer point identifies the best approach for the study to be carried out. The third layer of the onion focused on the methodological research options for the research to be carried out. The fourth layer gives an insight into the research strategy, while the fifth focuses on the time horizon. The last layer helps in analysing how the data for the research should be collated (Saunders et al., 2016).

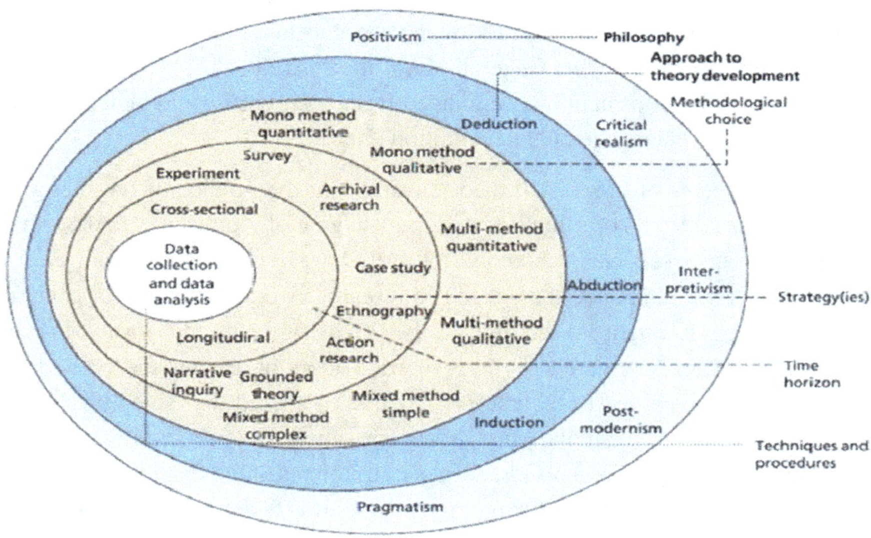

Figure 15: Research Onion (Saunders et al., 2016)

4.1. Research Philosophy

It is crucial to understand the philosophy underlining any study to be carried out. Philosophy is defined as a set of conceptions about the entity to be studied (Bryman, 2016). The philosophy of a study plays an essential role in the direction research goes. Saunders focuses on three major philosophies. According to Saunder 2016, there are various philosophies. The most common philosophies researchers use in their studies are: "Positivism, Realism, Pragmatism, Interpretivism" (Saunders et al., 2009).

In a positivist study, the research is limited to information collected and interpreted through objective means. This type of research study usually is factual with evidence as well as quantifiable. Positivism holds reality as stable. This ideology analyses that data that is not found based on positivism is invalid (Miller et al., 2010). It is assumed that it is feasible to study social life and develop a dependable understanding of its internal operations.

Positivism argues that sociology should be based on observation and that the concepts of social life ought to be built in a direct means based on verifiable truth (Corry et al., 2019). "The nineteenth-century French thinker Auguste Comte created and specified the following term in his books "The Course in Positive Approach" and "A General View of Positivism",". The researcher postulated that the information accumulated from positivism could benefit social adjustment and enhance the human condition (Harp, 2010).

The main concepts of positivism theory affirm that the science of reasoning is the same over all levels of scientific studies. The goal of inquiring is to describe, forecast, and uncover; research should observe human discoveries (Park et al., 2020). Positivism maintains that scientific research is not equivalent to general reasoning, and it ought to be judged by logic without any form of bias (Crossman, 2021). A researcher who is worried about observing and foreseeing results is perceived as a laboratory scientist bothered by scientific law's generalisation. For example, the 'scientific method' proposes and tests hypotheses with highly organised and generally quantifiable data. The research is not in any way affected by the researcher's values (Guerra et al., 2021). This process includes a typically wide range of measurable data and hypothesis testing (Guerra et al., 2021).

Realism is a philosophy that holds the scientific way to deal with data (McPhail et al., 2017). The fundamental assumption of the philosophy is what it really is. It is free from the conviction of the people (Emmel et al., 2018). The two types of realism are critical and direct realism. Direct realism perceives the world in a still way with no transition of any kind (Maloney, 2018). Critical realism accepts that change is a constant phenomenon (Buchanam and Bryman, 2009). In pragmatism, issues are managed directly (Simpson, 2017). This philosophy is keener on outcomes or truth as opposed to the standard related to ideology. Realism expresses that reality exists autonomously and that what a researcher detects is reality, although the researcher might be affected by world perspectives and encounters (Fletcher, 2017).

A researcher mirroring an immediate pragmatist position contends that what is experienced through our senses gives an exact picture of what it showcases (Aikin et al., 2017). Interestingly, a researcher mirroring a basic pragmatist position contends that what it is at the first experience through senses is along the line prepared abstractly by the mind (Allmark and Machaczek, 2018). For the critical realist researcher, this implies a need to discover what was experienced and the framework and connections that support such claims, which means examining the main concept (Allmark and Machaczek, 2018).

Suppose a study is focused on gathering an in-depth understanding of intuitive meanings rather than creating law-based generic findings. In that case, such a study is more likely to portray interpretivism's philosophy (Alharahsheh and Pius, 2020). This philosophy identifies with the research of the social phenomenon based on their daily situation. It centers around directing studies among individuals instead of upon objects, embracing a compassionate position to comprehend their social world, which means they provide for it from their perspective (Ban, 2019). In contrast to the positivism study, interpretive research examines findings in esteem bound, focusing on a specific area of a particular situation and people at a particular time (Alharahsheh and Pius, 2020).

Studies that incorporate pragmatism theory rely on practical consequences for its significance (Simpson, 2017). Because most of those studies acknowledged that conclusions could not be drawn from a single perspective, even though there are various representations of what reality is perceived. It does not imply that studies based on pragmatism theory utilize multiple data collection strategies and analysis procedures. Instead, the research design should empower credible, relevant and reliable data (Brierley, 2017). Ontology is one of the philosophical studies that is posited by Saunders research onions, it refers to a study that focuses on reality, while the second philosophy known as Axiology is the study of valuables and the effect the values to be acquired will have on research results (Saini, 2020). The last philosophy is epistemology, which involves collating adequate information to achieve a research result. Epistemology includes positivism, interpretivism, postmodernism, pragmatism and critical realism

(Saunders et al., 2016). Positivism is a philosophical study that generates law-related results for social existence, while interpretivism's philosophical study opposes the idea of positivism (Ryan, 2018). On the other hand, critical realism represents a subject that truthfully or directly avoids unrealistic or artistic conventions (Ryan, 2018). In this research, critical realism philosophy was used to connect the relationship between employee attrition in a non-profit organisation and how retention strategies can help minimise this issue.

Theory development can be achieved using inductive, deductive and abductive approaches (Saunders et al., 2016). The deductive approach moves from a general ideology to specific reasoning, whereby hypotheses are checked prior to ascertaining a study's result and results drawn from accessible facts. The Inductive approach follows a process of empirical perception prior to the analysis of results confirmation. The inductive approach starts with a specific ideology and grows into a general analysis to shape theories mostly through qualitative research. An Abductive approach is the process of creating new ideas and hypotheses based on unexpected facts, whereby researchers navigate from their preliminary theoretical insights to a new one (Saunders et al., 2016).

4.2.Justification for Methodology

Critical realism philosophy was used in this research because it simplifies the understanding of the research process and the issues to be tackled. Realism gives direct knowledge about a subject that can be easily related to by both the researcher and people who show interest in this research due to its realistic nature. Using critical realism philosophy methodology helped direct this research in a straightforward format as regards understanding the cause of attrition in non-profit organisations and the best retention strategies that will help curb the attrition challenges.

Trustworthiness and Utility of Research

Trustworthiness can be adopted to ascertain the reliability and validity of studies carried out using a quantitative research approach. However, this research is qualitative; the trustworthiness and utility will be well established through precise and consistent data analysis coupled with detailed research information that will prove and show credibility. Furthermore, this research will be a hundred per cent based on participants' narratives without any form of bias from the researcher. This will help understand that these research findings are credible, transferrable, confirmable and dependable (Gunawan, 2015).

The credibility aspect proves how confident the researcher of this study is with regards to the truthfulness of these research findings, which also shows how accurate the findings are. In other to make this concise, triangulation was also utilised. Regarding the transferability of these research findings, the findings from this research are transferable and can be useful in other sectors and not only the non-profit. The confirmability aspect also proves that the findings from this research were not biased but solely reliant on the responses of the study participants. This was proved through the detailed description of every step of the data analysis. The dependability aspect is to show that another researcher can achieve the same or related findings if this study was to be replicated.

The findings from this research will be well utilised in a well practical form to reduce employee attrition in a non-profit organisation.

Triangulation

Triangulation is a method that helps strengthen the rationality and reliability of research findings (Fush et al., 2018). As regards this research, triangulation was achieved by interviewing participants coupled with the collation of data through surveys because this will help in increasing data reliability and validity. In other to make this more reliable, elements of descriptive statistics were used alongside the descriptive NVivo analysis. Triangulation helps in establishing credibility and makes it easier for a study to achieve trustworthiness which is essential for this research.

Delphi Technique

The Delphi technique is the process of giving out a series of questionnaires and responses to experts in a particular field or sector and collating data from the group of feedback (Flostrand, 2017). The Delphi technique was also utilised in this study. The survey questionnaires were first sent out before finalising the interview questions because the findings received from the survey helped inform this research further. All participants were given opportunities to add to their already given responses when the feedback was further used to reanalysed some of the questions.

4.3. Research Approaches and Methodology Choice

One of the essential steps in carrying out research is to determine the best approach that will help achieve the best result for the study to be carried out. Saunders et al., 2016 explain three significant approaches the research can follow, which include deductive, abductive, and Inductive approaches. An Abductive approach is a process by which research will kick-start with unexpected ideas and be analysed through the research process (Osman et al., 2018). The deductive approach involves the development of hypotheses or theories that are already in use which will lead to the formulation of a method that will either dismiss or accept a past argument as valid or invalid (Osman et al., 2018). This approach is usually used to check or observe the result of past research expectations. The idea with this approach usually moves from general to a particular theory using the base to top means. It works very well with exploratory research and aligns well with quantitative technique research. The inductive research approach involves a direct format of study which moves from a particular to general theory. Inductive results are generated from the information and primary data collated (Steffen et al., 2018). The inductive research approach uses the top to bottom approach. This approach will not give a biased idea of the result before findings are carried out. The methodology layer of the Saunders research onions comprises mono-method quantitative and qualitative, multi-method qualitative and quantitative, mixed-method complex and simple methodological choices. The methodology layer features a fundamental but significant decision all researchers pass through when planning the research: this helps in deciding if the quantitative technique or qualitative techniques, a qualitative strategy or strategies, or a combination of the two methods should be utilised. A single strategy for data collection might be adopted by researchers, e.g., mono method qualitative or monomethod quantitative strategy.

Researchers can also use multiple data collection strategies with suitable analysis procedures when it comes to a multi-method quantitative or qualitative design. However, the use of both qualitative and quantitative data collection methods and analysis procedures is described as a mixed techniques configuration. Researchers can decide to pick quantitative methods to break down qualitative data which is acceptable as a mixed-method complex design (Saunders et al., 2016).

The inductive approach aligns well with the qualitative research technique, where research conclusions are determined from data collection. This research focused on the inductive approach and a few elements of the deductive approach. Saunders et al. (2016) encourage the use of both methods in other to achieve in-depth research findings. The reason for this decision is because this research is majorly focused on qualitative research methods with few elements of descriptive statistics to achieve a strategic retention framework as a means to reduce employee attrition in non-profit organisations.

4.4.Pilot Study

A preliminary study should be carried out in other to ensure the research direction is feasible, which is known as the pilot study (Hopkins, 2017). A pilot study was carried out using 10 per cent of the intended sample size for this research, and the process gave an idea of understanding the time constraint, cost and the possibility of what could be a hindrance to the study. This process also helps in providing an insight into what to improve on positively in other to achieve a detailed research result. Random respondent was selected in various organisational position. A top manager also volunteered to give an interview based on the initial draft of the interview questions. This step helped the researcher identify valuable interview questions that were included in the survey to enhance the research responses. The pilot study helped the researcher accept that the time allocated for the questionnaires was feasible enough. This process also helped in unravelling the fact that the surveys would aid the process of data collection as regards uncovering the issues leading to employee attrition in non-profit organisations adequately. The questionnaire was adjusted after the pilot study in other to formulate it into a more user-friendly format that will ease the process of data collection from respondents. This test run has helped improve this research direction by making it more objective focused. The result from this pilot study is shown in the appendix section of this write-up.

Variables	Number of Questions	Questions Removed
Career Development and Training	11	0
Working Environment and Work Practices	11	0
Job Role	7	0
Personal Values and Interpersonal Relationship	5	0
Employee Retention	14	0

Table 5: Pre-test Questionnaire

4.5.Research Strategy, Design and Procedure

This section explains the research strategy, procedure, and design used in this research. Research design helps outline the order research will follow to achieve an unerring result. Furthermore, this outline helps identify the most suitable methodology and techniques for achieving the research objectives (Sahay, 2016).

Scientists embrace various strategies depending on the type of research.

Saunders' research onion considers various research strategies, which include Survey, archival research, narrative inquiry, action research, experimentation, case study, grounded theory, and ethnography. (Saunders et al., 2016).

Experimental research is usually adopted in physical science situations. In contrast, the survey research strategy focuses on a small or large specific population to find answers to questions, usually in a social science setting (Saunders et al., 2016). A case study is a thorough investigation of a social unit whereby the subject matter of the research can be an establishment, individual, or group of people.

Action research is related to a specific venture and issue. Action research aims mostly to gather fast responses to issues or situations in a general public scenario. It studies the 'what', 'how', and 'why' of real-life scenarios (Saunders et al., 2016).

Grounded Theory is a subjective research study in social science. When the conventional logical strategy focuses on hypothesis, this technique embraces the framework of straightforward data gathering. All the data gathered are put in various codes to distinguish common elements. From the group of these codes, theories are developed (Khan, 2014). Ethnography is an extraordinary subjective research technique based on the cultural phenomenon of a particular subject matter (Adams, 2012). Archival research strategy implies a whole study would be dependent on research materials kept in specific archives from different researchers. This strategy provides access to an enormous amount of data (Saunders et al., 2016). The last layer is the time horizon. When the research relies on responding to an inquiry or addressing an issue at a precise time, it is called a cross-sectional time horizon, for example, a questionnaire or case study. On the other hand, when focusing on inquiry or issues requiring data accumulation for an extended period, such research time horizon is longitudinal.

Different components were put into consideration before the strategic approach for this research was determined. These components include the aim and objectives of this research, availability of resources, time constraint, the research approach and philosophy. An example is the ethnography system of research which is understood to align well with interpretivism and realism theory sampling, while positivism, on the other hand, aligns well with the positivism approach to reasoning (Glaser and Strauss, 2017). It has to be well analysed in other to use the one that best suits the research because some work better with the inductive while others are best for deductive methodology (Saunders et al., 2016). This study utilizes the interview and survey strategic approach, and it was analysed using qualitative data and a few elements of quantitative statistical data.

In other to achieve a successful research analysis, an adequate research design is essential. The research design is the process research will pass through to achieve its result (Turner et al., 2017). It gives an insight into the selection of research participants and the methodology of data analysis. Research design comprises descriptive, exploratory, and explanatory research design. An exploratory design process was used for this study because of its interview and survey qualitative approach. These procedures were adopted in other to carry out effective research.

4.6.Qualitative Questionnaire Approach

The qualitative questionnaire approach is the process of allowing research to create its reality through the research respondents' flexible or open responses (Brennen, 2017). The qualitative research method has become widely acceptable over time. Still, the researcher must carry out the study in a very analytical and explanatory way, whereby people who read the research will have a deep understanding of it (Herper, 2011). For qualitative research to be accepted as trustworthy and valid, it has to be concise, consistent and in-depth through its recording and systems used coupled with the analysis method. We use themes in our day-to-day activities to align or organise effectively (Castlseberry and Nolen, 2018). For example, the way our supermarkets order their products on display in various sections like the bakery, kitchen products, gardening products, etc. Thematic analysis is a huge qualitative analysis member in social science and will be utilised in this research because it is qualitatively based. Thematic analysis is a form of qualitative analysis method that helps identify, analyse, and report the correlation between the collected data for a study (Castleberry and Nolen, 2018).

The main advantage of qualitative research is that it helps researchers collate data directly from people who have experienced what the research area is all about first-hand (Basias and Pollalis, 2018). Methodological literature agrees that qualitative research includes various research designs such as case-study, ethnography, Narrative inquiry etc., which is usually characterised by specific design assumptions, sampling procedures, data collection and analysis protocols (Mohajan, 2018). Because qualitative research is usually open-ended, the data analysis is usually text-based (Korstjens et al., 2018). As a result, thematic analysis comes into place because it is very effective for text-based data analysis and other data types. Thematic analysis can be used across all qualitative designs (Terry et al., 2017). Thematic analysis is widely used because of its ability to work with various research questions and topics without jeopardising the data content (Maguire and Delahunt, 2017). This analysis allows flexibility to occur in contrast to the rigidness of quantitative data analysis, which is mostly number based. Usually, after collecting qualitative data through interviews, focus groups, or observations, researchers often struggle to make sense of the data collected. However, Thematic analysis helps in systematically analysing the qualitative data (Nowell et al., 2017). Thematic analysis helps identify and analyse patterns of meaning from collated data (Braun and Clarke, 2006).

One of the major advantages of thematic analysis is that it helps identify Important themes. Ordinarily, the result of thematic analysis primarily highlights the most crucial meanings presented in data (Sundlet et al., 2019). This analysis showcases the practical cognitive and symbolic dimension that exists in the data (Held et al., 2019). For example, when asking interview questions, people are expressive with their emotions which is usually non-existence in the quantitative data. For this research, it was essential to note employees' emotional expressions because it helps get in-depth originality to employees' responses and shows how much they are in support or against an ideology from the interview questions asked. The thematic analysis also helps set research information into the proper categories of themes that can be either implicit or explicit because it is a comprehensive process (Braun et al., 2021). The thematic analysis makes it easier to extract information and show the relationship between variables and evidence within the same study.

Braun and Clarke, 2006 argued that all qualitative analysis should be based on thematic analysis because of its ability to give research a clear direction from the get-go. In contrast, some authors maintained the ideology that thematic analysis is not a standalone method (Braun et al., 2021). Stating that because the thematic analysis applies to various qualitative methods, it is not a separate method; instead, it should be used as a basis for all research analysis (Braun et al., 2021). This ideology was debunked by other researchers who maintained the ideology that due to the comprehensive ability of thematic analysis, it is a robust method on its own (Kiger et al., 2020). A rigorous thematic analysis produces insightful research and trustworthiness (Castleberry and Nolen, 2018). Due to thematic analysis's flexibility, it can be modified to fulfil many kinds of research needs by providing an in-depth but complex amount of data (Kiger et al., 2020). The thematic analysis does not require rigorous technological and theoretical knowledge compared to other qualitative approaches (Catleberry and Nolen, 2018). As a result, it is a more accessible form of analysis and creates a non-complex understanding for people interested in reading certain research findings and results. Braun and Clarke further ascertain that thematic analysis effectively examines various research respondents' perspectives, showcasing their differences and what they have in common while discovering new research areas (Terryy et al., 2017). The thematic analysis also helps in summarising critical features of a huge amount of data due to its well-structured analysis in producing an organised final report (Nowel et al., 2017). No matter how excellent an analysis method is, there will always be a downside to it. Some of the limitations of thematic analysis were unraveled when compared to other qualitative research methods. The thematic analysis does not have substantial works of literature when compared to ground theory, ethnography and phenomenology (Gavin, 2008). As a result, a new researcher might find it challenging to carry out an in-depth thematic analysis because a direct analysis might not be robust compared to other forms of analysis. It should be noted that inconsistency might occur due to the variability attribute of the analysis when generating themes from researched data (Kiger and Varpio, 2017). Nevertheless, consistency could be achieved if an epistemological position is adopted and maintained (Braun and Clarke, 2021).

In the year 2006, Baun and Clarke wrote an article explaining how effective thematic analysis is. This analysis is user-friendly and flexible in its application to research (King and Brooks, 2018). It is very adaptive to any theory of choice. Some of the advantages of thematic analysis are (1) It gives academic freedom, whereby the researcher can apply it to any form of research without losing its validity and rigour and trustworthiness. (2) It is an accessible form of analysis, and researchers do not need a depth understanding of other qualitative approaches before using it. (3) Because this research has a time constraint, Thematic analysis is a suitable method due to its usability, ease and quick understanding. (4) Thematic analysis can analyse different research participants' perspectives with a detailed understanding of their similarities and differences and unveil unplanned ideas. (5) It makes qualitative data more structured to handle (King and Brooks, 2018).

There are various methods used in conducting qualitative research. Still, the five advantages mentioned above are why this researcher chooses to use the thematic analysis, coupled with the fact that it allows for rich and well-refined descriptive research data. Some researchers argued that thematic analysis's flexibility might make it less consistent. In other to make sure this does not happen, the researcher chose to utilise the thematic analysis under the umbrella of grounded theory (Vaismoradi et al., 2013).

Process Stage in Thematic Analysis	Description	Application to this Research	References
Data Familiarisation	Qualitative data can come in different forms. It can be written, recorded, pictorial and so on. Researchers need to familiarise themselves with their data regardless of the form used to harness it. Having a deep understanding of how data collated will be analysed helps the researcher structure the research process from the get-go since it will guide the researcher on what is essential.	The qualitative data for this research was both written and recorded. Therefore, this researcher already understands how data collated should be structured and analysed. As a result, this researcher decided to utilise NVivo analysis software (which helps analyse text-based data, recorded data, etc.) to analyse the collated interview data.	Salleh et al., 2017 Jackson and Bazeley, 2019
Generation of Initial Codes	This second phase becomes a reality after the researcher has familiarised themselves with their data. The most intriguing aspect of the data usually becomes the initial codes because they will keep passing a specific message from the data at large. Coding helps the researcher to give the required attention to essential data.	Researchers need to give importance to the whole data collated in other to be able to identify the right themes. For this study, the researcher chooses to use the interview question as codes for a structured and consistent result.	King and Brookes, 2018

Theme Search	This phase includes sorting collated data into themes. A theme helps analyse related data into a piece of more structured and understandable information. Themes bring together elements of data that might not have depth meaning as a piece of standalone details. A study research theme can be set inductively or deductively using the data collected.	This researcher generated the research theme Deductively coupled with inductive subthemes through the raw data collated; that way, any form of inconsistency loophole has been avoided.	Vaismoradi and Snelgrove, 2019
Review of Selected Themes	This stage involves the refinement of the selected themes. This second stage is crucial because it allows the researcher to ensure that the chosen themes match the data grouped with it. This process will provide the researcher with a platform to code or recode data that might have been mismatched or left out initially.	This phase helped the researcher of this study to have more constructive subthemes than it did initially, and as a result, the data analysis became more explicit.	King and Brookes, 2018
Defining and Naming Themes	This phase allows the researcher to give detailed information on all the individual themes identified by ensuring that each selected theme is self-explanatory. It gives a third party a summary of what the theme might be explaining.	At this stage, this study's researcher explains in detail the story behind each of the refined themes to ensure consistency.	Scharp and Sanders, 2019

Generating Report	A thematic analysis report must be concise, meaningful, logical and serve its primary purpose in the research analysis. This report must be written in a way that readers from various fields can make sense of it after it's been finalised. Keeping direct quotes from the participants will help avoid any issues regarding trustworthiness and validity. This phase also explains the correlation some of the new findings have in common with past research.	The last phase was achievable after the researcher had made sure that data aligned well with developed themes. As a result, this research includes essential excerpts from the participants to promote trustworthiness and validity. The literature review correlation also allowed this researcher to either argue, agree or buttress some of the existing literature while creating strategic frameworks that will enhance employee retention in non-profit organisations.	Kiger et al., 2020

Table 6: Stages of Thematic Analysis

The research considered the COREQ checklist (COnsolidated criteria for REporting Qualitative research) to ensure the research findings' transparency. This study focuses on the qualitative approach in carrying out its findings, and this was achievable by using open-ended questionnaires. Conducting Interviews was the major means of accumulating its intended data. Elements of descriptive statistics were included in analysing the supportive semi-structured questionnaire that was added to the research questions.

4.7.Data Collection

The methodological approach used for this research will determine the method of data collection. Data collection is a crucial stage for any research as it determines the authenticity of the research result been carried out (Saunders et al., 2016). The data collection for this research was achieved using interviews and self-completed questionnaires coupled with the reviewed secondary data collated from various research sources.

4.8. Sampling Method

The sampling method helped determine which sample size is enough for specific research to be carried out (Gentles and Vilches, 2017). The purposive sampling method was employed in this research to achieve in-depth knowledge of the factors leading to attrition in non-profit organisations. This study adopted purposive sampling because the selection of participants was deliberate in other to get the relevant information regarding the study at hand (Etikan et al., 2016). The sample size was between 20 (interview) and 80 (survey) participants. This number of participants was selected because it helped achieve saturation point for the purpose of this research. As such, extra participants in this scenario will not affect the results. These participants are from the top, middle and junior level management of two non-profit organisations in two different countries to have a broad knowledge about what leads to employee attrition in non-profit organisations. Participants were interviewed and backed up with an element of survey questions.

4.9. Primary Data Collection

Interviews and surveys questionnaires were used in collating the primary data for this research. Data collection was conducted in a non-profit organisation in UAE as a comparative analysis of another non-profit organisation in the UK.

Characteristics	Description
Job title	Open-Ended to avoid missing options
Nature of Job	Research and development, Human resources (HR), Engineering, General Management, Technical support, Procurement, finance, Industrial management, Marketing and others
Type of Employment	Full-time, Part-time and Volunteer
Experience	Open-Ended
Age	Less than 24 years old, 25 to 40 years old, 41 to 55 years old, above 55 years old
Gender	Male, Female and other
Marital Status	Single, Married, Divorce, Separate and Widowed
Education	Less than bachelor's degree, Master's degree, Doctorate and others
Position	Top-level manager, Middle-level manager, Supervisor, Entry level and others

Table 7: Demographic Characteristics of Respondents

Summary of Research Methodology

Research Philosophy	Critical Realism
Approach to Theory Development	Inductive approach with few elements of deductive approach
Methodological Choice	Qualitative Methodology with few Elements of Descriptive Statistics
Research Strategy	Case study and Survey Strategies
Time Horizon	Cross-sectional
Research Technique and Procedures (Data Collection and Data Analysis)	Interviews, Self-completed Questionnaires, Thematic Analysis and Statistical analysis.

Table 8: Summary of Research Methodology

(Influenced by Saunders et al., 2016)

	Data Sources		
Research Stages	Interview Participants	Self-Completed Questionnaire Participants	The approach to Data Collection
Research stage 1: Qualitative Case Study Research Data Collection	20 (10 from each organisation) Face to face and VoIP interview was conducted in gathering the qualitative data. The participants include the two organisations human resources, top management, middle management and junior level management. Each interview lasted for approximately 40 minutes.	Eighty participants partake in the survey, 50 from the UK non-profit organisation and 30 from UAE non-profit organisation.	Interviews and survey questionnaires were used to collate the primary data for this research. Data collection was conducted in a non-profit organisation in UAE as a comparative analysis of another non-profit organisation in the UK.
Research Stage 2: Data Analysis	Data collated from the interview was analysed using Thematic Analysis. This research utilises NVivo analysis software	The self-completed questionnaires were analysed using statistical elements like charts, tables and percentile analysis.	

(which helps analyse text-based data, recorded data and so on) in analysing and structuring the interview collated data.

Table 9: Research Stages

4.10. Ethical Consideration

The greatest challenge in research is not the data collection itself but the ethical consideration that involves carrying out the research (Ary et al., 2018). Ethical research guidelines must be strictly adhered to accordingly. This research has gone through the stage of ethical approval from the University of study, and it has been approved to be ethically fit for an investigation. The two organisations involved in the provision of primary data also gave their consent to participate after having a detailed knowledge of what the research entails. The privacy of the participants was protected at every stage of the research, and there was no form of compulsion in answering questions they were not interested in responding to.

4.11. Limitation

Every research methodology has a limitation. This research focused mainly on qualitative research methodology for its interview with descriptive statistics from surveys collated to help increase research reliability and validity. The limitation resulted from the time-bound nature of the study as the research has a time limit to submit it. Needless to say, this qualitative research was time-consuming because this research interview was mostly focused on the company's heads and managers with busy schedules. For future analysis, a quantitative methodology can be adopted, and if there is enough time, both methods can be utilised for further results.

This research is mainly focused on non-profit organisations. Data collection for this research was based on two non-profit organisations. Due to the sensitivity of the data collection, especially the interviews, details were mostly anonymously presented. Some of the respondents fear the effect their responses might have on their job and thus, decide to be partially sincere due to the sensitivity of the research.

Chapter Five

5. Results, Analysis and Discussion

This section analyses all the data collated from both the interview, self-completed questionnaire and past reviewed work. Data analysed was discussed in detail, leading to the provision of research results.

5.1. Qualitative Data

The qualitative data was collated by conducting face-to-face and VoIP interviews. The participants include the two organisations human resources, top management, middle management and junior level management. Open-ended questions were asked in this scenario. Some of the questions asked are the rate of employee attrition, retention policies in place, the function of top management in regards to retention, how performance is measured and evaluated, and training opportunities. Middle and junior level management were also questioned about their year of service in the organisation, their source of motivation, challenges, level of involvement, training, supervision and role feedback format. Ten participants were interviewed in the non-profit organisation in the UK, and the same population was interviewed at the chosen non-profit organisation in UAE. Data collected were transcribed using the NVivo tool. The data was organised using the research objectives as pointers, after which data collected was coded to make the analysis more logical because the result must be consistent and reliable.

5.2. Qualitative Results and Analysis

This section discussed the qualitative results and analysis of the study of the UAE and UK Non-profit organisations extensively.

The research group query usually shows the relationships between items within a research project (Bazeley and Jackson, 2013). This query was generated from coding in the NVivo app.

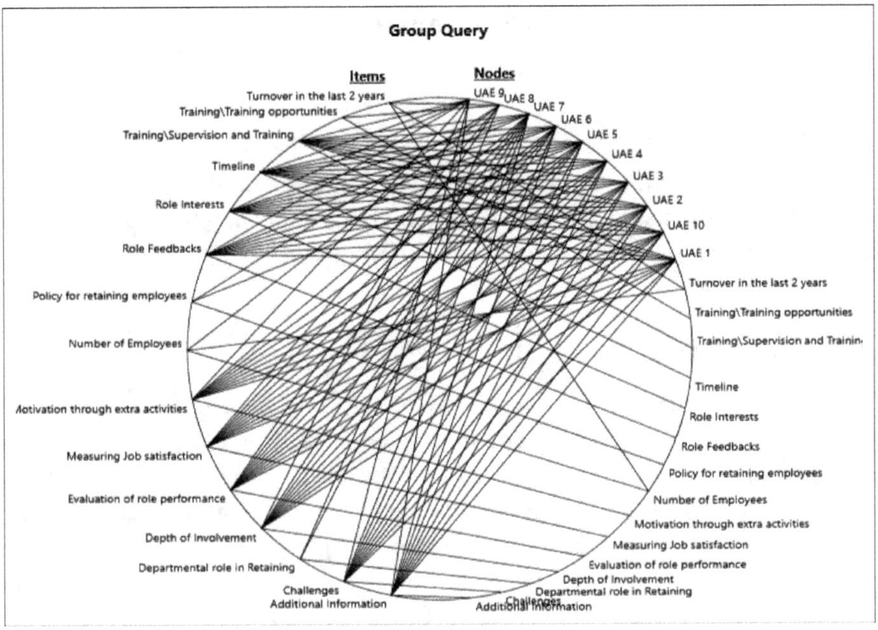

Figure 16: UAE NVIVO Group Query

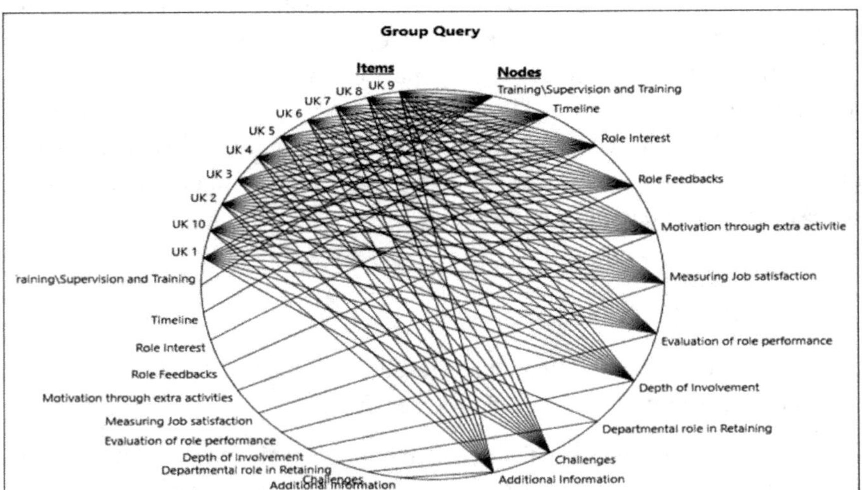

Figure 17: UK NVIVO Group Query

Theme Name	Description
Additional Information	This provides more explanations on what the organisation might be doing wrong or right as regard retention that was not asked in the listed questions
Challenges	Employees explained the challenges they face in their roles and place of work.
Departmental role in Retaining	What the department is doing to encourage employee retention.
Depth of Involvement	Employees explains how involved they are in planning their day to day task
Evaluation of role performance	Explains how employee's performance are evaluated.
Measuring Job satisfaction	Process of measuring employees job satisfaction
Motivation through extra activities	Shows if extracurricular activities will aid motivation.
Number of Employees	This gives the number of employees that works at the chosen non-profit organisations.
Policy for retaining employees	Policies in place to encourage employee retention.
Role Feedbacks	How employees receive feedbacks in their role.
Role Interests	Explains what employees enjoys or love most about their role and organisation.
Timeline	Shows how long employees have been working in the organisation.
Training:	Human resources management and Employees responses regarding training and supervision.
Supervision and Training	
Training Opportunities	
Turnover in the last 2 years	This shows the number of employees that left the organisation in the past two years.

Figure 18: UAE Codebook

This research data collection started with a demographic question for both its interviews and survey. However, some of the demographic information for the interview was not displayed for privacy purposes.

The national institute of health made a guideline of including minorities in funded projects in 1993 (Hammer, 2011). As a result, it has been a criterion to include research participants' demographic information when presenting a research report because this will help ascertains diversity in the research. Demographic information involves showing the age, gender, educational level, languages and sometimes ethnicity of participants depending on the research area, questions and expected results (Balkin and Sheperis, 2011). Without research participants demographic information, researchers tend to speculate that all research participants' interest is identical regardless of age, class, culture, etc. Getting this information will allow researchers to achieve a stance of universalism that showcases the apparent differences in research participants (Beins, 2017).

In conclusion, describing research participants demographic characteristics gives researchers and readers detailed information on the similarities and differences in research outcomes and why, which can also be used in secondary data for future purposes (Beins, 2017).

Theme 1 (UAE)	Question	Response
Employees	Number of Employees	30

Table 10: Number of Employee UAE

Theme 1 (UK)	Question	Response
Employees	Number of Employees	200

Table 11: Number of Employees UK

Theme 2 (UAE)	Question	Response
Turnover	Turnover in the last two years	8

Table 12: Employee Turnover UAE

Theme 2 (UK)	Question	Response
Turnover	Turnover in the last two years	25

Table 13: Employee Turnover UK

The attrition rate is a way of estimating the level at which employees leave an organisation over time (Alduayi and Rajpoot, 2018). Based on the tables above, the UAE non-profit organisation has had an employee turnover of 8 in the last two years. This researcher concluded from the data collected that the attrition rate at the UAE organisation is high considering the organisation's population and, in comparison, to the UK organisation. For the UK non-profit organisation, employee attrition is just a little bit over 10%. At the time of this research interview, the human resources respondent mentioned that the UK non-profit attrition rate was due to the restructuring going on at the time of data collection. The UK organisation has many volunteers working with them who leave at will, but they do not consider it employee attrition.

These two non-profits organisation have been in operation for just over ten years, even though some of the UK non-profit organisation employees have been working for the city council before the UK organisation took over and retained some of them. This researcher interviewed various participants with different years of experience at both organisations, as shown in the tables below.

Theme 3 (UAE)	Question	Response
Timeline	Years spent so far in the Organsation	9 months, 1 year, 3 years, 5 years, 6 years 7 years, 8 years and 10 years

Table 14: Years of Employment UAE

Theme 3 (UK)	Question	Response
Timeline	Years spent so far in the Organisation	2 years, 3 years, 7 years, 9 years, 12 years, 13 years, and 18 years

Table 15: Years of Employment UK

Theme four interview question is about what interest each of the participants in joining the organisation as an employee. The response to this question helped this researcher understand what attracted employees to these two organisations. It can also help the organisation retain their employees if the organisation maintains the attraction features. Learning what pulls skilled employees to an organisation will help an organisation maintain a competitive edge in their area of operation even though diverse strategies might be needed to attract various skilled workers (Alniacik et al., 2014). In most cases, employees are attracted to an organisation due to shared values because they give the employees what they need. In return, the employees give their best service to help the organisation grow or leave if their initial attraction to the organisation ends (Thomas and Letchmiah, 2017).

Theme 4	Question	Response (UAE)	Response (UK)
Role Interest	What do you like most about your work?	One of the participants mentioned that he likes the fact that there is a strong teamwork bond in the organisation, helping local communities, working with lots of varieties even though it's a small organisation and the cultural diversity in the organisation. Examples of direct responses "*I enjoy the teamwork and interacting with different people, working with lots of varieties. I enjoy doing*	According to the UK participants, most employees love working for the organisation because it's a charity organisation and their ability to make a difference in society with their respective roles. Examples of direct responses from employees: "*I like the fact that I work for a charity organisation and making a difference, I used to work for profit-making organisations, so this transition into non-*

research because I also work with the ministry that helps inform policy and liaise with students who come into the organisation for the purpose of research". "*I like the variety, there is a very wide variety of projects that we deal with, a lot of different stakeholders, different ages, different backgrounds, different countries and in different sectors. So, it's an open-ended organisation due to varieties*". This respondent explained that she also loves working in the organisation due to the variety of opportunities given to her by the organisation with further reasons "*I like many things about my job, first I like the fact that I am able to work on a variety of projects and not just one. We support education and support different audiences. We try to support as much as we can to help develop the community*". Based on participants responses, it was apparent that this organisation is doing well in implementing varieties of work for their employees and letting them make important decisions while connecting well with fellow employees.	*profit is really fulfilling, knowing I am helping different people daily. Money made in non-profits is reinvested into other causes instead of making someone wealthier. I enjoy how we work with different people. I also enjoy the fact that I am very much involved in the work that I do while getting the necessary support from my line manager. I initiate so many ideas in my role*". "*The adequate training opportunities and work-life balance*". "*A very supportive working environment and the fact that organisation's aim is giving back to society*".

Table 16: Employee's Role Interest

From Theme 4, it is apparent that most of the employees enjoy working with varieties of tasks which seems to be inevitable in the organisation. Some of the employees are encouraged to remain in the organisation long-term due to the kind of relationship that exists between them and how they all feel like a family with the same end goal towards the development of the organisation. It is interesting how both organisations had so much in common regarding why they are working in their various non-profit organisation, except for the work-life balance factor, which is somewhat missing as expressed by the employees in the UAE organisation.

Theme 5 interview question is about the challenges employees are facing at their various organisations. It is essential to know the challenges employees face in their organisation because this is one of the main problems that cause employee attrition. If organisations work around their employees' challenges at work, it might intrigue the employees to stay longer. De Cieri et al., 2005 take the stand that in other to keep up with a highly competitive edge, organisations should recruit and retain their valued employees while maintaining an excellent work-life balance strategy.

Organisations should implement policies that will prioritise the well-being and health employees and their families (Bray et al., 2013). "The National Institutes of Health and the Centers for Disease Control and Prevention formed the Work, Family and Health Network (WFHN) implemented an innovative multisite study". This research followed a comprehensive and in-depth empirical design (control groups, adaptive randomisation), targeting a psychosocial work setting (Bray et al., 2013). This study explains why it is essential to curb the challenges employees face at work in other to encourage retention.

Theme 5	Question	Response (UAE)	Response (UK)
Challenges	Do you find anything difficult about your role? Can you tell me about it?	Based on these three responses below and other responses, most of the participants complain about too many varieties of work with limited staff members, which makes their role very stressful. Examples of direct responses: "*Having conversations with people from different countries and the challenges is the language barrier, and I must talk to them and give feedback. Talent hunt is quite challenging, and because of this, some positions are usually open for too long*". "*Definitely. Is there a particular area you want me to focus on? Well, I think it's connected to the fact I mentioned earlier that the organisation operates in an open-ended format. Too many open-ended things here*	The UK participants complained that the organisation keeps adding more services to their tight schedule. Some of these new services might not be within the organisation budget because the organisation gives free will to their employees in regards to showcasing their talent or gift, which might not fit into the organisation's financial budget. As a result, some of these employees are always at loggerhead with the financial department representatives. Example of direct responses: "*I am used to the way things are done in the profit-making sectors because everyone already knows their role and what might be at stake if the necessary financial analysis is not carried out. But here is diversify and most of the*

	at the organisation, so sometimes there are challenges due to being too open-ended where some of us end up being spread a little too thin but still trying to maintain a high quality of product or services. Because quality is taken has a high priority. Due to this variety, it is usually difficult to maintain a balance of work and rest". "*I do not like the idea of not being able to measure efforts. Because it's a non-profit organisation, we tend to work in various environments depending on where the project to be carried out is*". Some of the participants also complain about the lack of work-life balance, which is essential.	*people are more passionate about their cause and talents without considering the financial constraints, and because I handle the organisation finances, it can sometimes be challenging to make them understand this. So, I usually have to explain to them in detail how it's important to be financially responsible and fulfil other important causes*". "*Not really because I have been here long enough to understand what is going on except for the fact that the organisation keeps adding in new services every now and then though it's interesting but it's also the challenging part*". "*Nothing aside from the poor management*".

Table 17: Challenges Faced at work

Both organisation employees complained about handling too many services at a time. The UK organisation employees further complained about how new services did not fit into the organisation financial budget. In contrast, the UAE employees complain about the lack of work-life balance, inability to measure efforts, etc.

Theme 6 question is to confirm if extracurricular activities will help motivate employees. For example, research conducted in the United States by the "National restaurant chain" in 2013 uncovered that extracurricular activities positively influenced employees' performance and helped to minimise employee attrition. Thus, whether extracurricular activities are practical is determined by the type of activities and the expected outcome (Tew et al., 2013).

The exchange of humour or having fun at work is said to lessen disagreement, boost creativity, enhance interaction, and improve employee retention. In addition, various research has established that the emphatic atmospheres associated with workplace fun do inspire employee commitment and turnover (Karl and Peluchette, 2006).

Favorable working conditions will more likely motivate workers and entice and retain them in organisations. Therefore, workplace relaxation exercises may be treated as part of the well-being of employees (Chan, 2010).

Theme 6	Question	Response (UAE)	Response (UK)
Motivation through extra activities	Will extra activities during break help motivate you?	Some participants agree that extra activities will help motivate them at work. At the same time, some said it will only increase their stress due to their already colossal workload and would prefer to go home immediately after work. Examples of direct responses: '*Yes, it will be great. It will help bring employees together*". '*We have a lunch time where everyone can come together and eat for a couple of hours, and I think that's a perfect way to interact with people. Because workdays are so intense in generally. I think there is a need for people to have some flexibility and space to eat together, and some might need to run errands, so I think adding more activities will be too much*". "*We do not have a lot of sporty people here; I think they will prefer to go home early instead. I also feel they might like to have some extracurricular activities once in a while*".	Example of direct responses: "*The organisation encourages employees to take breaks with the availability of drinks and snacks. I always encourage my team to take breaks as well. I use that opportunity to discuss their welfare and make sure they are doing alright. I do all this in other to keep them motivated, and that way, they would want to stay with the organisation. A friendly and conducive environment is important for employees to strive*". "*It might help, though; some employees will rather just go home to their families after work or go out with friends after work*". "*Yes, it will be good, especially if we get to meet people from other departments, which seems to only happen at Christmas parties*".

Table 18: Motivation through Extracurricular Activities

Based on the UAE and UK interview participants responses, some of the participants agreed that fun extracurricular activities would help motivate them to work better and stay longer in their various organisations. At the same time, some explained that it would not make much difference as they would prefer to have such activities with family and friends. Some UAE participants agree that extracurricular activities will be great, but they are already too tired to have fun due to their workload.

Theme 7 is about asking interview participants questions about how involved they are in planning their work. This question helped this researcher understand how much each organisation trusts their employees regarding decision-making and ownership in employees' various roles. The practical application of employee involvement is positively linked to perceived organisational accomplishment. More specifically, employee participation and empowerment plan and self-managing teams directly correlate to the managerial perception of organisational performance. Therefore, organisations are encouraged to utilise employee engagement strategies to enhance performance, competitiveness and growth (Sofijanova and Zabijakin, 2013). Furthermore, propelling decision-making power downward in organisations focuses on what employee involvement is all about (Lawler, 1999).

It is easier to attain organisational growth if everyone who works in an organisation adopts a mutual level of trust, which creates a platform for complete openness and collaboration (Thomas et al., 2009).

Theme 7	Question	Response (UAE)	Response (UK)
Depth of Involvement	How involved are you in planning the work you do?	This organisation gives most of its employees' ownership in their various roles. Example of direct responses: "*I work with the management team at the beginning of every year to set the organisational goals. But it's up to the managers to bring those goals into reality. I do not keep track of everyone's work, but my personal assistant does when necessary. So far, the goals are met. I do not have to worry about how*". "*I am very involved. I am the one in charge of planning any program to be handled, so I plan the programs and projects to be executed; after that, I will pass it on to the top management for their decision. So, I am very involved in planning the work I do*". "*The organisation entrusts me with various roles. I collaborate with all the departments because I set the departmental goals and partake in the follow up*".	This organisation also gives most of its employees' ownership in their various roles. Some of the direct responses: "*I am very involved, but I have a collaborative nature, so I also involve and carry my superiors along in anything I do. I share the necessary information with them coupled with the fact I am a great team player because I like to be very open with my work in case, I choose to do some things differently, they will understand why that is important*". "*I participate in drafting organisation business plans and plan my day-to-day activities, and also have like five line-managers answer to me so yeah, I will say I am very much involved*". "*I plan what I do with considering what the target is for the month*".

Table 19: Level of Involvement in planning

The two organisations are doing well in giving their employees power over their involvement in their various roles. Just as stated above, this factor usually makes employees feel accepted. As a result, they will be able to put in their best by setting their own goals based on the organisational goals.

Theme 8 talks about how employees' performance is evaluated. Organisations need to measure their employees' performance because it will help both the organisation and employees set their goals accurately and work effectively.

Organisations should clarify performance indicators that will enable the achievement of organisational goals (Grafton et al., 2010).

Most strategies relating to performance measurement innovations emphasise the role of performance measures in influencing managers' awareness of the long-term consequences of their actions by stimulating supervisors to pursue practical strategy implementation and informing the evaluation and development of organisational capabilities (Kaplan et al., 2001).

A performance analysis report is an essential information for an array of managerial decisions. It also serves as a catalyst in identifying problems and relevant solutions, helps concentrate on crucial processes, and is a valuable data source for organisational knowledge, which will enable the implementation of adequate strategies (Chenhall, 2005). To achieve adequate development in any organisation, such an organisation needs to have the ability to measure performance (Lohman et al., 2004).

Theme 8	Question	Response (UAE)	Response (UK)
Evaluation of role performance	What method is in place to evaluate employees' performance?	Most of the employees said there is no specific structured way of evaluating role performance, but few methods are in place to ensure all employees meet their set targets annually. Examples of direct responses: *"There is no specific method, but if an employee is lagging, they will be called to order by the HR or sent an email depending on how serious". "At the beginning of every year, we have an annual goal and performance settings. We have touch base meetings with managers, and we evaluate performance as the project progresses". "We have performance evaluation retreats; I cannot really remember. But we do like a grade-based things like 80, 60, 70 per cent or more or less based on job goals and accomplishment. We also have 5 grading formats like significantly below expectations, below expectations, meet*	Most of the UK employees mentioned that their role performance was evaluated through annual goals reviews. *"Annual review is the main thing, but if an employee needs to be addressed prior, we do make sure of that". "Organisation analyse if yearly goals were met". "Through yearly goals analysis to confirm targets are met".*

expectations, above expectations, and significantly above expectations to analyse our performance at the end of each year. Then the management decides on bonuses based on this performance".

Table 20: Role performance evaluation

Employees from both organisations explained that their organisations measured performance through yearly appraisals and ensured they met their organisation and individual roles goals. They further explained that if any employee is lagging in their role, the management will call such an employee to order.

Theme 9 is about receiving feedback. Without good feedback, employees and management will not understand what they need to adjust in their roles and why.

Most of the time, employees avoid feedback because of the fear of being criticized because most employers focus more on their employee's mistakes and not on what the employees are doing right; that is why employees rarely seek them even when needed (Knesek, 2015).

Efficient feedback is a crucial aspect of a productive work setting. It gives a tool for evaluating employees' performance and serves as a pointer for supporting workers' progress, understanding new responsibilities, and a basis for self-reflection, which will, in turn, enhance productivity (Prayson and Rowe, 2017).

Accurate and timely feedback gives people the ability to work on their shortcomings. In addition, it helps them understand what they are doing well because this understanding will, in turn, help performance and productivity (Noble et al., 2019).

Theme 9	Question	Response (UAE)	Response (UK)
Role Feedbacks	How do you receive feedback in your role?	In this organisation, based on the interview responses, receiving recurrent feedback is subjective. It depends on the activeness of whom employees report to. Most of the employees only get detailed feedback twice a year through the organisation appraisal. Examples of direct responses: *"I get daily feedback on ongoing projects, sometimes we communicate through email. The organisation also operates a 6-month appraisal to analyse organisation goal and project progress".* *"I produce research papers and reviews and am in charge of changes to be made. I rarely receive feedback, but we do have the annual goal review where we get to conclude if the goals set for the year were achieved and reflect on what has been done. Occasionally I get feedback emails directly from the director on projects involving many people".* *"I usually do a one-on-one form of feedback, but the formal feedback occurs twice a year in the form of an appraisal and all".*	In contrast to the UAE organisation, employees rarely receive daily feedback. The UK employees receive recurrent feedback but mostly through emails. *"I am always asking my line manager for feedback; we do have regular meetings. I also get feedback from my subordinates because that way, we would have a better working relationship. Feedbacks give a clearer picture of a different and better way of doing things". "The organisation is fond of sending emails as a channel for both positive and negative feedback". "Both formal and informal from the director and those who report to me. Because if something goes wrong along the way, we do not wait until the formal feedback; instead, we sort it as soon as possible".*

Table 21: How Feedback is received

The UAE employees mentioned that they rarely get active feedback aside from the quarterly feedback analysis if the yearly goals are near completion or achieved. Some UAE employees further explain that they only get feedback outside the quarterly appraisals when something is not going right and not otherwise. On the other hand, the UK respondents mentioned that they do get active feedback through email but mostly criticism. One of the UK employees mentioned that he was stressed because he felt like the organisation did not appreciate his effort. After all, they only focus on his mistakes.

Theme 10 is about measuring employees job satisfaction. Top, middle and low-level employees were asked if the organisation actively measures job satisfaction.

Research regarding job satisfaction started in the 1920s and 1930s during the employment crises of the great depression due to the widespread job dissatisfaction at the time, where emotion was identified as the essential factor (Sessa and Bowling, 2020).

Numerous studies have shown the importance of job satisfaction, which proves its attribution to most individual and organisational behaviour, including performance, organisational productivity, and employee attrition (Judge et al., 2020).

Theme 10	Question	Response (UAE)	Response (UK)
Measuring Job satisfaction	Are there processes in place to measure job satisfaction of your employees?	Based on participants responses, this organisation does not have any structured process for measuring job satisfaction. Examples of direct responses: *"I will not call it that, but we have annual goal settings, and we have organisation, departmental and individual goals checked with progress. There is a system to know if people are getting the professional development they like on a yearly basis. Non as regards satisfaction, though, but they can tell managers if anything is wrong but in a non-structured way. No formal system in place".* *"We did in the past in form of surveys, but we have not done any in a while though we plan to do another one this year. So, I will say we do, but not in a systematic way that we ought to. In terms of job satisfaction, we offer things like the number of sick days for employees and*	Like the UAE organisation, the UK organisation does not have any current structured way of measuring employee satisfaction. Both organisations rarely have an idea if their employees are happy or not. *"Yes, employee engagement survey and appraisal system are very much in use in this organisation". "Yes, the organisation do measure job satisfaction, but more in an informal way. It used to be very much active a few years ago, unlike now". "Non that I know of. Except the survey they did years back".*

			so on". *"I think they follow through the job evaluation and see if the goals set are achieved and try to understand why it isn't if not. We do like a survey. We have both internal and external reviews to determine promotions, so nothing specific to job satisfaction".*

Table 22: Measuring Job Satisfaction

Both the UK and UAE organisation does not have a distinct method of measuring employee satisfaction. One of the UAE respondents further explains that there used to be a system in place in the past where they could air out their worries. However, the organisation shut it down because they could not correct all that the employees complained about and did not keep all their promises of what would be done. This respondent further buttresses this fact by suggesting that if the organisation allows employees to air out their worries in a timely fashion, the organisation will rectify mistakes without being overwhelmed.

Theme 11 is about asking respondents the role their department plays in retaining employees in the organisation.

Based on the competition rate in organisations today, one crucial means to retain employees is to have adequately engaged workers. Factors such as job nature, effort recognition, teamwork, collaboration between departments, benefits, and fair company policies contribute to employee engagement which is why it is essential for organisation management to create a platform that will encourage trust and career fulfilment (Abraham, 2012).

Organisational culture, goals and departmental influence go a long way in encouraging employee retention in an organisation (Wheeler et al., 2006).

Organisations are increasingly striving to entice proficient employees in numerous professional areas; thus, organisations that interest the most skilled talent will have a clear advantage in the marketplace. Managerial collaboration in organisations is essential for successfully designing and implementing the employer branding policy (Maheshwari et al., 2017).

Theme 11	Question	Response (UAE)	Response (UK)
Departmental role in retaining	How will you describe the role your function	Based on participants' responses, this organisation starts its retention process	"We encourage employee engagement and make sure employees are well

unit plays in retaining your employee?	from the hiring stage by employing the right set of employees. They give employees the right set of training to make them relevant in their role to avoid employee attrition. Examples of direct responses: "As a new HR coordinator, I think by hiring the right employees, creating the right culture and by being more flexible to the requests of employees". "I am part of the administration team, so we support employees and set up necessary training for them to get better at their roles".	trained in other to perform their role effectively. Employees are also free to give feedback. I personally do have open conversations with my teams to discuss feedback and adjust where necessary".

Table 23: Department role towards employee retention

Most of the respondents mentioned that they encourage employee retention by being good to their colleagues. Both the UAE and UK human resources respondents mention that they encourage employees through adequate training, career advancement, and feedback for their employees and colleagues. The UAE respondents further explain that they keep retention strategies in mind from the recruitment stage by ensuring they employ the right employees for various roles from the get-go.

Theme 12 is about the policy the two organisations have in place in regards to retaining employees. Organisations need to have adequate policies or strategies to retain their employees, making it easy for such organisations to keep track of what is working and what is not.

In a free market-driven economy, it is not possible to retain everyone. However, businesses should attempt to retain those workers that contribute significantly to the organisation. As a result, employee attrition would be limited. However, organisations need to understand that employee retention starts from the hiring stage (Dey, 2009).

Organisations with satisfactory employee retention strategies such as good salary packages, policies encouraging job security, employee's involvement in decision-making, and considerations for employees' family welfare will encourage retention and intensify employee performance. The implication organisations that fail to put the right retention policy or strategies in place face is the inability to keep a skilled and motivated workforce hence experiencing continuous employee attrition and reduced organisational performance (Gberevbie, 2008). To sustain organisational growth, organisations need to retain their performing employees, thereby protecting their knowledge bank (Dey, 2009).

Theme 12	Question	Response (UAE)	Response (UK)
Policy for retaining employees	What are the policies in place to retain employees in the organisation?	This organisation does not have any retention policy in place but participates in various activities like training, professional development programmes, reasonable pay rate, employee getaway, and so on that will encourage their employees to stay long-term. Examples of direct responses: "No specific policy per se, but we offer a professional development budget every year for all employees at all levels and offer training to everyone. We have an annual staff retreat where we all go away for one night. We spend a lot on training employees, and we provide lunch to everyone. We give employees the opportunity to execute a personal project. So, I will say no specific policy but a combination of lots of things we do to make our employees feel very comfortable". "We do not have any specific policy for employee retention, but we make sure to offer a competitive salary package, benefit, and professional development programs".	The UK organisation does not have any specific policy towards retention aside from various attributes that encourage their employees to stay. "We do not call it retention policy per se, but it works in retaining our employees. We allow our employees to discover and express their talent using the company resources. This organisation also helps their employees in regard to career advancement coupled with adequate training and effort recognition".

Table 24: Policy for retaining employees

Both the UK and UAE organisations explained that they do not have any specific policy for employee retention. However, they retain their employees using various strategies like training, career advancement, further studies provisions for employees, reasonable pay rates and bonuses. One of the UAE organisation respondents further adds that the organisation usually pay for their employee yearly travel expenses, especially for employees who are far away from their families.

Theme 13 focuses on training and supervision questions; respondents were asked if they receive adequate training and supervision in their various roles. Employee development and training program should encourage career development. Both the organisations and their employees will benefit from this (Jehanzeb and Bashir, 2013). The organisation is responsible for ensuring that employees have the proper expertise and skills required for a job. Employees' skill set needs should be prioritised timely because this will help an organisation maintain its competitive edge in its industry ((Rodriguez and Walters, 2017).

It is also crucial for organisations to evaluate how successful their employee training and development programs are in a timely fashion (Jehanzeb and Bashir, 2013). Employee performance influences the success of an organisation. As a result, organisational leaders must understand the effect training and development programs has on their workers performance because it supports employees towards achieving organizational goals, boosts their morale and overall abilities (Rodriguez and Walters, 2017).

Theme 13	Question	Response (UAE)	Response (UK)
Training	Do you get enough supervision and training in your role?	All participant answered yes to this question. According to the participant's comments, this organisation organises adequate training for its employees and supervises their work. Even though all the participants answered yes to this question, some employees said the organisation can still do better in the aspect of supervision and training.	*"This organisation invests in their employees through learning and development, and this gives us the ability to do our jobs better. The organisation also offers seminars and conferences, which helps a lot, and they also give employees the opportunity to showcase what they learnt".*
		"I get a lot of supervision in my first year, I was assigned a coach who gives me advice on the way I lead and challenges I face every 4-6 weeks. That's one of the things this organisation does well by providing professional development and necessary training".	*"Most of the time, but the organisation can always do better".* *"The professional development is really great, and we receive training opportunities all the time".*
		"This is one unique and great thing about my organisation because they support a lot and give the necessary professional development and training. We get to develop our area of interest. Each employee is flexible in determining any training they would like to partake in". "Yes, I do get supervision in some areas of my work while I do not on others. The company supports whatever training we all need".	*"Yes, the training is really good, and I get to learn new things all the time".*

Table 25: Employee's Training and Supervision

Both the UK and UAE respondents have the same responses for theme 13. Participants from both organisations explained that they do get adequate training and supervision that helps them in carrying out their roles accurately. However, participants from both organisations also mentioned that the organisations could do better in the training area, which was more apparent with the UK participants.

Theme 14 focuses on additional information. The theme was used to ask participants if they had further information or queries regarding encouraging employee retention. Some participants suggested that the extracurricular idea is excellent even though extra resources might be needed to achieve it. The UAE respondents lament about being stretched too thin and would be happy if the organisation could prioritise work-life balance and employ enough working staff. The UAE respondents further mentioned that accurate measurement for job satisfaction should be in place to encourage retention). Furthermore, the UK respondents are not happy that their organisation does not pay them for work done outside their role and are discouraged from staying in the organisation due to its recurrent restructuring.

Theme 14	Question	Response (UAE)	Response (UK)
Additional Information	Is there anything you would like to share with regard to this interview?	Examples of direct response: *"The organisation focuses on accountability, which is not too good because they focus only on the goals. They have no idea if employees are happy or not. They need more employees, and it will be good if they reduce working hours because one employee is usually overburdened with too much workload. People burn out due to stress and too much work. Some of the employees do not feel empowered, and some people leave due to frustration".* *"Though the work has been intense so far, but I have received enough support. I feel the organisation should have a structured way of measuring job satisfaction and some enhanced form of acknowledgement. Also, too many tasks with a limited amount of time, it's not sustainable for people to work so hard for so long, and this might be the reason why people leave due to the intensity of workload, though it's noble they try to serve the*	*"Not really though the extracurricular activity for employees would be a great idea but then resources need to be managed".* *"The organisation's frequent restructuring and rate of redundancy is really alarming, and this is affecting most employee's loyalty to the organisation".* *"The organisation does not pay their employees for extra task performs and sometimes it is difficult to know who to explain a problem to hierarchy wise".*

public as much as possible but it's quite challenging on the employees". Some of the employees asked me to advise the top-level management to encourage employee engagement and hire more employees to reduce employee workload.

Table 26: Additional Research Responses

Summary of Interview Response

The UK non-profit organisation has 30 employees with eight employee's turnover, while the UAE non-profit has 200 employees with 25 employee's turnover at the time of data collection. The UAE organisation participants have spent between 9 months to 10 years in the organisation, while the UK participants have spent between 2 to 18 years in their organisation.

When asked what participants liked most about their jobs, the UAE participants mentioned teamwork, varieties, cultural diversity, career advancement, helping local communities, and making a difference. In contrast, the UK participant mentioned work-life balance, making a difference in society, working with different people, and training opportunities.

When this researcher asked participants about what they find challenging in their roles, the UAE participants mentioned language barrier, open-ended tasks, no work-life balance, and lack of structured format in measuring efforts. In contrast, the UK participants mentioned continuous service adds on, financial constraints and organisation recurrent restructuring.

The researcher asked further if extracurricular activities will help motivate participants at their jobs. Most of the participants said yes but gave more insight. Participants from the UAE did not forget to mention that they are stretched at their day-to-day activities already and adding extracurricular activities might increase their stress level instead of relieving it. However, if the organisation could prioritise work-life balance, then extracurricular activities could work as a motivation factor. The UK participants agree that extracurricular activities would motivate them because they will mingle with employees from other departments. In contrast, some of the participants said they would prefer to go home to family and friends.

Research participants were also asked how involved they are in planning the work they do in their various roles. Most of the UAE participants mentioned that they were very much involved in planning their roles because the organisation gives them ownership in completing their tasks, and the same applies to the UK participants.

When this researcher asked how employees' performance is evaluated by the organisation from the participants, it became apparent that the UAE organisation does not have any structured method in place but is measured through other processes like annual appraisals and so on. While the UK organisation primarily focuses on appraisals as well to determine if organisational goals are met.

Participants were further asked how they receive feedback in their roles. The UAE participants receive timely feedback on their various roles, but the reoccurrence usually depends on whom the employees report to. In contrast, the UK participants receive recurrent feedback but mainly through emails, and they do not like the feedback email strategy.

Job satisfaction is always an essential factor when it comes to employee retention. When the UAE participants were asked if there is any method to measure job satisfaction, most of the answers were no, but they would love it if the organisation started doing it again like they did years back. In contrast, the UK participants explained that it is mostly done informally but making it formal for everyone would be a great strategy.

Participants were further asked about the role their departments play in regard to retention. The UAE organisation human resources answered the question by saying they start by employing suitable candidates and giving them the required training and development to perform better in their roles. Some of the participants also mentioned that they encourage retention by treating their colleagues fairly and with respect. The UK participants also mentioned that training is one of the strategies they use in retaining employees in addition to employee engagement and a flexible feedback process.

This researcher asked further if there was any organisational retention policy in place. Both organisations explained that they do not have any retention policy in place. However, they have various strategies like training, career development, reasonable pay rates and the likes to encourage retention.

Research participants were asked if they get enough training and supervision in their various roles. According to the participant's responses, both organisations seem to be doing well in these aspects, even though some of the UK participants said their organisation could do better.

At the end of the interview, each participant was asked if they have further information to share. Some UAE participants mentioned that the organisation needs a structured way to measure job satisfaction, prioritise work-life balance, and employ more staff. In contrast, the UK participants mentioned that they are tensed from the continuous restructuring of the organisation, financial constraints and lack of clear hierarchy regarding positions.

Figure 19: Research Word Cloud

Word cloud is a visual way of showcasing the visual communication between words (Lohmann et al., 2015). This visualisation shows the frequencies of words in a document. This word visualisation is primarily straightforward and attractive. Word cloud shows an overview of the most or highest frequency of words in data analysis (Heimer et al., 2014). The word cloud figure above shows how the word "employee" was more apparent than other words because it is what this research is mostly about. Employees are the focus of understanding why attrition or retention will occur in an organisation.

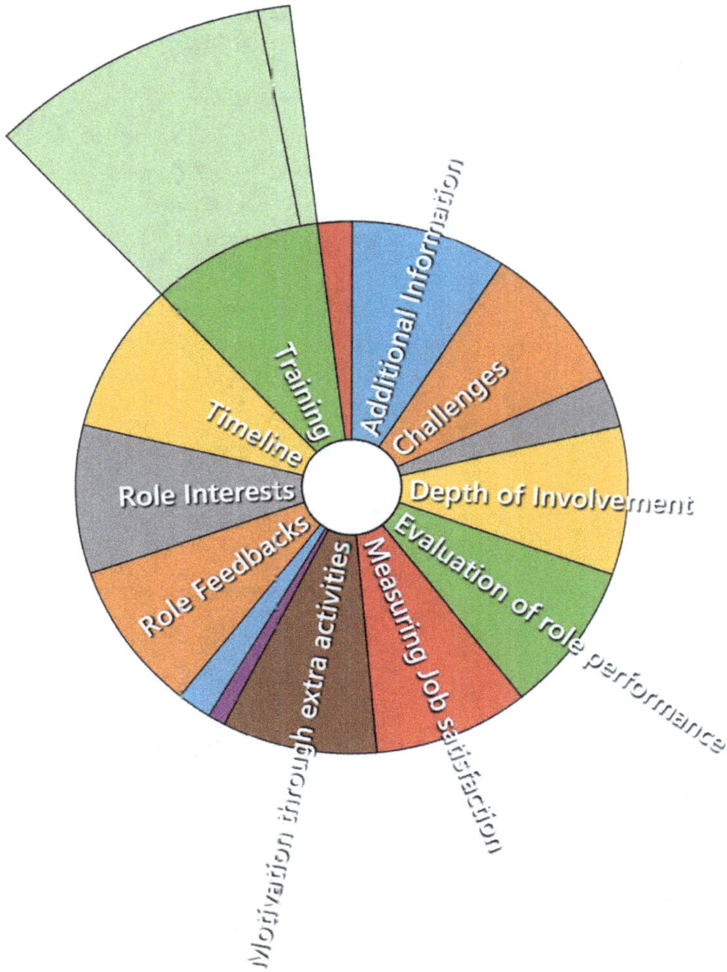

Figure 20: Coding themes based on number of coding references

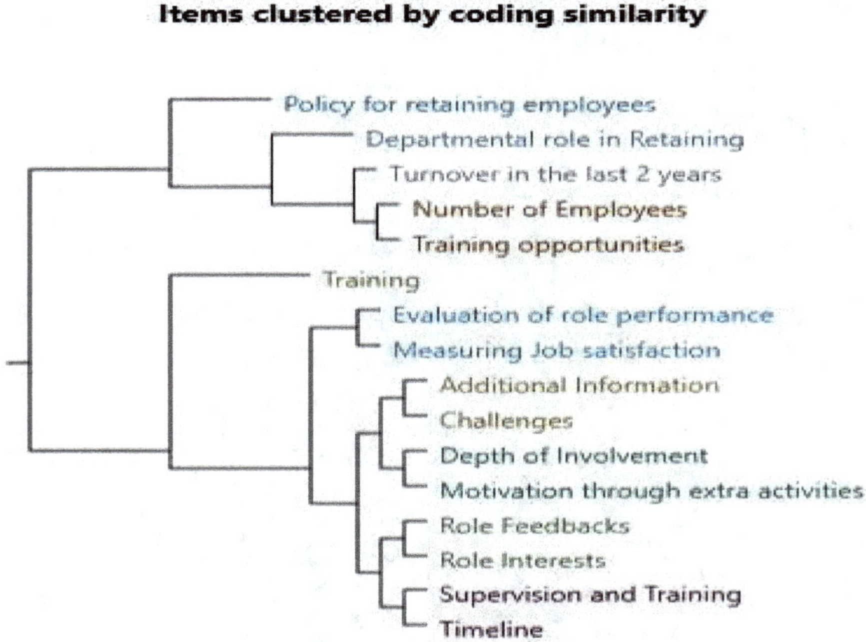

Figure 21: Cluster Analysis

Cluster analysis is an algorithm that allows related objects to be classified together (Wierzchon et al., 2018). This analysis produces a cluster set, even though each cluster is distinct from one another but shares a lot of similarities (Kassambara, 2017). It is usually classified into the two most compact clusters (Edwards et al., 1965). For example, the cluster analysis above shows the similarities between variables that impact employee attrition and retention in a non-profit organisation in the United Arab Emirates. This cluster analysis used directional lines and colours to show the relationship and similarities between various components in a tree format diagram.

5.3.Empirical Testing of Theories in the Secondary Data

This section tests the theories mentioned in the literature review to see how much the employee's responses fit.

Theories and Models	Questions	Responses
Herzberg Two Factors Theory	Are there processes in place to measure job satisfaction of your employees	Some of the Top management employees explained that there is a process in place. In contrast, the middle-level employees argued that there is no process that measures Job satisfaction and that it was carried out years ago and not recently. Some of the low-level employees explained that the organisations stopped the measure of job satisfaction process because employees used that opportunity to express their pains and lack of satisfaction. Still, the Top management could not achieve fulfilling their promises or rectify the issues raised by employees, and as a result, they stopped doing it. For example, Direct quote response from one of the top management employees ("We do like surveys to ask questions based on employee's satisfaction. But we usually do it on a one-on-one informal formats"). Direct quote response from one of the middle-level management employees ("I think they follow through the job evaluation and see if the goals set are achieved and try to understand why it is not achieved if not achieved. We do like a survey. We have both internal and external reviews to determine promotions, so nothing specific to job satisfaction"). Direct quote response from one of the low-level management employees ("No, the organisation tried conducting employees job satisfaction program 2 years ago, but it did not turn out well because employees were asking for more and complaining over multiple things. I believe if they do it consecutively, it will reduce hard feelings from employees and employees will be able to express themselves early enough, and the necessary actions can be carried out").

Social Exchange Theory	How will you describe the role your function unit plays in retaining your employee?	The top-level management explained that they support their employees and make sure that their employees get the necessary training required for them to perform well in their various roles. The human resources department explained that they achieve this by first interviewing the right set of employees for the job and then create the right organisational culture. The human resources further clarify that they prioritise their employee's requests and try to be flexible as much as possible. Example of a direct quote "As an HR coordinator, I think by hiring the right employees, creating the right culture, and being more flexible to employees' requests". "We encourage employee engagement and make sure employees are well trained in other to perform their role effectively. Employees are also free to give feedback. I personally do have open conversations with my teams to discuss feedback and adjust where necessary".
Vroom Expectancy Theory	Role Interest and Motivation through extra activities	Example from direct response "I like many things about my job. First, I like the fact that I am able to work on a variety of projects and not just one. We support education and support different audiences. We try to support as much as we can to help develop the community". "I like the fact that I work for a charity organisation and making a difference, I used to work for profit-making organisations, so this transition into non-profit is really fulfilling, knowing I am helping different people daily. Money made in non-profits is reinvested into other causes instead of making someone wealthier. I enjoy how we work with different people. I also enjoy the fact that I am very much involved in the work that I do while getting the necessary support from my line manager. I initiate so many ideas in my role". The employees explained in detail what motivates them at their job. Some of the employees said Teamwork, helping local communities, working with lots of varieties and the fact that the organisation is culturally diversified motivates them. Some employees also mentioned that interacting with different people, doing research that helps inform policy and

		liaising with students who come into the organisation for research motivates them. Some explained further that the ability to make a difference, influencing a lot of things, supporting as much as they can to help develop the community and the family-like working environment coupled with the remuneration benefits helps motivates them.
Maslow Theory	Measuring Job satisfaction	Example of direct response "I will not call it that, but we have annual goal settings, and we have organisation, departmental and individual goals checked with progress. There is a system to know if people are getting the professional development they like on a yearly basis. Non as regards satisfaction, though, but they can tell managers if anything is wrong but in a non-structured way. No formal system in place". Most of the employees explained that there is no form of measure in place to confirm if their needs are met formally. The interviewee also analysed that the UAE organisation tried conducting employees job satisfaction programs a few years ago, but the process did not turn out well because employees were asking for more and complaining about multiple things. The employees believed that if the organisation measures job satisfaction consecutively, it will reduce hard feelings from employees, and employees will be able to express themselves early enough, and the organisation can carry out the necessary actions. Some of the middle-level management team explained that they would not call the measure in place job satisfaction measure, but they have annual goal settings where organisation, departmental and individual goals are checked with progress. There is a system to know if employees are getting the professional development, they like every year. Non as regards satisfaction, though, but

		employees can tell managers if anything is wrong but in a non-structured way because there is no formal system in place. Some of the top-level management team explained that they measured Job satisfaction in the past in the form of surveys, but they have not done any in a while though they plan to do another one for the coming year. The top-level management team concurred that they do measure job satisfaction but not in a systematic way that they ought to. In terms of job satisfaction, they offer things like off sick days for employees for better performance and so on. But some of the employees said they do not like the idea of the organisation not being able to measure efforts because the organisation is a non-profit organisation. Employees tend to work in various environments depending on where projects need to be carried out.
Equity theory and Employee Motivation	Challenges at work	Example of direct response "Having conversations with people from different countries and the challenges is the language barrier, and I must talk to them and give feedback. Talent hunt is quite challenging, and because of this, some positions are usually open for too long". "I am used to the way things are done in the profit-making sectors because everyone already knows their role and what might be at stake if the necessary financial analysis is not carried out. But here, it is diversified, and most of the people are more passionate about their cause and talents without considering the financial constraints, and because I handle the organisation's finances, it can sometimes be challenging to make them understand this. So, I usually have to explain to them in detail how it's important to be financially responsible and fulfil other important causes". The employees of this organisation ascertain that there is equality regarding how the organisation treats all

		their employees.
McClelland Human Motivation Theory	Depth of Involvement at Work	Example of direct response "Highly involved, I am on the leadership team, so if I am not directly involved, then I am usually somehow connected, or my team is connected to many of the organisation activities. Since the organisation is not huge most of us are usually involved in planning and implementing activities". "I am very involved, but I have a collaborative nature, so I also involve and carry my superiors along in anything I do. I share the necessary information with them coupled with the fact I am a great team player because I like to be very open with my work in case, I choose to do some things differently, they will understand why that is important". The need for power, achievement and affiliation was apparent in these two organisations coupled with its dominance. Some of the employees explained that the organisation entrusts them with various roles. At the same time, they collaborate with all the departments because some of the employees are empowered to set the departmental goals and partake in follow up. The employees enjoy the fact that they are highly involved in their work, while the ones who are always told what to do seems to complain about the top-level management. Most of the top-level management team confirms that they are extremely involved in the work they do. These employees coordinate various research and interact with the CEO and executives on organisational goals and are involved in all levels of the organisation's plans. Some of the employees further explained that they

		are highly engaged because their roles involve finding issues and resolving them. Few of the middle-level employees explained that they have the power of planning any program to be handled, so they design the programs and projects they will execute, after which they will pass it on to the top-level management for their decision.
Job Coupling	Challenges: Employee compatibility with Organisation	Example of direct response "I do not like the idea of not being able to measure efforts. Because it's a non-profit organisation we tend to work in various environments depending on where the project to be carried out is". Not all the employees seem to be comfortable with the way things are in the organisations. Some employees explained that the organisation focuses on accountability, which they explain is not too good because they focus only on the goals. They have no idea if employees are happy or not. The employees explained that the organisation needs more employees, and it would be good if they reduce working hours because one employee is usually overburdened with too much workload. An interviewee further explains that People burn out due to stress and too much work. Some of the employees do not feel empowered, and some people leave due to frustration.
Job Embeddedness	Challenges	Example of direct response "Definitely. Is there a particular area you want me to focus on? Well, I think it's connected to the fact I mentioned earlier that the organisation operates in an open-ended format. Too many open-ended things here at the organisation, so sometimes there are challenges due to being too open-ended where some of us end up being spread a little too thin but still trying to maintain a high quality of product or services. Because quality is taken has a high priority. Due to this variety, it is usually difficult to maintain a balance of work and rest". "Expectations sometimes do exceed staff allocation and financial issues". Job fits, relationships, and sacrifice seem to be a bit of a challenge in this organisation because some of the employees explained that they are stretched too thin and end up

		carrying out roles that were not in their job description as a result of limited employees.
Zinger Retention Model	Challenges: Employee engagement	Example of direct response "The organisation focuses on accountability, which is not too good because they focus only on the goals. They have no idea if employees are happy or not. They need more employees, and it will be good if they reduce working hours because one employee is usually overburdened with too much workload. People burn out due to stress and too much work. Some of the employees do not feel empowered, and some people leave due to frustration". Some of the employees asked this researcher to advise the top management to try and encourage employee engagement because it is lacking in the organisation.
ERC Retention Model	Challenges: Varieties of work	Example of direct response "It can be stressful sometimes to juggle many tasks due to few numbers of employees". Employees explained that these organisations operate too many open-ended activities, especially the UAE organisation. So, as a result, some of the employees sometimes face different challenges due to these open-ended issues where some of them end up being spread a little too thin while still trying to maintain a high quality of products or services. Because quality is considered a high priority, due to these varieties, it is usually tricky for employees to maintain a balance of work and rest.
Integrated Retention Model	Policy for retaining employees	Example of direct response "No specific policy per se, but we offer a professional development budget every year for all employees at all levels and offer training to everyone. We have an annual staff retreat where we all go away for one night. We spend a lot on training employees, and we provide lunch to everyone. We give

	employees the opportunity to execute a personal project. So, I will say no specific policy but a combination of lots of things we do to make our employees feel very comfortable". The top-level organisation management explained that there is no specific retention policy in place. But both organisations offer professional developments budget every year for employees at all levels and provide training to everyone. The UAE organisation have an annual staff retreat where all employees go away for one night. The top management also analysed that they spend a lot on training employees, and the UAE management provide lunch to everyone. They allow employees to execute a personal project, give them a competitive salary package and benefit. So, they concluded that there is no specific policy in place but a combination of lots of things they do to make their employees feel very comfortable.

Table 27: Empirical Test of Theories in the Literature Review

Further Summary of Interview Findings

In the UAE non-profit organisation, thirty per cent of the total employees have left their job in this organisation in the past two years, which is a high rate of employee attrition (UAE chosen Non-profit organisation report, 2019). The interviewed employees have spent 1-10 years in the organisation. While in the UK non-profit organisation, employee attrition is just a little over 10% at the time of this research interview.

Some of the UAE employees explained that they face challenges like language barriers issues with people they must render their services by communicating with them and giving necessary feedback because they are usually from various countries. The participants also explained that the talent hunt is quite challenging, and as a result of this, some positions are usually open for too long. Due to this issue, some of the employees have to Juggle many tasks which they do not seem to be comfortable with. The UK non-profit organisation participants might not have language barrier issues. Still, they also struggle with juggling too many tasks because of the continuous add on of service from their organisation which they explained is stressful to cope with.

Through this research interview, some of the middle-level management struggles with not having all the answers to a few issues at hand. At the same time, top-level management has high expectations of always being number one. The employees feel there should be an improvement in the administrative and human resources section of the organisation.

Some of the employees enjoy their job and feel connected to the organisation because the organisation provides bonuses, celebrates their birthdays, and gives necessary holidays. Both organisations also offer professional development in addition to travelling opportunities for UAE employees. Employees retreats are also available, and that is appreciated as extracurricular activities by some of the employees.

The researcher asked the employees if extracurricular activities would help ease their stress. Some of the employees agree that it will encourage employee engagement which seems to be lacking, while others feel it might add to the already exhausting job.

The top-level management explanation as regards extracurricular activities was that some of the employees are more of an introvert and sees break time as a time to unwind and be by themselves, to relax since they have been engaged all day.

One of the employees in UAE said the organisation have a lunchtime setting where everyone can come together and eat for a couple of hours which he feels is a perfect way to interact with fellow employees. This employee further explains that because workdays are usually intense in general that this ideology of extracurricular activities will work only on an occasional basis. Few employees ascertain those extracurricular activities will help the organisation, but the varieties will depend on individuals because different things motivate different people. Some might prefer an hour break or time off work while some prefer the flexibility as regards their jobs.

Some of the employees said the organisation is not doing so well as regards giving feedback. In contrast, others feel the twice in a year goals analysis feedback is enough, coupled with the fact that the organisation do call its employee's attention to things not done right. Some of the employees argued that the organisation shouldn't only give recurrent feedback when things are not right but should always give positive feedback when something is going great.

The top management team explained that the organisation do have an annual goal review where they get to conclude if the goals set for the year were achieved and reflect on what has been done and that employees occasionally receive feedback emails.

But some of the top management teams feel because they operate an open office policy that enables employees to share anything with them at any time, it is unnecessary to give recurrent feedback since employees are free to come in for one. Some of the managers also explained that they do face to face feedback, formal review through writing reports and meetings with fellow managers who will, in turn, pass the necessary information to their team. Regarding the evaluation of performance, some of the employees explained that there is no specific method in place. Still, if an employee is lagging, they will be called to order by the human resources department or sent an email, depending on how serious.

The top management team explained that their employees have an annual goal-setting format that they follow. These are the organisational and departmental goals, and they all have their individual goals. So, they meet with their managers quarterly to review the plans and see if they met them or not and discuss them. Then the management discusses bonuses and other things earned by the employees at that stage. Top management further explained that at the beginning of every year, they have annual goal and performance meetings where they have touch base meetings with managers and evaluate performance as the projects progress.

The UAE organisation also operates a five grading formats like significantly below expectations, below expectations, meet expectations, above expectations, and significantly above expectations to analyse their employee's performance annually. Then the management decides on bonuses based on this performance.

From the interview conducted, the researcher concluded that some of the employees are happy with the way the organisation operates while others are not. The unhappy employees are more of the middle and low management team. The Top management team feel they are doing most things right, but the middle and low-level employees do not share the same thought. For example, the top management thinks the variety of roles given to their employees will motivate them, but the employees said this ideology stresses and burns them out. The employees believe the organisation should hire more people so that the workload won't be too much for them to handle because too many tasks with a limited amount of time are not sustainable for people to work so hard for so long. Some of the employees from both organisations ascertain that this might be the reason why people leave due to the intensity of workload; though it is noble, they try to serve the public as much as possible, but it's quite challenging for the employees. The employees also do not feel appreciated enough for the services they render for these organisations and insist that feedback should not only be given for terrible situations. Some of the UAE employees said the organisation should do something as regard language barrier issues because they need to work with people from various countries; the organisation should find a way to bridge this gap.

The UAE and UK employees are happy with the organisation's support concerning career development and training because a few employees who are happy to stay back in the organisation said this is one of their primary driving forces. Still, they want a structured way of measuring job satisfaction and some enhanced means of acknowledgement. The UK participants complained that the issue of recurrent restructuring in the organisation is quite discouraging and that, as a result, the idea of job stability is threatening. The UAE organisation helps its local community by hiring fresh graduates, primarily through an internship, so some of the top management teams feel the employees leave to further their studies and explore greener pastures.

5.4.Descriptive Statistical Analysis

In addition to the qualitative data analysis, this research adopted elements of statistical analysis to increase the level of research validity and reliability in other to produce consistent results and answers to research questions. The statistical analysis was generated from the conducted employee's self-completion survey questionnaire.

Descriptive statistics are mathematical figures that help summarises collated data by illustrating the relationships and what occurs in a data set (Thompson, 2009). Descriptive statistics also makes it easy to compare one group of data with the other (Lawless and Heymann, 2010). For example, it will be beneficial for the comparative analysis of the UAE and UK non-profit organisations used in this study. This type of statistic explains the set of characteristics that influences research results (Thompson, 2009). The frequency distribution is the first set of analysis carried out on the data set most of the time because of its valuable method for defining nominal and ordinal data levels (Kaliyadan and Kulkarni, 2019). Because this research is majorly qualitative complex statistical analysis was not adopted.

The data for this section was gathered with an online-based questionnaire, started by gathering demographic-related questions from employees. This helped the study analyse the group each of the respondents falls into. In the light of the theories and models that were studied in-depth and explained in the literature review, various questions relating to career developments and training were considered as this also analysed basic salaries, bonuses, annual leaves, accommodation, allowances, health care and so on. Under this factor, promotion opportunities, internal transfer flexibility, the adequacy of training opportunities, transfer to or within another affiliate, culture and leadership style were considered. Employee work-life balance was also investigated, and this entails flexibility of employee's schedule, convenient means of transportation, supervision, comfort experienced in the working environment, sincerity in performance appraisals, and the professional skills of organisation supervisors.

Questions relating to work challenges, frequency of meetings, innovation opportunities, involvement in decision making, learning opportunities, professional experiences and the likes were also responded to by the employees.

Factors like teamwork, organisation location, work pressure and job stability were part of the questions asked as regards why employees decide to stay in their current position.

Employees in these two organisations were also asked about factors they think impact retention and options like a salary increase, bonuses, employee welfare, promotion, and flexibility in job roles were considered. Furthermore, factors like regular training opportunities, flexible working hours, involvement in decision making, a flexible day off, motivating working environment, communication, supervision guide, and organisation vision were also considered. The descriptive statistic aspect of the data was analysed using statistical frequency, mean, and a few statistical data analysis tools.

Descriptive Statistical Comparative Analysis of UAE and UK Chosen Non-profit Organisations

This section shows the descriptive statistical comparative analysis of UAE and UK Non-profit organisations. This data was collated using a self-completed questionnaire through an online survey (Zoho). This questionnaire was mainly directed at the Middle and low-level employees because most of the Top-level employees have been interviewed, which allows saturation point to be reached. Eighty participants partake in the survey, 50 from the UK non-profit organisation and 30 from UAE non-profit organisation. This section helps draw a conclusion based on the proposed and developed factors contributing to employee attrition and the best strategies to help enhance retention. This section analysis started with demographic questions. Demographic information involves showing the age, gender, educational level, languages and sometimes ethnicity of participants depending on the research area, questions and expected results (Balkin and Sheperis, 2011). Without research participants' demographic information, researchers tend to speculate that all research participants' interest is identical regardless of age, class, culture, etc. Getting this information will allow researchers to achieve a stance of universalism that showcases the apparent differences in research participants (Beins, 2017). Describing research participants demographic characteristics gives researchers and readers detailed information on the similarities and differences in research outcomes and why, which can also be used in secondary data for future purposes (Beins, 2017).

S/N	Responses	Frequency	Per Cent
1	Complete	17	53
2	Incomplete	14	44
3	Disqualified	1	3
	Total	32	100

Table 28: Population response rate (UAE)

S/N	Responses	Frequency	Per Cent
1	Complete	28	55
2	Incomplete	22	43
3	Disqualified	1	2
	Total	51	100

Table 29: Population response rate (UK)

The tables above show the number of participants in the survey aspect of the research data collection. This researcher will call this a strong turnout considering the population of the company employees. For the UAE organisation, only one of the responses was disqualified, while a few had one or two questions skipped, but 53 per cent of the participants answered all the questions. While for the UK organisation, only one response was also disqualified with few questions skipped, and 55 per cent of the participant population answered all the questions in the questionnaire.

Choices	Response per cent	Response Count
Top Level Manager	9.9%	2
Middle-Level Manager	13.64%	3
Supervisor	13.64%	3
Middle Level staff Members	40.91%	9
Entry Level Staff Member	18.18%	4
Other (Executive)	4.55	1

Table 30: Employment Role (UAE)

Choices	Response percent	Response count
Top Level Manager	2.78%	1
Middle-Level Manager	22.22%	8
Supervisor	8.33%	3
Entry Level	38.89%	14
Other (Please specify)	27.78%	10

Table 31: Employment Role (UK)

Based on the second survey question about employee’s current role in the organisation, the tables above show that the highest number of participants in UAE are from the middle-level staff members with a response of 40.91%, followed by the entry staff member of 18.18% and 13.64% responses from both the middle-level managers and supervisors. Finally, 9.09% of responses are from top-level management plus one response from the company's senior executive.

In contrast, the highest number of participants in the UK are from the entry-level staff members with a 38.89% response rate, followed by the 27.78% rate from other departments and 22.22% from the middle-level management. 8.33% of the responses are from supervisory roles, with 2.78% responses from the top-level management.

These roles variety responses were robust, considering that most top-level management and executives participated in the research interview.

Choices	Response per cent	Response Count
Research and Development	18.18%	**4**
Program Delivery	31.82%	**7**
Technical Support	0.00%	**0**
Procurement	0.00%	**0**
General Management	4.55%	**1**
Marketing	18.18%	**4**
Human Resource	0.00%	**0**
Finance	4.55%	**1**
Customer Service	0.00%	**0**
Administrative Support	9.09%	**2**
Other (Please specify) - 1.External Collaborations & Outreach 2.Engagement/managing editor 3.Education	13.64%	**3**

Table 32: Nature of Job (UAE)

Choices	Response per cent	Response count
Research and Development	0.00%	0
Human Resource	11.11%	4
Engineering	0.00%	0
General Management	11.11%	4
Programming	5.56%	2
Technical Support	2.78%	1
Procurement	0.00%	0
Industrial Management	2.78%	1

Marketing	0.00%	0
Finance	5.56%	2
Others ((1.) Front of house (2.) Customer Service * 6 (3.) Library Assistant (4.) Sales*2 (5.) Beauty Therapist (6.) Operational (7.) Programming (8.) Receptionist (9.) Leisure (10.) Project Manager *2 (11.) Administration (12.) Sports and Exercise Delivery (13.) Gym Work (14.) Library (15.) Programming)	61.11%	22

Table 33: Nature of Job (UK)

The third question was based on the nature of employee's job. The tables above show the categories of job nature and the percentage of participant that falls under each. For UAE, 31.82% of the participants are from the program delivery department, while 18.18% are from the research and development department,18% are from the marketing department, and 4.55% are from the finance department. In addition, 9.09% of the participants are from administration support. While 13.64% of the participants are from other departments: the external collaborations & Outreach, Engagement/managing editor and education department.

For the UK non-profit organisation, 61.11% of the participants are from the above listed "other" department in the table, 11.11% from human resources and 11.11% from the general managers. 5.56% of the participants are from both programming and finance, with 2.78% from both industrial management and technical support. All the departments in both organisations participated in this research, and a saturation level was reached.

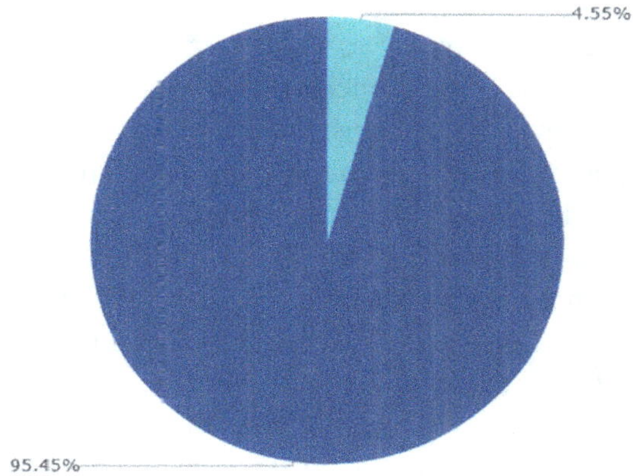

Figure 22: Employment contract (UAE)

● Part-time Employee ● Full-time Employee ● Volunteer

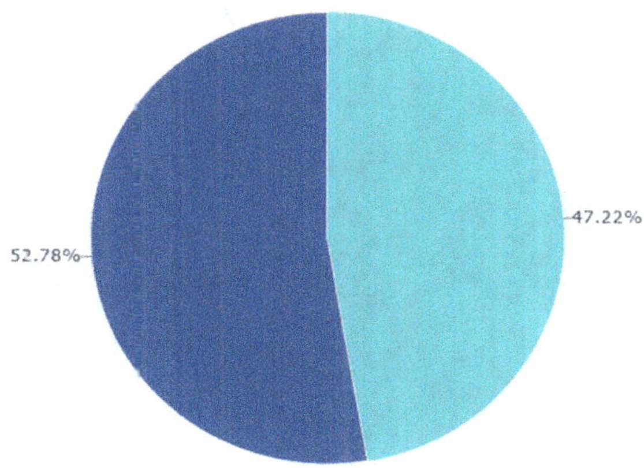

Figure 23: Employment contract (UK)

● Part-time Employee ● Full-time Employee ● Volunteer

The fourth survey question talks about the kind of employment contracts research participants operate because this question helps understand if the type of employee employment contracts affects employee attrition in the organisations.

The figures above show the percentage of employment contracts from research participants. For the UAE organisation, 95.45% of employees in the organisation are full-time employees, while 4.55% fall under the part-time employee category. None of the participants is a volunteer staff which explains that the organisation either has a limited number of volunteers or none at all. For the UK organisation, 52.78% of the survey participants are full-time employees, while 47.22% of the employees work part-time. Compared to the UAE employment results, it shows that the UK non-profit organisation has almost equal numbers of employees working full time and part-time, which shows high employment flexibility, unlike the UAE with 95% full-time employees. These results also show that employees in UAE have more employees who are more tied to their jobs than the UK organisation. Employment flexibility usually makes it easy for employees to quit an organisation (Lambert et al., 2012).

How many years have you been working in this organisation	Number of Employees
Less than 2 Years	**5**
2-5 Years	**11**
6 – 10 Years	**5**
>10 Years	**0**

Table 34: Years of Employment (UAE)

How many years have you been working in this organisation	Number of Employees
Less than 2 Years	**11**
2 - 5 Years	**15**
6 - 10 Years	**6**
>10 Years	**4**

Table 35: Years of employment (UK)

Survey question five was about the number of years participants have worked with the UAE and UK non-profit organisations. For the UAE organisation, five of the participants have been with the organisation for less than two years. At the same time, eleven of the employee participants have been in the organization for two to five years. Five of the survey participants has been working in the organisation for six to ten years. None of the employees has been with the organisation for more than ten. At the time this data was collected, the UAE organisation was ten years and a few months old. These responses show that majority of the employees have been with the organisation for two to five years. For the sake of data analysis, this researcher would like to add that the five participants who have stayed in the organisation for more than six years are top-level managers and executives.

For the UK organisation, eleven of the employee participants have been working in the organisation for less than two years. Fifteen of the participants have been in the organisation for two to five years. Six of the participants have been working in the organisation for a period of six to ten years. At the same time, four of the survey participants from the UK organisation has been with the organisation for more than ten years.

The above tables and analysis show that this research has a participant representing all years of company employment. As a result, it was easier to get reliable responses from all levels and employees with long and limited experiences.

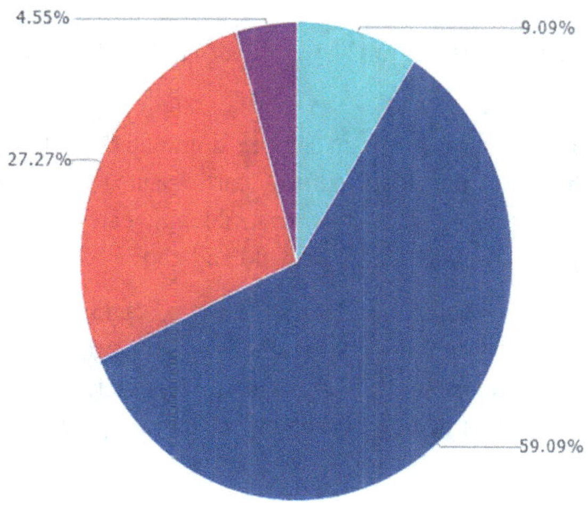

Figure 24: Age group (UAE)

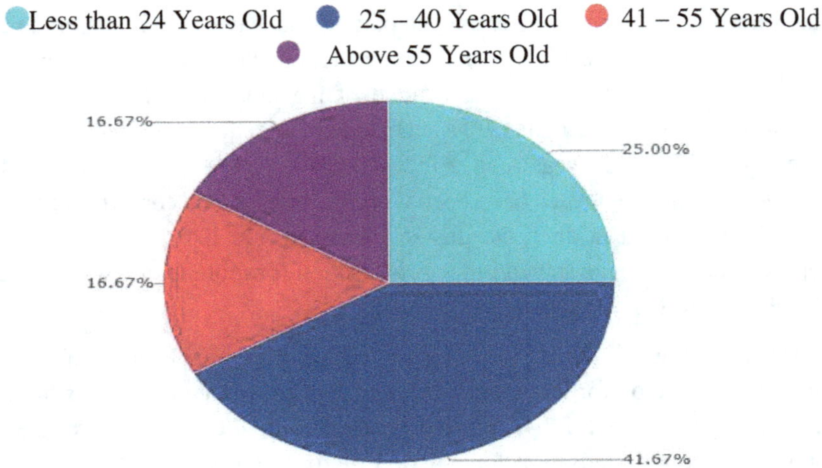

Figure 25: Age group (UAE)

Less than 24 Years Old 25 – 40 Years Old 41 – 55 Years Old Above 55 Years Old

The diagrams above shows that the UAE non-profit organisation is more dominated by the 25 to 40 age group, with 59.09% of the total survey participants. Followed by 27.27% of 41 to 55 years old. 9.09% of the participant's population falls below 24 years old. And 4.55% above 55 years of age group.

The UK non-profit organisation is also more dominated by the 25 to 40 age group, with 41.67% of the total survey participants. 25% of the survey population falls under the below 24 years old age categories, followed by 16.67% of participants for both 41-55-year-old and above 55 years old group.

With this analysis, it can be concluded that the two organisations shared some similarities in regards to the 25 – 40 years old employee group, which is usually the most active age range in the workforce. However, the UK has more percentage below 24 years of age participant when compared to the UAE age group range result.

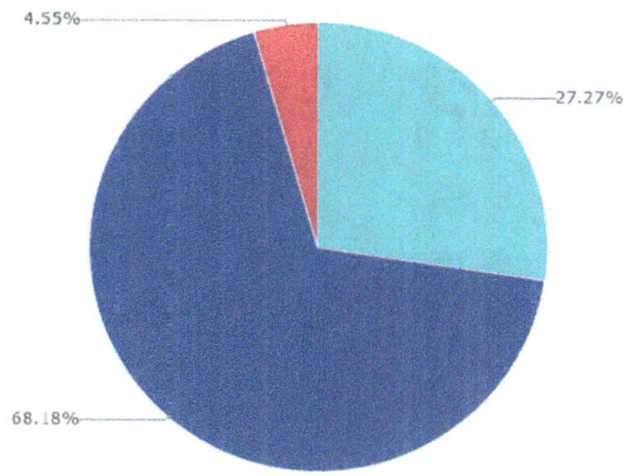

Figure 26: Gender (UAE)

● Male ● Female ● Other (Please specify)

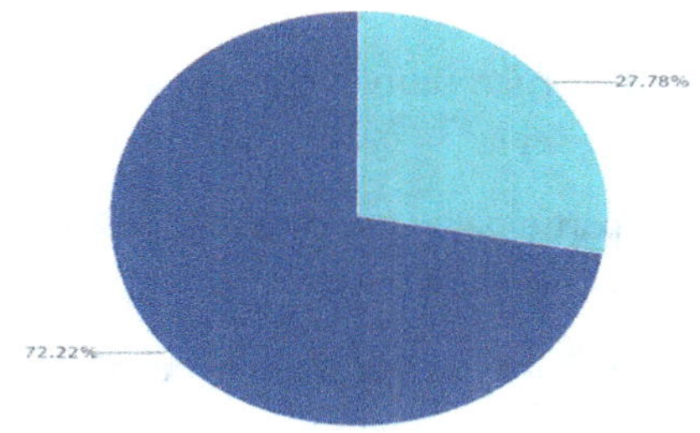

Figure 27: Gender (UK)

● Male ● Female ● Other (Please specify)

Based on the figures above, the two non-profit organisations participants are female gender, with 68.18% for the UAE and 72.22% for the UK. This is followed by 27.27 % males in UAE and 27.78% males in the UK, with a 4.55% unknown gender in the UAE.

This research shows that more females than males dominate both non-profit organisations. This uniqueness also helped in increasing the validity of the comparative analysis of both organisations.

Choices	Response Per Cent	Response Count
Single	36.36%	8
Married	63.64%	14
Divorce/Separate	0.00%	0
Widowed	0.00%	0

Table 36: Marial status (UAE)

Choices	Response Per Cent	Response Count
Single	38.89%	14
Married	50.00%	18
Divorce/Separate	11.11%	4
Widowed	0.00%	0

Table 37: Marital status (UK)

For the UAE non-profit organisation, 63.64% of the survey participants are married, while 36.3% are single.

50% of the UK survey participants are married, 38.89% are single, and 11.11% with a divorce or separate marital status.

Both organisations have more married employees than single or divorced from the analysis above. This is because employees with married marital status tend to stay in an organisation longer for family stability than singles or separated, and this can encourage employee retention to a certain degree (Nadler and Kufahl, 2014).

Choices	Response per cent	Response count
Less than bachelor's degree	22.73%	5
Bachelor's Degree	22.73%	5
Master's Degree	40.91%	9
Doctoral Degree	13.64%	3

Table 38: Level of Education (UAE)

Choices	Response percent	Response count
Less than bachelor's degree	50.00%	18
Bachelor's Degree	33.33%	12
Master's Degree	16.67%	6
Doctoral Degree	0.00%	0

Table 39: Level of Education (UK)

The tables above show participants' levels of education from the UAE and UK non-profit organisations. 40.91% of the UAE participants have a master's degree, with 22.73% for both bachelor's and below bachelor's degree holders and 13.64% doctoral degree holders.

In the UK organisation, 50% of the participants have a bachelor's degree, with 33.33% with a bachelor's degree and 16.67% with a master's degree.

From the analysis above, participants in the UAE are more educated when compared to UK organisations. None of the UK participants has a doctorate with a high percentage of below bachelor's degree compared to UAE.

Tables 13 and 14 analyse factors that influence participants in joining the organisation as an employee. The response to this question helped this researcher understand what attracted employees to these two organisations. It can also help the organisation retain its employees if it maintains the attraction features. Learning what pulls skilled employees to an organisation will help an organisation maintain a competitive edge in their area of operation even though diverse strategies might be needed to attract various skilled workers (Alniacik et al., 2014). Employees are attracted to an organisation due to shared values because they give the employees what they need. In return, the employees give their best service to help the organisation grow or leave if their initial attraction to the organisation ends (Thomas and Letchmiah, 2017).

Row	1	2	3	4	5	Average rating	Response count
Basic Salary	33.33% (7)	52.38% (11)	9.52% (2)	4.76% (1)	0.00% (0)	1.86	21
Bonuses	19.05% (4)	19.05% (4)	28.57% (6)	28.57% (6)	4.76% (1)	2.81	21
Annual Leave	42.86% (9)	23.81% (5)	23.81% (5)	9.52% (2)	0.00% (0)	2	21

Accommodation Allowance	23.81% (5)	28.57% (6)	14.29% (3)	23.81% (5)	9.52% (2)	2.67	21
Health Care	42.86% (9)	19.05% (4)	23.81% (5)	9.52% (2)	4.76% (1)	2.14	21
Others (Please Indicate Below)							5

Table 40: Factors influencing Decision of employment (UAE)

Average rating: 2.30

Additional factors mentioned by UAE participants as reasons behind joining the organisation: Prestige organisation, Foundation aligned with my personal values and that the work would allow me to make a positive difference in the local community and contribute something to the world. I work as a researcher in development, and the size of the organisation meant that I would be more involved and have more opportunities than elsewhere while still maintaining a decent standard of living -not always possible in development—the name of the organisation and its influence in Ras Al Khaimah.

Row	1	2	3	4	5	Average rating	Response count
Basic Salary	12.90% (4)	25.81% (8)	19.35% (6)	32.26% (10)	9.68% (3)	3	31
Bonuses	9.68% (3)	12.90% (4)	12.90% (4)	16.13% (5)	48.39% (15)	3.81	31
Annual Leave	16.13% (5)	19.35% (6)	25.81% (8)	19.35% (6)	19.35% (6)	3.06	31
Accommodation Allowance	9.68% (3)	6.45% (2)	6.45% (2)	3.23% (1)	74.19% (23)	4.26	31
Health Care	9.68% (3)	6.45% (2)	9.68% (3)	12.90% (4)	61.29% (19)	4.1	31
Others (Please Indicate Below)							4

Table 41: Factors influencing Decision of employment (UK)

Average rating: 3.65

Additional factors mentioned by UK participants as reasons behind joining the organisation: Type of job, Flexible Working Hours, Good social events and relationships with staff, staff benefits, for example, free gym

Table 13 and 14 above talks about the factors that influence employees to join the UAE and UK non-profit organisation. Using the indication from Strongly agree, agree, unsure, disagree to strongly disagree.

For the UAE non-profit organisation, most of the employees agree that "basic salary" is one of the reasons for working in the organisation, with 33.33% strongly agreeing responses and 52.38% agree responses. Only 9.52% of the respondents were unsure, and 4.76% disagreed.

5% of participants agree and strongly agree that "bonuses" are one of their influencing factors towards joining the UAE organisation, while 28.5% of respondents were both unsure and disagree. In addition, 4.78% strongly disagreed with the idea of being influenced by a company bonus.

42.8% and 23.8% of the survey participants strongly agree and agree, respectively, that "annual leave" influences their decisions towards joining the UAE non-profit organisation. On the other hand, 23.8% of the respondents, 23.8%, were unsure, while 9.52% disagreed.

23.8% of UAE respondents strongly agree, and 28.5% agree that "accommodation allowance" influences the decision towards joining the non-profit organisation. However, 14.2% of respondents were unsure, while 9.52% of respondents disagreed.

42.86% and 19.0% strongly agree that the "health care" provision helps influence their decision to join the UAE non-profit organisation. 23.81% were unsure, while 9.52% and 4.76% of the respondents disagreed and strongly disagreed, respectively. Some of the respondents shared further information that they joined the organisation because of its prestige and influence. Some of the employees also joined the organisation because of the foundation values that match theirs, the size of the organisation and available opportunities in the organisation.

In contrast, the UK non-profit organisation mostly disagree that salary influences their decision to join the UK non-profit organisation, while 32.26% disagree and 9.68% strongly disagree. Only 12.90% and 25.81% strongly agreed and agreed, respectively, while 19.35% of the respondents were unsure.

Regarding bonuses, 48.39% of the UK respondents strongly disagree that bonuses help influence their decision to join the UK non-profit organisation, while 16.13% disagree. 12.90% of the respondents agree, while 9.68% strongly agree, with 12.90% of unsure respondents.

25.81% of the UK respondents were unsure if "annual leave" influenced their decision to join the non-profit organisation, while 19.35% agreed and 16.13%bstrongly agreed about being influenced by the annual leave package. 19.35% strongly disagree and disagree, respectively.

74.19% of the UK respondents strongly disagree with having joined the organisation by the accommodation allowance provision, while 3.23% disagree. 9.68% and 6.45% of the UK respondents strongly agreed and agreed, respectively, that accommodation allowances influenced their decisions of joining the organisation, while 6.45% of the respondents were unsure.

61.29% of the UK respondents strongly disagree that health care provision influences their decisions in joining the organisation. Only 9.68% and 6.45% of the UK respondents strongly agree and agree that the organisation's health care provision influences their decision to join the organisation. 9.68% of these respondents were unsure, while 12.90% disagreed. Some of the UK respondents further explained that the nature of the job, flexible Working Hours, good social events and relationships with staff, staff benefits, and free gym membership are part of the factors that influenced them in joining the organisation.

From the analysis above, the UAE employees are more driven to join the organisation because of salary, annual leave, health care provision, and accommodation allowance when compared to the UK organisation. The UK respondents mostly joined their organisation for factors that will help increase employee engagement and job flexibility.

Understanding that different organisations have different factors for retaining their employees will help an organisation customise their influencing factors towards employing the right employees as a steppingstone towards retention.

Tables 15 and 16 below analyse why research participants decided to stay in both organisations after joining to work there. According to Schabracq, 2003 most employees remain in their organisation longer if their well-being and health are a priority to the organisation, alongside the respect employees get from the organisation, making the working environment safe and conducive. Organisations can extend employees life cycle in an organisation if the satisfaction level is high with a good leadership style and the required level of employee engagement (Cattermole, 2019). If organisations can discover early reasons why their skilled worker might want to leave, it will give them an edge to rectify the issues and keep their key employees (Ghosh et al., 2013).

Row	1	2	3	4	5	Average rating	Response count
Promotion Opportunities	23.81% (5)	9.52% (2)	19.05% (4)	33.33% (7)	14.29% (3)	3.05	21
Internal Transfer Flexibility	19.05% (4)	19.05% (4)	9.52% (2)	38.10% (8)	14.29% (3)	3.1	21
Adequate Training Opportunities	38.10% (8)	33.33% (7)	23.81% (5)	4.76% (1)	0.00% (0)	1.95	21
Transfer to Another Affiliate	19.05% (4)	9.52% (2)	33.33% (7)	23.81% (5)	14.29% (3)	3.05	21
Culture that exist in the Organisation	23.81% (5)	33.33% (7)	28.57% (6)	14.29% (3)	0.00% (0)	2.33	21
The Management Leadership Style	28.57% (6)	19.05% (4)	33.33% (7)	14.29% (3)	4.76% (1)	2.48	21
Others (Please Indicate Below)							2

Table 42: Factors that influence staying with the organisation (UAE)

Average rating: 2.66

Additional factors mentioned by participants as reasons behind staying in the organisation: The challenge in finding another work and the transfers, the relationship that has been built already, the above options are things that would influence me to stay but are currently lacking.

Row	1	2	3	4	5	Average rating	Response count
Promotion Opportunities	16.13% (5)	9.68% (3)	16.13% (5)	32.26% (10)	25.81% (8)	3.42	31

Internal Transfer Flexibility	16.13% (5)	22.58% (7)	19.35% (6)	16.13% (5)	25.81% (8)	3.13	31
Adequate Training Opportunities	12.90% (4)	32.26% (10)	16.13% (5)	9.68% (3)	29.03% (9)	3.1	31
Transfer to Another Affiliate	9.68% (3)	12.90% (4)	29.03% (9)	12.90% (4)	35.48% (11)	3.52	31
Culture that exist in the Organisation	19.35% (6)	29.03% (9)	22.58% (7)	9.68% (3)	19.35% (6)	2.81	31
The Management Leadership Style	12.90% (4)	32.26% (10)	9.68% (3)	22.58% (7)	22.58% (7)	3.1	31
Others (Please Indicate Below)							3

Table 43: Importance of factors influencing employment (UK)

Average rating: 3.18

Additional factors mentioned by participants towards retention: Currently training to be a teacher. This job is to get me through my training year.

Tables 15 and 16 show that the UAE and UK participants mostly disagreed that job promotion is one of the reasons they stayed in their organisations. The UAE participants mostly disagree about being motivated to stay by internal transfer flexibility, with a percentage of 38.10% (disagree) and 14.29% (strongly disagree). In contrast, the UK participants maintain an almost equilibrium percentage in this regard.

Both organisations were encouraged to stay due to adequate training opportunities. In terms of organisational culture, the UAE organisation are motivated to stay, while the average percentage of the UK participants agree to be motivated by the organisational factor. The UAE participants seem to be encouraged by their organisation's leadership style. In contrast, an equal number of the UK participants agreed and disagreed with being motivated to stay in their organisation based on the practised leadership style.

Tables 17 and 18 analyse the factors that make employees commit to their organisations long-term. According to Shahid and Azhar, 2013, it is easier for employees to commit to an organisation if they share mutual goals; thus, organisations should practice achieving a committed and engaged workforce. Organisations should adopt a good culture that portrays good values and beliefs to encourage employees to stay long-term and enhance employee retention (Westover et al., 2010).

Choices	Response per cent	Response count
Financial Rewards	11.11%	2
Promotion Opportunities	0.00%	0
Training and Personal Development	38.89%	7
Work-life balance	22.22%	4
Good Working Relationships	22.22%	4
Other (Fulfilling work)	5.56%	1

Table 44: Important factor that influences commitment towards the organisation (UAE)

Choices	Response per cent	Response count
Financial Rewards	3.45%	1
Promotion Opportunities	3.45%	1
Training and Personal Development	10.34%	3
Work-life balance	31.03%	9
Good Working Relationships	37.93%	11
Other (Please specify)	13.79%	4

Table 45: Important factor that influences commitment towards the organisation (UK)

Additional factors mentioned by participants regarding retention: My role is something I enjoy, and I'm knowledgeable about. None of the other factors, Love of books and my communities, good maternity pays, Works around my current life circumstances.

The UAE non-profit organisation considers the training and personal development of its employees as highly important, as acknowledged by 39% of the respondents as a reason they enjoy working with the organisation. The work-life balance and good working relationships trail with about 44% of the respondents equally influenced by them.

With the UK non-profit, the working relationships keep the majority of the employees happy and as a reason to extend their commitment to the organisation. 38% of the respondents enjoy good working relationships with their colleagues, while about 31% hold the position that work-life balance drives their commitments.

The analysis shows that while financial rewards and promotion opportunities may be considered, some of the factors influencing employee commitment to the organisation include work-life balance, good working relationships, training and personal development, all of which are crucial toward keeping the employees' commitment.

Row	1	2	3	4	5	Average rating	Response count
Schedule Flexibility	5.56% (1)	50% (9)	5.56% (1)	33.33% (6)	5.56% (1)	2.83	18
Convenient means of Transportation	11.11% (2)	16.67% (3)	27.78% (5)	33.33% (6)	11.11% (2)	3.17	18
Supportive Supervisor	16.67% (3)	50.00% (9)	16.67% (3)	16.67% (3)	0.00% (0)	2.33	18
Excellent IT Support	11.11% (2)	27.78% (5)	33.33% (6)	16.67% (3)	11.11% (2)	2.89	18
Comfortable Working Environment	33.33% (6)	44.44% (8)	22.22% (4)	0.00% (0)	0.00% (0)	1.89	18
Fair Performance Appraisal	22.22% (4)	38.89% (7)	33.33% (6)	5.56% (1)	0.00% (0)	2.22	18
Supervisor's Professional Skills	16.67% (3)	33.33% (6)	44.44% (8)	5.56% (1)	0.00% (0)	2.39	18
Others (Please Indicate Below)							1

Table 46: Factors influencing staying in the organisation (UAE)

Row	1	2	3	4	5	Average rating	Response count
Schedule Flexibility	44.83% (13)	27.59% (8)	13.79% (4)	6.90% (2)	6.90% (2)	2.03	29
Convenient means of Transportation	20.69% (6)	34.48% (10)	13.79% (4)	13.79% (4)	17.24% (5)	2.72	29
Supportive Supervisor	37.93% (11)	20.69% (6)	17.24% (5)	10.34% (3)	13.79% (4)	2.41	29
Excellent IT Support	17.24% (5)	24.14% (7)	20.69% (6)	24.14% (7)	13.79% (4)	2.93	29
Comfortable Working Environment	24.14% (7)	48.28% (14)	3.45% (1)	17.24% (5)	6.90% (2)	2.34	29
Fair Performance Appraisal	24.14% (7)	27.59% (8)	27.59% (8)	17.24% (5)	3.45% (1)	2.48	29
Supervisor's Professional Skills	31.03% (9)	24.14% (7)	17.24% (5)	17.24% (5)	10.34% (3)	2.52	29
Others (Please Indicate Below)							1

Table 47: Factors influencing staying in the organisation (UK)

For tables 19 and 20. Most employees of the UAE non-profit organisation employees, with over 55%, hold the position that schedule flexibility is one of the major reasons they chose to continue to stay with the organisation. The convenient means of transportation does not seem to be much of an important reason why the employees remain with the organisation as only about 28% are influenced by it. Over 66% of the employees consider a supportive supervisor a key reason to maintain one's loyalty to the organisation. However, 61% do not see a significant influence of IT Support on their continuing engagement with the organisation. Comfortable Working Environment and Fair Performance Appraisal also stand out as important factors, with over 77% and 71% of the employees respectively placing significant consideration on them. Meanwhile, the employees' perception of the Supervisor's Professional Skills towards their continuous stay in the organisation is divided into equal halves.

Lastly, similar to the UAE non-profit organisation, the UK non-profit organisation's employees place significant importance on Schedule Flexibility and a Comfortable Working Environment toward their continuous stay with the organisation, with over 72% agreement for each of the factors. The excellent IT support is also considered the least important factor to remain with the organisation amongst the UK non-profit organisation. Only about 41% of respondents consider it a reason to stay with the organisation. The convenient means of transportation seem to be more important to the UK non-profit, with over 55% of the employees continuing their engagement with the organisation. Supportive Supervisor and Supervisor's Professional Skills with over 58% and 55% respectively of the respondents considered them significant to keep their loyalty with the organisation. Of course, Fair Performance Appraisal, as expressed by over 51% of the respondents, is yet relatively another factor to reckon with in the UK non-profit organisation.

This analysis corroborates the importance of work-life balance for employees' commitment with an overwhelming consistent agreement by the two organisations to the impacts of schedule flexibility towards continuous employment with the organisations.

Tables 21 and 22 below also analysed factors influencing employees to stay in their organisation.

Still, the factors that influence employees continuing loyalty to the UAE non-profit organisation, according to the study, show significant consideration for learning opportunities and professional experiences, with a whopping 88% of the respondents holding the same position on the two factors. Similarly, over 72% of the respondents hold the position that their roles in the organisation meet with their personal interests and the challenging nature of the role and the innovative opportunities within the organisation influence their staying with the organisation. Still, 55% of the participants agreed that their involvement in decision making and the organisation's culture that facilitate the ability to work under little or no supervision encourage them to sustain their services with the organisation.

The UK non-profit organisation employees consider important their role as it fits into their personal interests, with over 68% of the participants agreeing to the position. The ability to work under little or no supervision is also elevated among the factors that influence the UK non-profit employees to stay with the organisation, according to 62% of the respondents. In the same vein, 55% of the study participants believe that the learning opportunities and the professional experiences they derive from the organisation are critical factors to their continuing engagement with the organisation. Meanwhile, more than 72% of the participants are either unsure or consider it not important to involve them in decision-making as a factor to keep them with the organisation. Similarly, only about 44% of the respondents see their challenging role as a factor to maintain loyalty to the organisation, as 68% of them are not influenced or not sure if they are influenced by the innovative opportunities in the organisation.

Irrespective of the organisation, the culture that supports and facilitates the ability of an employee to work under little or no supervision and ensures that employees' roles align with their personal interests tends to make the employee stay longer with the organisation.

Row	1	2	3	4	5	Average rating	Response count
Challenges at Work	16.67% (3)	55.56% (10)	27.78% (5)	0.00% (0)	0.00% (0)	2.11	18
Job Meeting Personal Interest	27.78% (5)	44.44% (8)	22.22% (4)	5.56% (1)	0.00% (0)	2.06	18
Innovative Opportunities	11.11% (2)	61.11% (11)	22.22% (4)	5.56% (1)	0.00% (0)	2.22	18
Involvement in Decision Making	27.78% (5)	27.78% (5)	33.33% (6)	5.56% (1)	5.56% (1)	2.33	18
Ability to Work under Little or No Supervision	27.78% (5)	27.78% (5)	33.33% (6)	5.56% (1)	5.56% (1)	2.33	18
Learning Opportunities	38.89% (7)	50.00% (9)	11.11% (2)	0.00% (0)	0.00% (0)	1.72	18
Professional Experiences	38.89% (7)	50.00% (9)	11.11% (2)	0.00% (0)	0.00% (0)	1.72	18
Others (Please Indicate Below)							1

Table 48: Factors influencing staying in the organisation (UAE)

Row	1	2	3	4	5	Average rating	Response count
Challenges at Work	10.34% (3)	34 48% (10)	31.03% (9)	20.69% (6)	3.45% (1)	2.72	29
Job Meeting Personal Interest	37.93% (11)	31.03% (9)	17.24% (5)	10.34% (3)	3.45% (1)	2.1	29
Innovative Opportunities	10.34% (3)	20.69% (6)	34.48% (10)	31.03% (9)	3.45% (1)	2.97	29
Involvement in Decision Making	10.34% (3)	17.24% (5)	31.03% (9)	20.69% (6)	20.69% (6)	3.24	29
Ability to Work	31.03%	31.03%	6.90% (2)	24.14%	6.90%	2.45	29

under Little or No Supervision	(9)	(9)		(7)	(2)		
Learning Opportunities	13.79% (4)	41.38% (12)	13.79% (4)	17.24% (5)	13.79% (4)	2.76	29
Professional Experiences	20.69% (6)	34.48% (10)	24.14% (7)	17.24% (5)	3.45% (1)	2.48	29
Others (Please Indicate Below)							0

Table 49: Factors influencing staying in the organisation (UK)

Tables 23 and 24 below show that teamwork retention strategy is one of the factors influencing participants from both organisations to stay. 85.71 % of the UK participants considered work-life balance as one of the main factors keeping them in their organisation, while half of the UAE survey participants said the same. This analysis also shows that the UK organisation implements a work-life balance strategy better when compared to the organisation in UAE. A higher percentage of both organisations participants agreed that one other factor influencing them to stay in their organisations is the organisation's location. The UAE participants are not motivated when it comes to working pressure, likewise with the UAE organisation but will lower percentage of disagrees compared to UAE. This analysis also shows that UK participants are discouraged by the lack of job stability in their organisation. In contrast, 70% of UAE participants mentioned that they were encouraged by the job stability in their organisation.

Row	1	2	3	4	5	Average rating	Response count
Teamwork	29.41% (5)	41.18% (7)	29.41% (5)	0.00% (0)	0.00% (0)	2	17
Work-life Balance	23.53% (4)	29.41% (5)	17.65% (3)	23.53% (4)	5.88% (1)	2.59	17
Organisation Location	23.53% (4)	35.29% (6)	29.41% (5)	5.88% (1)	5.88% (1)	2.35	17
Reduce Work Pressure	11.76% (2)	35.29% (6)	23.53% (4)	17.65% (3)	11.76% (2)	2.82	17
Job Stability	23.53% (4)	47.06% (8)	23.53% (4)	5.88% (1)	0.00% (0)	2.12	17
Others (Please Indicate Below)							1

Table 50: Factors influencing staying in the organisation (UAE)

Row	1	2	3	4	5	Average rating	Response count
Teamwork	25.00% (7)	46.43% (13)	10.71% (3)	10.71% (3)	7.14% (2)	2.29	28
Work-life Balance	53.57% (15)	32.14% (9)	3.57% (1)	10.71% (3)	0.00% (0)	1.71	28
Organisation Location	35.71% (10)	39.29% (11)	14.29% (4)	10.71% (3)	0.00% (0)	2	28
Reduce Work Pressure	17.86% (5)	35.71% (10)	21.43% (6)	14.29% (4)	10.71% (3)	2.64	28
Job Stability	32.14% (9)	14.29% (4)	17.86% (5)	25.00% (7)	10.71% (3)	2.68	28
Others (Please Indicate Below)							0

Table 51: Factors influencing staying in the organisation (UK)

Tables 25 and 26 analysed which retention methods employees' participants agree will encourage employee retention if adopted.

Organisations should understand what leads to employee attrition in their organisations and adopt various employee retention strategies (Sandhya and Kumar, 2011).

Organisations need to know which retention strategies suit their organisation and avoid a shoe fits all retention method (Presbitero et al., 2016). Adopting robust retention strategies will encourage employee retention if organisations are consistent and practice good organisational culture (Dechawatanapaisal, 2018).

Row	1	2	3	4	5	Average rating	Response count
Salary Increase	47.06% (8)	41.18% (7)	0.00% (0)	5.88% (1)	5.88% (1)	1.82	17
Bonus Increase	29.41% (5)	41.18% (7)	17.65% (3)	5.88% (1)	5.88% (1)	2.18	17
Improved Employee Welfare	64.71% (11)	35.29% (6)	0.00% (0)	0.00% (0)	0.00% (0)	1.35	17
Promotion	23.53% (4)	17.65% (3)	41.18% (7)	17.65% (3)	0.00% (0)	2.53	17
Flexibility in Job Roles	41.18% (7)	29.41% (5)	23.53% (4)	5.88% (1)	0.00% (0)	1.94	17
Frequent Training Opportunities	17.65% (3)	76.47% (13)	5.88% (1)	0.00% (0)	0.00% (0)	1.88	17
Participation in Decision Making	17.65% (3)	64.71% (11)	11.76% (2)	5.88% (1)	0.00% (0)	2.06	17
Flexible Working Hours	76.47% (13)	5.88% (1)	11.76% (2)	5.88% (1)	0.00% (0)	1.47	17
Flexible Day Off	58.82% (10)	17.65% (3)	11.76% (2)	11.76% (2)	0.00% (0)	1.76	17
Motivative Working Environment	76.47% (13)	11.76% (2)	11.76% (2)	0.00% (0)	0.00% (0)	1.35	17
Improve Internal Communication	52.94% (9)	41.18% (7)	5.88% (1)	0.00% (0)	0.00% (0)	1.53	17
Supervisor Guide	41.18% (7)	35.29% (6)	23.53% (4)	0.00% (0)	0.00% (0)	1.82	17
Organisation Vision	41.18% (7)	41.18% (7)	17.65% (3)	0.00% (0)	0.00% (0)	1.76	17
Others (Please Indicate Below)							0

Table 52: Retention methods (UAE)

Row	1	2	3	4	5	Average rating	Response count
Salary Increase	28.57% (8)	17.86% (5)	28.57% (8)	14.29% (4)	10.71% (3)	2.61	28
Bonus Increase	21.43% (6)	14.29% (4)	21.43% (6)	28.57% (8)	14.29% (4)	3	28

Improved Employee Welfare	32.14% (9)	32.14% (9)	14.29% (4)	10.71% (3)	10.71% (3)	2.36	28
Promotion	21.43% (6)	35.71% (10)	14.29% (4)	14.29% (4)	14.29% (4)	2.64	28
Flexibility in Job Roles	32.14% (9)	42.86% (12)	14.29% (4)	7.14% (2)	3.57% (1)	2.07	28
Frequent Training Opportunities	28.57% (8)	39.29% (11)	10.71% (3)	10.71% (3)	10.71% (3)	2.36	28
Participation in Decision Making	25.00% (7)	35.71% (10)	17.86% (5)	10.71% (3)	10.71% (3)	2.46	28
Flexible Working Hours	50.00% (14)	28.57% (8)	14.29% (4)	3.57% (1)	3.57% (1)	1.82	28
Flexible Day Off	32.14% (9)	35.71% (10)	17.86% (5)	10.71% (3)	3.57% (1)	2.18	28
Motivative Working Environment	42.86% (12)	32.14% (9)	0.00% (0)	17.86% (5)	7.14% (2)	2.14	28
Improve Internal Communication	28.57% (8)	35.71% (10)	17.86% (5)	3.57% (1)	14.29% (4)	2.39	28
Supervisor Guide	10.71% (3)	53.57% (15)	14.29% (4)	14.29% (4)	7.14% (2)	2.54	28
Organisation Vision	10.71% (3)	32.14% (9)	28.57% (8)	14.29% (4)	14.29% (4)	2.89	28
Others (Please Indicate Below)							1

Table 53: Retention methods (UK)

Both organisation's participants accepted that a salary increase retention method would encourage them to stay longer in their organisation, with a higher percentage of 88.24 from UAE and 46.43 (agree) and 28.57% (unsure) from the UK. This analysis shows that the participants in UAE would be more motivated by salary increase when compared to the UK participants. Less than an average of the UK survey participants agrees that a bonus increase would encourage retention. In contrast, 70 per cent of the UAE participants agree that an increase in bonus would encourage employee retention. All the survey participants agree that improved employee welfare would encourage retention, coupled with a higher percentage of the UK participants accepting that improved welfare would boost their retention mindset.

Only 41.18% of the UAE survey participants accepted that promotion would boost retention, while higher percentages of the UK employee participants agreed that promotion would boost retention.

Both organisations participants agreed that flexibility in job roles would encourage them to stay long-term in their organisation. Frequent training opportunities seem to be a big deal to participants from both organisations based on the high acceptance percentage.

Higher participants from both organisations mentioned they would be encouraged towards retention if they participated in decision making and had flexible working hours.

All UAE participants want a motivative working environment, while a higher percentage of UK participants share the same view.

Both organisations also want improvement in internal communication towards enhancing employee retention.

The supervisory guide retention method seems to be an essential factor for the UAE participants because none of the participants disagree with the method. In contrast, 64.28% of the UK participants agreed that a supervisor guide would enhance employee retention.

More than 80% of the UAE participants accepted that the organisation's vision would help enhance employee retention, and 43% of the UK participants supported the same idea.

Conclusion (Statistical Analysis)

All the analysis above shows how vital employee retention methods are to both organisations and their employees. The statistical analysis shows how important salaries, bonuses, training, supervision, work-life balance, culture, management leadership style, health care, promotion, work relationship, IT support, working environment, and other factors affect retaining employees long-term. This analysis also shows that one shoe does not fit all for various organisations when allocating retention strategies. These research findings show that the UK and UAE participants have both differences and similarities regarding what motivates and would enhance their long-term stay in their various organisations.

Chapter Six

6. Conclusions and Recommendations

This section is vital because it helps the researcher draw a conclusion from the data collected. This section also helps establish the consistency, similarities, and differences between past studies and this research.

All the findings from the data collection phase were interpreted, and the link between the findings and the research objective was established. The research questions were answered at this phase of data analysis. This chapter has demographic details of employees, employee retention factors, and the effects and relationship these retention factors have on employee retention.

6.1. Inference from Questionnaire and Interview

These results were derived from the questionnaire and interviews conducted from the non-profit organisations in the UK and UAE.

6.1.1. Demographic Characteristics

The research population comprises employees working in non-profit organisations in the United Kingdom and the United Arab Emirates. Job title, nature of Job, type of Employment, experience, age, gender, marital status, education and employee position were considered under the demographic of employees for this study. This study's results analysis comprises 20 respondents for interviews, ten from each organisation and 45 completed surveys alongside 36 partially completed surveys from both organisations. The respondents include top and middle-level managers, supervisors, middle level and entry-level staff members. The 20 interview participants were majorly from top management, middle-level management, and human resources management. This process gave the researcher a broad research result by getting detailed research responses from all levels of the UAE and UK organisations.

6.1.2. Examples of Some of the Differences and Similarities between Past Studies and this Research

This section showcases some of the similarities and differences between this study and past studies on employee attrition and retention.

According to a study by Zin et al. (2012), intrinsic and extrinsic motivational factors, e.g., career development, effort recognition, training, organisation interpersonal relations, and organisation policies, are said to influence retention. This study shows that this ideology is very true because most participants attest that the abovementioned strategies keep them in their various organisations.

According to Herzberg's (1959) two-factor theory, Job satisfaction can encourage employee retention. This study supported this theory because the research participants hold job satisfaction in high esteem regarding employee retention.

Victor Vroom's expectancy theory shows that the level of productivity is based on an individual's perception of motivation (Parijat and Bagga, 2014). This theory was analysed using expectancy, Valence and Instrumentality variables. This theory shows that people are motivated due to expected results through their determination, expected reward, or value placed on task outcome.

These three variables give a direct pointer: effort equals performance, which equals reward and the importance of the reward. The most critical factor in the Vroom theory is "individual perception". These research findings prove this theory as realistic because each of the research participants has a different perception of what motivates them, coupled with the importance some participants place on being recognised after getting something done.

Job coupling theory emphasises that the comfort of employees is what makes them commit fully to their jobs. This theory is grand because it prioritises employees' compatibility with the organisation they work with. The theory further explained that If employees' goals and careers are compatible with organisational culture, retention can be ascertained. According to this study's results, employee retention is not ascertained because of the organisation and employee compatibility since employees sometimes might leave for a better organisation with a growth perspective in their career even though the organisation culture compatibility will motivate such employees for the time being (WeiBo et al., 2010).

The ERC retention model explains that organisations can stimulate their employees by giving them varieties of work to do while providing the required resources needed to achieve the task alongside enough support (Shahin, 2014). Participants of this study agree that they enjoy working with varieties. However, they feel overburdened because it is too much workload since the organisation does not allocate various tasks flexibly. The organisation gives their employees varieties of tasks due to limited employees.

6.1.3. Cross-examination of Findings from Interview and Survey

Dimensions	Questions	Identified Factors in Interviews		Survey Assessment	
		UAE	UK	UAE	UK
Role Interest and Motivation	What employees love most about their role, and reasons for staying in the organisation? and Important factors toward retention	Teamwork, helping local communities, Organisation causes, varieties, Cultural Diversity, alignment of organisation and personal value, company size, the challenge in finding another work, the relationship that has been built already,	Organisation cause, Training opportunities, work-life balance, Helping local communities, Flexible working hours, Staff benefit, Free wellness access, Good social events		
	Basic Salary			✓	✓
	Accommodation allowance			✓	✓
	Flexible working hour			✓	✓
	Work-life balance			✓	✓
	Teamwork			✓	✓
	Health care			✓	✓
	Bonuses			✓	✓
	Annual leave			✓	✓

Promotion Opportunities	Ş	Ş
Adequate training opportunities	Ş	Ş
Internal Transfer Flexibility	Ş	Ş
Transfer to Another Affiliate	Ş	Ş
Culture that exists in the Organisation	Ş	Ş
The Management Leadership	Ş	Ş
Schedule Flexibility	Ş	Ş
Convenient means of transportation	Ş	Ş
Supportive supervisor	Ş	Ş
Excellent IT Support	Average	Average
Comfortable Working Environment	Ş	Ş
Fair Performance Appraisal	Ş	Average
Supervisor's Professional Skills	Average	Ş
Job Meeting Personal Interest	Ş	Ş
Innovative Opportunities	Ş	Ş
Involvement in Decision Making	Ş	Ş
The ability to Work under Little or No	Average	Ş

Supervision		
Learning Opportunities	Ş	Ş
Professional Experiences	Ş	Average
Organisation Location	Ş	Ş
Reduce Work Pressure	Average	Ş
Job Stability	Ş	Average
Describe your best experience with the organisation, which has strengthened your commitment and loyalty to it	Appropriate funds for professional development, the opportunity to travel, the work and mission of the organisation and the 'fit' with career interests. Being given increasing responsibility and trust to run personal projects. Professional development opportunities, good co-workers, interesting work itself. Family-type of organisation, where people care for each other. Lots of benefits, the team is working hard to improve the brand. Ability to add value and make a difference Good maternity provision.	Promotion, Trust, Further training, and development opportunities. Knowledge and development, learning from more experienced people and being treated with respect. Opportunities to build positive working relationships which contribute to the development of the company. Trusting employees to bring in a completely new vision. Variety in day-to-day work. Making a lot of lifelong friends. The overall friendliness and support from the company. Flexible working and working from

Meals out and retreats. There is a culture of giving opportunities and support for professional and personal development. Empathy. Opportunity and responsibility to design and implement research projects with a good level of autonomy.	home arrangement. Flexible working, which allows work-life balance. Commitment to providing inclusive public services and doing demonstrably good things for the people. Having feedback from happy customers.
Work relationship. Good support and Cooperation. Prestigious organisation.	Welcoming behaviour of all the staff. Free training courses.
The Foundation helps employees to grow personally and professionally.	Having a good boss, opportunity to learn new things, friendly staff regardless of position.

Challenges	Challenges and worst experience with the organisation	Too many varieties of work with limited staff members, language barrier, Scarcity in talent hunt, organisation operates in an open-ended format, not been able to measure efforts, work life balance	Concurrent add-on of new tasks, poor management, projects financial constraints, restructuring and redundancies.	Management style that prioritises personal interests or preferences over the organisation itself, Irresponsible spending of funds, Organisation unrealistic expectations of how quickly things can be completed, failure to advance within the organisation and promises not being followed through on. Too little flexibility, having to work extra hours just a little too often, Leadership culture, Work/life balance, there are organisational culture dynamics that are quite challenging to navigate. Lack of appreciation of supportive effort, Lack of working hours flexibility, Difficulty in getting holidays approved, long working hours, Lack of trust, inconsistency in staff salary range.	The training element needs some work. End of year reviews is discouraging. Inadequate recognition of high performance. Management lacks listening skills and dealing with difficult customers. Toxic working environment, poor morale, terrible communication, and bad management. Pressure on funding to maintain services, Unreasonable expectations, and inadequate staffing levels to support the service as it should be delivered. Camera in the staff room. Salary not consistent with the role. Lack of acknowledgement for tasks well done but constant criticism of mistakes. Frequent changes of personnel, Doing jobs

				outside current role with little training and no extra pay or support. Cuts to staff lead to doing more work thus, more stress and sometimes be expected to work when the levels of staffing are unsafe. no policy of who to contact when something happens. Restructure and redundancies
Motivation through extra activities	Will extra activities during break help motivate you?	Average	Average	
Depth of Involvement	How involved are you in planning the work you do?	This organisation gives the majority of its employees ownership in their various roles	This organisation also gives the majority of its employees ownership in their various roles	
Evaluation of role performance	What method is in place to evaluate employee's performance?	Most of the employees said there is no specific structured way of evaluating role performance, but few	Most of the UK employees mentioned that their role performance was evaluated through	

		methods like Quarter and annual appraisal are in place to ensure all employees meet their set targets annually.	annual goals reviews.		
Role Feedbacks	How do you receive feedback in your role?	Based on the interview responses, receiving recurrent feedback is subjective. It depends on the activeness of whom employees report to. Most of the employees only get detailed feedback twice a year through the organisation appraisal.	The UK employees rarely receive daily feedback, and when they do, it's mostly through emails.	Average	Ş
Measuring Job satisfaction	Are there processes in place to measure job satisfaction of your employees?	Based on participant's responses, this organisation does not have any structured process for measuring job satisfaction.	Like the UAE organisation, the UK organisation does not have any current structured way of measuring employee satisfaction.	Ş	Ş

Policy for retaining employees	What are the policies in place to retain employees in the organisation?	This organisation does not have any retention policy in place but participates in various activities like training, professional development programmes, reasonable pay rate, employee getaway, and so on that will encourage their employees to stay long-term.	The UK organisation does not have any specific policy towards retention aside from various attributes that encourage their employees to stay.		
	Please indicate how effective you think the following retention methods are?				
	Salary Increase			Ş	Average
	Bonus Increase			Ş	Ş
	Improved Employee Welfare			Ş	Ş
	Promotion			Average	Ş
	Flexibility in Job Roles			Ş	Ş
	Frequent Training Opportunities			Ş	Ş
	Participation in Decision Making			Ş	Ş
	Flexible Working Hours			Ş	Ş
	Flexible Day Off			Ş	Ş
	Motivative Working Environment			Ş	Ş
	Improve Internal Communication			Ş	Ş
	Supervisor			Ş	Ş

	Guide Organisation Vision			Ş	Ş
	Others (Making employees feel valued with regular feedback and acknowledgment of work. Realistic expectations)				Ş
Training	Do you get enough supervision and training in your role?	All participant answered yes to this question. According to the participant's comments, this organisation organises adequate training for its employees and supervises their work. Even though all the participants answered yes to this question, some employees said the organisation can still do better in the aspect of supervision and training.	The UK participants also answered yes to this question. According to the participant's comments, this organisation organises adequate training, seminars, conferences, and platforms to showcase what has been learnt.	Ş	Ş

Table 54: Cross-examination of findings from Interview and survey

Indicators: Ş Denotes a positive opinion while Ş Denotes a negative opinion

6.1.4. Factors Identified from Interviews

Work-Life Balance

Work-life balance is one of the factors UAE participants complained bitterly about; apparently, some of them felt they were living to work instead of working to live and maintain a balance. It was a cultural shock for some of the employees who relocated to the UAE from other countries. In contrast, the UK participants are happy about the standard work-life balance in their organisation due to schedule flexibility, accurate leave and time for personal life commitments.

Teamwork

These two organisations showcase the importance of teamwork in an organisation because the majority of the employees were influenced to remain in the organisation because of the established teamwork factor.

Task Varieties

Working with varieties is also one factor that encourages some of the interview participants to stay in their various organisations. Still, the UAE and UK participants complained that it's getting too much and causing work-related stress. The participants mentioned that it would be more appreciated and enjoyable if task varieties were maintained on a moderate level.

Job Fulfilment

More than 90% of the research participants love their jobs because they were able to make a difference in people's lives and society at large. This factor is usually attributed to working in a non-profit organisation where financial gain and career progression is not the only aim of such employees. These research participants explained that this factor gives them a fulfilling life and career.

Training and Development

Training and development are one factor that cannot be overemphasised, especially when it comes to the UAE and UK organisations used as a case study for this research. Almost all the research participants mentioned that this is one of the main factors that keep them in their various organisations. Luckily both organisations are doing well above average in this regard.

Measuring Effort

Some of the UAE participants complained bitterly about not being able to measure effort because the UAE organisation operates in an open-ended format. The employees cannot always tell or forecast what activities they would be involved in or instructed to carry out. Even though the UK organisation keeps having add-on service which increases their employee's workload, the employees still have a clear idea of their various roles and activities.

Poor Management

Poor management was also one of the factors that came up during the interview, which was more apparent in the UK organisation. The research participants complained that the organisation does not carry them along in decision-making. They are usually lost when various changes happen, which seems to be a reoccurring issue.

Motivation through Extracurricular Activities

Most of the research participants accepted that motivation through extracurricular activities would encourage them towards retention because of its ability to improve employee engagement and would be a good idea if they are not already burned out from work-related stress.

Job Role Ownership

These research participants mentioned that one of the factors that encouraged them to stay in their various organisations is the ownership they have in regard to planning and making solid decisions in their roles. Both organisations give their employees the power to use their processes and initiatives in achieving tasks results; so far, the organisation's set goals are met.

Criticism with Limited Positive Feedback

This factor was identified when this researcher asked questions regarding feedback. Both organisations do not have a structured means of giving feedback to their employees. Some of the UK participants said the organisation is proactive when it comes to criticising what they didn't do right but doesn't give the same energy when it comes to a job well done. As a result, they are usually discouraged.

Measuring Job Satisfaction

This factor appears to be important to this research respondents. Most UAE research respondents mentioned that they would be happy if their organisation has a structured way of measuring job satisfaction. As a result, they will have the ability to air out their worries in an accurate and timely fashion for solutions. Some participants mentioned that aside from too much workload, this factor is one of the other reasons for employee attrition.

Organisational Culture

The UAE organisation's top management explained that maintaining the right organisational culture is one of their primary strategies for retaining their employees. The UK respondents also emphasised that there might be bad management. Still, the culture regarding job flexibility and work-life balance are key factors keeping them in the organisation.

Employee Engagement

From the UK and UAE participants responses, employee engagement is a vital factor in employee retention. Most of these respondents mentioned that they love how they act as one big family amongst their colleagues. The two organisations also ascertain that employee engagement is one of their retention strategies, including maintaining an open office policy, even though some participants mentioned that there is room for improvement regarding bringing employees together.

Understaffing

Research participants from both organisations confirm that this factor is one of the primary reasons their colleagues leave for other organisations. The UAE participants explained that the organisation needs to employ more staff because they are usually frustrated by too much workload and limited deadlines. While the UK respondents further explained that their organisation keeps increasing their workloads instead of hiring more employees for newly introduced services.

Appreciation

Appreciation is another factor that becomes apparent during this research process. Research interview participants feel underappreciated and mentioned that the organisation rarely acknowledges their efforts and sees their achievement as a norm.

Compensation for Extra Work

Research respondents mentioned that their organisation does not compensate them for additional workload. Employees carry out tasks outside their role responsibilities without any form of extra pay or compensation. Due to this, the employees mentioned they are not encouraged or motivated.

6.1.5. Factors Identified from Survey

This researcher achieved the survey results through a self-completed questionnaire ranging from strongly agree (positive) to disagree (negative) The researcher also gave respondents options to give answers outside the open-ended questions for more accurate and realistic responses.

Factors like Basic salary, teamwork, health care, bonuses, annual leave, promotion opportunities, adequate training opportunities, Internal transfer flexibility, organisational culture, supportive supervisor, comfortable working environment, Job meeting personal interest, learning opportunities and organisation location were positively agreed upon by research participants from the two case study organisations used for this research to be factors aiding retention and the reason why they stick to their organisations.

In contrast, factors like Flexible working hours, work-life balance, transfer to another affiliate and convenient means of transportation were disagreed upon by the UAE case study as reasons why they stick to their organisation because they are factors missing in the organisation.

Factors like accommodation allowance, the management leadership style, adequate feedback, innovative opportunities and involvement in decision making were disagreed upon as the reason the UK case study participants stuck to their organisation because these factors are missing in the UK organisation.

Furthermore, factors like excellent IT skills were on an average rating for both organisations. In contrast, the ability to work under little or no supervision, adequate feedback, work supervisor's professional skills, and reduced work pressure was averagely agreed upon as the reason why the UAE case study participants stuck to their organisation. The UK case study participants averagely agreed-upon factors like Fair performance appraisal, professional experiences, and job stability are why they stick to the UK organisation because they are not well maintained.

Survey participants were given an open opportunity to state the factors that make them loyal to their various organisations and their worst experiences in these organisations.

The UAE participants mentioned that the following factors are the reasons they are loyal to their organisation: Appropriate funds for professional development, the opportunity to travel, the organisation's work and mission, and the 'fit' with career interests. Increasing responsibility and trust to run personal projects. Professional development opportunities, good co-workers, interesting work itself. Family-type of organisation, where people care for each other. Lots of benefits, where teams are working hard to improve the brand. Ability to add value and make a difference, including good maternity provision. Workers retreat and meal out.

Empathy. Opportunity and responsibility to design and implement research projects with a good level of autonomy. Good support and Cooperation and organisation being a prestigious organisation.

In contrast, the UK case study participants are loyal to their organisation because of the factors below: Promotion, Further training, and development opportunities. Ability to learn from more experienced people and being treated with respect. Opportunities to build positive working relationships which contribute to the development of the company. Trusting employees to bring in a completely new vision. Variety in day-to-day work. Making a lot of lifelong friends. The overall friendliness and support from the company. Flexible working and working from home arrangement. Flexible working, which allows work-life balance. Commitment to providing inclusive public services, doing demonstrably good things for the people, and having feedback from happy customers. Opportunity to learn new things, having a good boss, friendly staff regardless of position.

Research participants mentioned factors that make their job challenging coupled with their worst working experiences. The UAE participants mentioned the following factors as their worst experiences and reasons they find their job challenging: Management style that prioritises personal interests over the organisation itself, Irresponsible spending of funds, Unrealistic expectations of how quickly employees should complete tasks, failure to advance within the organisation and promises not fulfilled. Too little flexibility, having to work extra hours just a little too often, Leadership culture, Work-life balance, and organisational culture dynamics are quite challenging to navigate. Lack of appreciation of supportive effort, Lack of working hours flexibility, difficulties in getting holidays approved, Lack of trust, and inconsistency in employee's salary range.

Furthermore, the UK participants mentioned the following factors as their worst experiences and reasons they find their job challenging: Training element needs some work, end of year reviews is discouraging. Inadequate recognition of high performance. Management lacks listening skills, dealing with demanding customers: bad management, toxic working environment, poor morale, and terrible communication.

There is pressure on funding to maintain services, unreasonable expectations, and inadequate staffing levels to support the service as it should be delivered. Camera in the staff room. Salary not consistent with the job role.

Lack of acknowledgement for tasks well done but constant criticism of mistakes. Frequent changes of personnel, doing jobs outside current role with little training and no extra pay or support. Cuts to staff lead to doing more work and more stress and sometimes being expected to work when the levels of staffing are unsafe. No policy on who to contact when something happens, and the issue of consistent restructuring and redundancies.

Participants from both organisations agreed that factors like Improved employee welfare, flexibility in job roles, frequent training opportunities, participation in decision making, flexible working hours, a flexible day off, improved internal communication, supervisor guide and a clear organisation vision will increase their loyalty in their various organisations which will, in turn, encourage employee retention.

The UAE participant acknowledges that salary and bonus increases coupled with job promotion will encourage retention.

6.2.Results: Answers to this Study Research Questions

After a depth investigation through interviews and surveys and research in this area, answers to these research questions 1, 2, 3 and 4 are apparent.

Factors identified in the interview are supported by the factors identified in the surveys. Table 6.1 showcased a cross-referencing of results derived from both interviews and surveys while results from interviews and surveys were individually sorted. Results from proposed retention factors derived from the literature review become apparent while new retention factors were derived in the process of this study. These new factors can be used alongside the proposed elements.

Future studies can also consider more retention factors that this research might not have looked into due to time constraints.

6.2.1. Answer to Research Question 1 (What are the policies governing non-profit organisations?)

Organisational policies are tools of action created to guide, protect and direct organisations accurately while fulfilling their goals and mission (Young, 2013). Non-profit organisations, also known as NPOs, are a form of organisation that is not profit dependent because they are created solely to improve the welfare of people in other to achieve a specific set of goals (Butler and Wilson, 2015). NPOs are usually referred to as charitable or philanthropic Organisation because it is regulated under the federal tax code, which exempts them from paying tax. The sole reason for its establishment is to serve the public through social services, educational empowerment, policy advancement, etc. NPOs usually get their financial strength from donations or through various fundraising programmes (Butler and Wilson, 2015).

NPO's disclosure of information policy is one of the most critical policies required for it to be in operation because members, media, contributors and the general public will always request to review records; especially because of NPO's tax-exempt criteria, which always makes it open to public inspection which varies depending on the type of NPO (Roslan et al., 2017). That's why every NPO need to be up to date with their state and federal statutory requirement laws. That way, the organisations can formalise the law process into their organisation system, and the strategy regarding record reviews will be available to every concerned body (McMillan, 2008). The second policy governing the NPO is the Financial Crime policy. The US usually relies on the Sarbanes-Oxley Act (SOX), especially to protect whistleblowers who might have in any way disclosed any financial discrepancies occurring in an organisation (Zhang, 2007). The UK version of this act is the Financial Reporting Council (FRC), while the UAE utilises Dubai International Financial Centre (DIFC). However, these laws are more applicable to public companies, but two significant aspects, which involve retaliating against whistle-blowers and destruction or concealment of certain organisation information, are relevant to NPOs (Eaton and Michael, 2007). Another policy governing the NPOs is the State issue policies. All NPOs need to understand and be up to date with their state laws guiding the not-for-profit organisations which showcases their obedience to duty by adhering to every law required (Buckles, 2011). This law varies from state to state, and it would help guide legal, personnel and transactional issues (Wright et al., 2011). The state issue policies also help guide registration for various activities like fundraising, open meetings etc. (McMillan, 2008).

Another important policy is the Accounting and Financial Policies. All NPOs must have a financial system that must be designed to provide relevant information to meet legal, management, and fiduciary requirements (McKinney, 2015). These policies also ensure that NPOs focus on their missions and not maximise profit or shareholders' revenue (McMillan, 2008). NPOs usually get their revenues from donations, sponsors or grants while providing services for free or at a very subsidised rate but without the intent to make a profit (Fischer et al., 2011). NPOs usually navigate within their mission, liquidity target, financial management and legal regulatory (Zietlow et al., 2018).

6.2.2. Answer to Research Question 2: What are the factors that lead to employee attrition in such organisations?

The table below answered the second research question by explaining various factors causing employee attrition. These factors include environmental factors, work-life balance, organisation and employee's relationship, employee's compatibility with organisation, economic condition, job satisfaction and motivation, leadership style, hiring skilled workers and job security. These factors are some of the major reasons employees leave their place of work.

Factors Leading to Employee Attrition	Explanation
Environmental Factor	The environmental factor is a crucial reason why employees might quit their jobs. The policies and rules practised in a workplace can determine if an employee will be comfortable staying in an organisation long-term (Alhassan et al., 2016). Policies like career advancement and promotion opportunities and policies practices in an organisation would substantially influence retention (Yang et al., 2012). Though some studies argue that the more training opportunities an employee has, the more equipped they are to leave. Some employees also quit their jobs due to non-conducive environments, social harassment, gender discrimination and emotional-related stress (Mackusick and Minick, 2010). Al Mamun and Hasan (2017) cited that firms attempt to create a good work environment with proper remuneration that makes leaving unnecessary for its employees. (Klijn and Tomic, 2010) stated that employers have to be innovative in creating a growth-enabling, work-friendly environment and also employers have to devise a reward system aside from the already agreed upon salary; for instance, recognition award, paid vacation for a job well done, amongst others; all of which stimulates the need to do more.

Organisational Relationship	The kind of relationship an employee has with an organisation can also determine if retention will be on the high side or not (Aguenza and Som, 2012). Most employees always have social networking outside the organisation they work with, and this gives them the opportunity to compare their benefits and salary to employees in other organisations (Cloutier et al., 2015). However, due to the relationship they have with their current organisation and co-workers, it will make it a bit difficult for them to decide to leave for another organisation also because they are unsure if the new organisation is going to have the same friendly attributes and benefits their current place of work possess. Thus, maintaining a strong relationship with employees is very beneficial (Moynihan and Pandey, 2008).
Employees Relationship	Most employees like to work in an organisation where teamwork improves their knowledge because this has a natural way of boosting their self-esteem, which in turn makes them perform better (Vasquez, 2014). This relationship is mostly extended outside the organisation, and due to the long-term friendship, they might have established, employees will find it a bit challenging to leave (Nwokocha and Iheriohanma, 2012). (Christenen and Rog, 2008) opined that NPOs should not be out to employ the highly referred hands but rather to establish harmony between the employees and employers so that workers will be willing to stay.
Employee compatibility with the organisation	Watson and Abzug (2005) termed this creating 'fit and embeddedness'. Compatibility between organisational goal and value has a positive effect on organisational retention capabilities. If an employee feels that their goals and value align with the organisation they work with, they tend to stay longer in such an organisation because it makes them feel fulfilled. This factor is mostly referred to as person-organisation fits (Monynihan and Pandey, 2008). For example, if an employee is interested in medical research and they are opportune to work in an organisation with similar goals, such an employee will most likely stay longer in the organisation; that is why organisations need to employ people who are in sync and ready to work towards the same end goal as the organisation due to their likelihood to stay longer in the organisation (Starks, 2007).
Economical Condition	Economic and labour market condition is one of the factors underpinning job retention because this can affect an employment decision as regards what job is worth maintaining (Kelchtermans, 2017). In a study carried out by Cotton and Tuttle (1986), it was explained that if the economic condition is favourable, it is more likely for an employee to quit their job due to numerous options available. Another study also shows that if an employee stays in a job for a long time, it is likely for them not to leave due to age constraints (Hom and Xiao, 2011).

Job Satisfaction and Motivation	A low level of retention is associated with low satisfaction of staff members, which leads to the high cost of selection and training, which then leads to poor customer satisfaction and generally low organisational performance (Anzazi, 2017). When high achieving staff members are underpaid in an organisation, they seek validation outside the firm and end up leaving the firm (Singh and Loncar, 2010). Studies by some authors like Priyasad and Weerasinghe, 2017 identified that employees often mentioned factors like salary above the market rate, warm working environment, good work interaction and job security as reasons for them to remain in their workplace. It is paramount for organisations to acknowledge their employee's skills and efforts as this will improve their satisfaction level with the organisation (Omonijo et al., 2015). Most employees compare their efforts and how they are seen and appreciated by employers to their colleagues, they most times strive to meet up with their colleague's output in other to receive similar recognition (Hassan, 2013). Motivation is also affected by the capacity of executing and understanding a task, and such individual motivation will reduce if they don't achieve both their intrinsic and extrinsic expectation after the completion of a task (Vroom et al., 2005). If employers strategize employees' needs effectively, it will drastically reduce the rate of employee attrition. These needs are self-actualisation, self-esteem, love-belonging, safety and physiological need. Employee needs could be at any of these levels at a point in time (Mcleod, 2007).
Leadership style	Great leadership makes it easier for employees to achieve career fulfilment and development, which encourages retention due to the fact that an organisation's leadership style can either make an organisation prosper or ruin its progress (Trush, 2012). Most employees would want to work in an organisation with a great leadership style practice. Transformational leaders are unique leaders due to their zeal for helping their followers, in this case, employees, to achieve their potential and goals by prioritising their needs (Fitzgerald and Schutte, 2010).
Work-Life Balance	An effective work-life balance is one of the best strategies for employee retention (Maphanga, 2014). Employees are usually happier when they know that their jobs will not hurt their lives outside of work. Anticipating that staff should consistently work for an extended period and be available even outside work hours will deter their passion for working efficiently (Balakrishnan, 2014). (Bacha, 2016) Also, it mentioned that current staff in an

	organisation known for attrition would most likely work more hours as a result of the extra workload that would have been carried out by the workers who left. Such a situation will increase work stress levels, leading to low performance and frequent leave-permit requests by employees and will encourage more employees to resign if they cannot cope with the workload.
Hiring Skilled Workers	Armstrong (2010) emphasises that the ability, skills and knowledge of people is a huge determinant of their value; thus, employing people with high values will help an organisation maintain its competitive position in its various industry. It is the role of every organisation to recruit skilled and knowledgeable workforce to achieve its required success to remain valuable in their business sector because attrition plays an enormous role in productivity and the kind of services provided (Tanwar and Prasad, 2016). It is quite challenging getting skilled employees recurrently, coupled with the financial constraint it will have on any organisation that keeps hiring new and efficient workforce (Kwenin, 2013). In other to avoid this, if a suitable human resources management practice is in place, the rate of attrition will be reduced (Slattery and Rajan, 2005).
Job Security	WeiBo et al. (2010) Explain that the reoccurrence of attrition in an organisation discourages new entrants of talented employees. Skilled employees will rather want to work in an organisation that has a promising job security standard for retaining its staff. The longer employees stay in an organisation, the less the level of attrition or turnover.

Table 55: Factors leading to employee attrition in NPOs

6.2.3. Answer to Research Question 3: What are the successful employee retention strategies for non-profit organisations?

Research question 3 considered detailed retention strategies that are already in place to curb employee attrition in a non-profit organisation

The table below answered the third research question regarding successful retention strategies that are already in place to minimise employee attrition. These sets of strategies start with the organisation attracting suitable candidates in their organisation through the job requirement and organisation culture detailed in the onboarding process. Other strategies are Job embeddedness, professional guidance, the relationship between employers and employees, worker's pay and benefit, effort acknowledgement and reward, an integrated system for retaining employees, initiating innovation and many more, including retention theories like Zinger and ERC retention model.

Proposed Retention Strategies	Explanation
Great start with informed direction	A brief but in-depth introduction about the job requirement, development plans, pay scale, and the organisation culture before starting the recruiting procedure would help kickstart attracting the right candidate for a role (Craig, 2015). All fresh recruits should be aimed at progress from the beginning (James and Mathew, 2012). The recruitment method should clarify what an employee's aim should be and shed light on the organisation's practice and ways of doing things, coupled with how they can contribute and flourish in the organisation (Chan and Kuok,2011). This process should be put into consideration from the onset because it will be a form of guidance for all employees (Sandhya and Kumar, 2011). Strategies for employee retention could be considered from the start of the recruitment process by explaining clearly in the job application what is expected from an individual and what the organisation has to offer (Nicholson et al., 2011). This strategy will help narrow down the number of qualified employees in the selection process while influencing the formal interview, where the expectations and offer will be reinforced again for in-depth understanding. Utilising psychometric evaluation devices during the employment process will assist selection representatives in ensuring that the applicant's conduct and competency will align well with the organisation's goals and expectations (Sangeetha, 2010). It is effortless for any organisation to strive in its industry if suitable candidates are selected. Organisation goals will be met, and employees will also be satisfied, thus encouraged to stay long term (Sangeetha, 2010).
Job embeddedness	Job embeddedness is one of the models that exhibit factors supporting employee retention. This model exhibit three factors which are job fits, relationships and sacrifice (Reitz and Anderson, 2011). These three factors have to do with alignments that exist between an organisation and its employee, such as the same end goals, having the required skill and a conducive working environment (Van et al., 2013). The impact a job has on the relationship of an employee, most especially external relationships (Robinson et al., 2014). Sacrifice has to do with the effect attrition will have on an employee; leaving an organisation is easier for an employee if they have not created a long-lasting relationship with their colleagues (Young et al., 2013).
Professional Guidance	Assigning a knowledgeable member of staff to mentor a new intake will give an excellent start for new employees (Waterman et al., 2011). This strategy will give a warm gesture to new employees because it will make new employees feel welcomed. New employees will learn from their senior colleagues while they share their fresh perspectives to help grow the organisation (Latham et al., 2011). An excellent mentorship program should be in place, and this will guide employees on how things are done while understanding the organisation's vision (Hallam et al.,

2012). Considering these, they will be able to absorb into the current work culture consistently. Some research explains that it takes a while for a new employee to be ultimately profitable in his/her new job (Baron and Morin, 2010). On a more extensive scale, a great job onboarding plan connects recruits to their colleagues from day one, which might be the beginning of a substantial learning curve (Allen and Shanock, 2013).

Relationship between Employers and Employees

Employers should maintain a certain level of relationship with their employees because this is one of the strategies for retention (Anis et al., 2011). Such connection makes it easier for workers to be open and articulate their needs and also helps employers in figuring out issues early enough (Das and Baruah, 2013). Excellent relationships with employees can be achieved without really crossing professional boundaries.

Establishing trust between the management and their employees usually boosts employee's performance (Chitsaz-Isfahani and Boustani, 2014). They are bound to accomplish the organisational set objectives if they have confidence in their employers.

The absence of transparency in leadership communication usually leads to a high rate of attrition in most organisations (Tillott et al., 2013).

If an organisation has not actualised an employee's engagement program, there is a good chance that employees do not trust the organisation as much as organisations might suspect they do (Adi, 2012).

For any organisation hoping to earn trust, it is essential to develop a good rapport, motivate, give credits alongside constructive criticism, and avoid being biased (Abraham, 2012). Nobody wants to feel excluded in their place of work. Every employee wants to feel needed in their various roles knowing they are achieving the organisation's goals (Bhattacharya, 2015).

Employers should practice having conversations with every one of their employees through strategic meetings or individually and solicit their ideas within the organisation (Yoerger et al., 2015). Then, listen, and take adequate notes of what they state.

Zinger Retention Model

Zinger's retention model emphasised the benefit of connection and engagement amongst organisations, employees and customers in achieving any form of organisational goal. In other for any organisation to maintain a certain level of a retention strategy. Such an organisation will have to learn the process of making sure its employees are all involved in decision-making because the relationship that exists between teams at various levels will determine the level of productivity, as well as achieving organisational goals (Kaur, 2017).

Worker's pay and Benefit

For any organisation to maintain its competitive edge in retaining key employees, it is a necessity to not only pay their staff well but also give them generous bonuses (Osibanjo et al., 2014). That incorporates pay rates, rewards, medical insurance and pension packages. These packages should be explained to all new employees from the get-go (Michael et al., 2016). Employers can also be helpful to their employees by providing services that will make them feel more comfortable in the organisation, for example, availability of lunches, discounted gym membership and the like. Employees feel elated when given access to different benefits at their place of work (Ahmad et al., 2013). To maintain retention status in an organisation, employers can think outside the box by offering unique benefits like stock options, monetary awards and many more to encourage their employees (Ahmad et al., 2013). Skilled workers are more likely to leave a workplace with a low pay rate (Scott et al., 2012).

Employee Retention Connection (ERC) Retention Model	According to the ERC model, the three key factors in achieving retention are leadership, work stimulation, leadership and effort recognition. This model explains that organisations can stimulate their employees by giving them varieties of work to do while providing the required resources needed to achieve the task alongside enough support. Employee's decisions should also matter while giving them feedback on work done with necessary acknowledgement and appreciation for a job well done (Shahin, 2014). Leaders with a motivational style of operating also encourage employees due to their ability to be able to open to new ideas. Such leaders usually lead by example and share insights with others in other to have a shared end goal, and this will help to instil a sense of belonging in others because shared values will aid positive outcomes on any task handled. Organisations should prioritise the benefit and importance of recognising employees' efforts. If an employee excellently executes a task, the organisation should acknowledge the employee's effort because this will boost the employee self-esteem and ability to do better on other tasks. This act of appreciation and acknowledgement will also encourage other employees to do better in their various job to be appreciated (Khan and Ahmad, 2019).
Cultivating cooperation	In situations where employees work in a group, employers should ensure that every member of the group contributes their ideas without making any one of the members feel irrelevant (Brunetto et al., 2013). Individual work should also be encouraged by the organisation. This strategy will make workers feel relevant in their workplace, thus intrigued to stay (Hussein and Rehman, 2013). Employee engagement is setting aside time to connect with employees. Employee engagement can dramatically affect the viability of any organisation (Bhat and Bharel, 2018). At the point when an organisation's workforce feels connected, it gives them a reason to help and perceive how they are adding value to the organisation (Balakrishnan et al., 2013). Organisations can draw the best out of their workforce by permitting employees to express their ideas, giving them the necessary opportunities to grow (Singh et al., 2016).
Effort Acknowledgement and	All individuals feel the need to be acknowledged and appreciated for their efforts (Tarera and Ngirande, 2014). Acknowledgement

Reward	encourages people to do more and better. Making this a culture in an organisation encourages employees' zeal to work harder. Both vast and little efforts should be appreciated (Alfandi and Alkahsawneh, 2014). Organisations should ensure that when demonstrating any form of gratitude towards an employee, they should clarify how the employee's role impacts the organisation positively (Abstein and Spieth, 2014). Various methods of reward programs can be put in place to encourage employees' efforts. Promoting deserving employees plays a substantial role in making them feel appreciated and the need to put in more effort in their role with a longevity plan (Osibanjo et al., 2014). Every promotion is always supported with more training and career advancement, which is another form of strategy to make employees stay long term. Employers should ensure they treat their workers right, recognise their effort and reward them accordingly (Saleem and Affandi, 2014).
Recognise Employee's Achievements	Recognising and celebrating employee achievements is another essential retention strategy (Alnaqbi, 2011). For example, celebrating employees' anniversaries in the organisation or executed projects makes employees feel like an essential part of any organisation. Organisations can practice a culture whereby employees will be celebrated yearly for their efforts and contribution to the organisation (Schwartz et al.,2011).
Integrated System for Retaining Employees	The integrated retention model uses five different approaches in explaining the system used to retain key employees. Employee retention connection will help an organisation maintain a competitive position and maintain a tremendous cultural balance. The first approach is to understand the form of motivational processes used in an organisation coupled with its retention culture. These can be achieved through surveys or focus groups to help analyse organisational driving forces and what needs improvement (Hughes and Rog, 2008). The second approach involves designing exciting role opportunities. If employees can work with variety in their roles with the required resources, it will excite them to go to work every day because they know every day won't be the same. They will get to learn and develop their values continuously. Allowing employees to make decisions and give feedback will make them feel involved, which will encourage retention (Kaur, 2017). The third approach is to equip leaders, for example, managers and supervisors, with motivational skills so they can practice the motivational style of leadership towards employees. This skill will give them the ability to have a shared vision with others and focus on improving employees' capabilities. Superiors who display a motivational form of leadership will help promote organisational change because they know the value of acknowledging and rewarding employees' contributions. These superiors are perceived as role models and imitated by their followers (Ibrahim, 2019). The fourth approach has to do with encouraging employees'

career development. Organisations should continue to train their employees with skills that will be beneficial to them and the organisation. In addition, organisations should give employees mentorship opportunities to help them get better in their role and feel elated, knowing they can deliver their role better (Kaur, 2017).

The fifth and last approach to employee retention connections emphasises building an award and recognition scheme that will suit each organisation's cultural belief. Organisations should let employee performance be a determinant of the kind of recognition or award that will be presented. This process will stand as a motivational channel to encourage employees toward retention in an organisation (Chen and Hsieh, 2006).

Keep employees Inspired	Most employees values varieties. That is why it is so essential for organisations to stimulate their employees with varieties of tasks and the opportunity to make a difference (Zaniboni et al.,2013). Employers should also encourage projects that will unify their employees who share the same vision towards the organisational goal (Hutto, 2017). The degree of organisational relationship with its workforce is directly corresponding to the organisation's potential for progress (Haider et al., 2015). Inspiration is a crucial segment that drives a specialist to perform sufficiently in any event (James and Mathew, 2012).
Initiating Innovation	One other method of encouraging retention is by innovating information technology devices to collate data regarding employee satisfaction and needs anonymously (Lichtenthaler, 2011). Surveys will be sent out to employees to fill anonymously. Acting on the employees' feedback from these data will not only make the company better but also make the employees feel valued (Cloutier et al., 2015). In situations where complaints or worries cannot be rectified, Organisations should try to communicate about them and not just ignore them (Sandhya and Kumar, 2011).
Have a Backup plan for attrition	sometimes it is unavoidable to lose skilled workers. Due to this fact, it is always good for organisations to be ready for it, thus having a backup plan (Yang et al., 2012). An example of such a plan is making sure more than one primary employee is handling a significant role; just in case the primary employee leaves, there will be someone to take their place and keep it running (Oladapo, 2014). Organisations can also do this by including some protective measure clause in their employment contract and giving enough time to find a replacement if the key employee must leave (Chen, 2019). Organisations that have these kinds of plans do not usually lose their shareholders and stakeholders because the business will continue to run as expected, and their efforts will not go unnoticed (Steingold, 2017).
Organisation Transformation	Organisations require some changes or transformations at a point in time. Organisations should learn the importance of carrying their employees alongside whenever any form of transformation occurs. For example, if a merger occurs, the organisation should inform its employees as soon as possible to avoid getting wrong information from an external source (Mendes and Stander, 2011). Crucial information can be passed through group meetings if not

individually, because change is unavoidable even though it can be daunting. For an organisation to stay afloat, they need to continuously develop new initiatives to reinforce quality (Knight, 2014).

Employees' mentality can be affected negatively by companies going through many changes at a time (Hussein and Rehman, 2013).

Employers usually feel that their employees can easily adapt to any situation. However, we all like to think about employees as tough individuals, capable of adjusting as necessary. However, without adequate prior communication, employees might lack the required confidence on staying in their job, thus leaving for other organisations (Hussein and Rehman,2013).

Flexible Working Hours and Conducive working Environment:

Organisations can encourage retention by giving their employees the opportunity of flexible working hours (Idris, 2014). Doing so makes employees feel in charge of their schedule, and this help reduces stress and improves productivity. If employees are given enough time to recharge their energy, it gives them more energy and zeal to do better at their work, and this can be achieved through enough in-between breaks while at work (Grobler and De Bruyn, 2012). Some organisations do so by offering working from home opportunities for a few days of the week to their employees (Idris, 2014). Employees strive better in a pleasant working environment. If an environment is not conducive to working, most employees will be discouraged and opt for better organisations with a better working environment. This can be as a result of toxic leaders and relationships or the physical environment itself as regards the infrastructure (Kossivi et al., 2016). Furthermore, if people sense danger, they might find it difficult to concentrate at work (Bibi et al., 2018).

Work-life balance

Inadequate work-life balance can have a strong effect on individual mental health. A great work-life balance is an effective means of retention strategy (Maphanga, 2014). Employees will be happy to know that their jobs will not hurt their lives outside of work. Anticipating that staff should consistently work for an extended period and be available even outside work hours will deter their passion for working efficiently (Balakrishnan, 2014). A stable work-life balance is essential, and individuals need to realise that their employers comprehend they have lives outside of work. Organisations should urge their employees to take some time off when necessary and offer opportunities for vacations (Sorensen and Mckim, 2014). Organisations should prioritise giving their exhausted employees breaks from work. Alternatively, practice getting everyone out of the office for a walk. Assess how organisation schedules affect employees' work-life balance (Idris, 2014).

Career Advancement

Giving employees the required training in other to help them advance in their various fields should be a necessity for organisations (Alias et al., 2014). Most organisations do this by paying for seminars and short courses for their employees. Further studies paid for by employees are also a strategic means of achieving this. Every employer should make investing in their employees a priority (Foday, 2014). For any organisation to compete effectively in its industry, it has to give its employees

	the required skills and chances to learn new things and explore their range of abilities. Organisations should learn to align employees' career advancement needs with organisational requirements (Chen, 2014).
Yearly Audits	Organisations should not overlook yearly auditing as this will help to analyse employees' performance as well as examine the organisation's long- and short-term goals (Cascio, 2014). The auditing process also allows employers to discuss future progress with their employees. Organisations should learn not to make unrealistic promises to their staff because failure to fulfil such promises might affect the trust the employees have in them (James and Mathew, 2012).
Employee's Health	Making sure employees are keeping fit both physically and intellectually is a great strategy; this process will also help employees perform excellently in their role, which is excellent for any organisation (Sears et al., 2013).
Correspondence and criticism	Maintaining an open correspondence is a conventional method for depicting a training that is fundamental to employee retention (Cloutier et al., 2015). Employees should find it easy to share their thoughts and concerns and be able to ask questions in return for a clear and concise response (Cloutier et al.,2015). If clarifying issues as soon as possible are prioritised, it will make it easy to achieve organisational goals. Employees feel safe if they are heard in an organisation (Olckers et al., 2012). Employers should understand the benefit of constructive criticism because if employees receive destructive criticism, it demoralises them and affects their future efforts in the organisation (Singh et al., 2013). Issues that are not in any way serious can also be ignored by employers in other to give the employees a sense of importance towards issues that are crucial to the organisation. Constructive criticism encourages employees to do better at their work, and it also allows them to perceive criticism as a means to grow (Thompson, 2011). Positive feedback ought to be offered often to encourage employees with the required assurance to help them accomplish their best work. In any case, corrective and constructive feedback is essential as well, especially when there is a need to address an issue or concern (Whitaker et al.,2012). We all realise that employees need feedback to improve and accomplish their possible best, both positive and valuable criticism (Tran et al., 2012). Positive feedback ought to be offered often to motivate employees and give them the assurance they need to accomplish their best work. In any case, constructive and corrective feedback is also essential, especially when there is a dire issue that should be stopped from growing (Whitaker et al.,2012). Employers should become more mindful of the number of negative remarks they are pointing out to employees in comparison to positive remarks (Van and Kluger, 2011).

Table 56: Successful Employee Retention Strategies for NPOs

6.2.4. Answer to Research Question 4: What strategic framework can be recommended in this context to enhance employee Retention?

The table below answered the fourth research question by recommending suitable strategic frameworks to help enhance retention.

This section was answered by first stating the aim of the research, the research model guide, and the creation and development of a suitable strategic framework to help enhance employee retention in non-profit organisations and bridge the research gap.

Recommended Strategic Framework to Enhance Retention in this Context

Dimensions	The Identified Strategic Framework Can Enhance Employee Retention in NPOs
Research Aim	The research aims to identify the key factors leading to employee attrition in non-profit organisations and recommend effective strategies that will help enhance employee retention in non-profit organisations. This research considers various strategies that non-profit organisations can utilise to reduce these challenges. This research first analysis why employee attrition was taking place. After studying multiple works of literature, this study unravelled recommendations and results that would help fill the literature gap on employee attrition in non-profit organisations. This is especially due to limited research on employee attrition in the non-profit organisation sector because most studies focus on profit-oriented organisations. This study integrated various perspectives like the working environment, work-life balance, organisation culture, career progression, training and development, effort acknowledgement and reward, employee engagement, leadership style, job satisfaction, motivation etc. This study also focuses on two non-profit organisations in two different countries (UAE and UK), which have not been investigated before in relation to attrition and retention.
Research Model Guide	This research utilised various models and theories to examine the factors affecting employee retention from diverse and multiple perspectives. This study developed a theoretical framework model that comprises employee attrition factors specific to NPOs and various strategies to enhance retention in NPOs and bridge the gap of limited research on retention and retention in NPOs.
Creation of a suitable strategy framework to enhance retention in NPOs and Bridge the gap in NPOs' Employee Attrition and Retention study	This research developed and reviewed a strategic retention framework that bridges the gap of limited research on Employee attrition and retention in non-profit organisations. While various theoretical retention frameworks have been developed for the FPOs (For-profit Organisations), this research chose well-established studies, models and theories and test run them in the NPO sector, thus creating other strategic frameworks to enhance employee retention in the non-profit sector.

Developed Retention Framework	From the result of this study, factors causing employee attrition in the Non-profit organisation were discovered, after which adequate retention strategies were recommended. Other studies can use the developed model as a suitable tool to analyse employee retention in NPOs and other sectors.

Table 57: Recommended Strategic Framework to enhance employee retention

6.3.Contributions

The aim of this research is to identify the key factors leading to employee attrition in non-profit organisations and recommend effective strategies that will help enhance employee retention in non-profit organisations. This research followed a variety of multidisciplinary approaches of various ideologies that causes employee attrition from work-life balance, culture, leadership style, salary, alignment of career goals, employee engagement, job satisfaction, motivation, feedback, appreciation, compensation, training and development etc.

In other to guide this empirical study, this research developed a theoretical framework.

Considering existing studies, this research considered more than seventy different proposed factors critical to both the UK and UAE non-profit organisations. This research was the first to consider choosing the UAE and UK non-profit organisations on employee attrition and retention. This research chose a qualitative approach supported by elements due to its exploratory nature. The study also carried out a self-completed survey to underpin the issue of employee attrition in NPOs. Data collated was analysed, and the results achieved provided detailed answers to the research questions. This section showcased theoretical and practical research contributions, research limitations, and suggestions for further studies. At the end of this chapter, recommendations were made and concluding comments were also expressed in detail.

This researcher carried out this research to provide a practical understanding of employee attrition in NPOs; thus, the choice of research method has led to the improvement of some retention theories and the development of new ones. As a result, this research has contributed to theory, methodology and practice, which has filled a gap in employee attrition and retention research in NPOs. This research will be beneficial to various organisations and researchers, especially in the non-profit sector.

6.3.1. Contribution to Theory

This study contributed to existing theories on employee retention, cross-cultural leadership, motivation, Information technology retention strategies and their processes.

6.3.1.1. Contributions to the Employee retention for non-profit Organisations- Asia (UAE) and Europe (UK)

Very few studies have been done in the non-profit sector regarding employee attrition and retention (Word and Park, 2015), and none have been carried out in the chosen case studies.

Employee attrition is a recurrent issue facing non-profit organisations.

This study found various research on employee attrition and retention in profit-oriented organisations. Literature like (Dei Mensah, 2014); (Parijat and Bagga, 2014); (Muogbo, 2013); (Reitz et al., 2010); (Kaur, 2017); and many others were considered in discovering the factors causing employee attrition in the non-profit sector. Most retention strategies created by other studies focused on profit-oriented organisations, while this research focuses on NPOs.

This research utilised various employee attrition and retention theories, models, and strategies to have in-depth information on NPOs ' employee attrition. As a result, multiple factors affecting the non-profit were discovered with practical recommendations. The interviews and survey carried out unravelled practical issues facing the Non-profit sector. Most theories and research focus on human resources management when it comes to the issue of employee attrition and retention. Yet, this research focused on all departments in the organisation and discovered that each department in an organisation has one or more roles they play regarding employees leaving or staying in an organisation.

This research can be used as a guide for other researchers when unfolding the causes of employee attrition in any organization. By not just focusing on the human resources department, profit-oriented organisations and understanding that the work culture in the UK has been different from UAE non-profits which is one of the gaps this research has bridged.

6.3.1.2. Contribution to Cultural difference in the non-profit Organisations

This research contributes to cross-cultural difference analysis. Understanding that employees are essential resources in any organisation is paramount because keeping them in the organisation long-term has a lot to do with positive organisational culture (Anitha, 2016). Different organisations exhibit and practice different organisational cultures, especially when they exist in different environments, usually referred to as the local culture, in contrast to the generic cultural value shared by human beings at large (Kawar, 2012). A study shows that westerners (e.g., USA, Europe) are more analytical. At the same time, Asians are more holistic in terms of cognitive differences, which strongly affects their social differences (Varnum et al., 2010). This research identifies the cultural issues affecting the two case studies. As Kawar, 2012 mentioned, there is a massive cultural difference in the UAE and UK chosen case studies, especially regarding employee retention. The UAE organisation does not integrate work-life balance as a necessity, thus letting the employees work tirelessly. In contrast, the UK non-profit case study sees work-life balance as a priority for their employees. During the interview session, some British-born workers in the UAE confirmed that the in-balance in their work-life occurred as a cultural shock for them when they started working in the UAE. This study discovered that cultural practice is critical for the success of any NPOs, thus, closing the gap in employee attrition.

6.3.1.3. Contribution to Retention Strategies in the non-profit Organisations

This research contributes to the retention strategies that can help reduce employee attrition in non-profit organisations. It is a fact that for any organisation to achieve growth and stability, successful employee retention strategies have to be in use (Cloutier et al., 2015). Organisations need to keep revisiting their retention strategies to ensure the comfort and satisfaction of their employees (Deery and Jago, 2015)

This study identified outstanding strategies that will encourage employee retention in NPOs. This research uncovered many factors causing employee attrition in NPOs and how organisations have knowledge of several retention strategies but fail to utilise them. As a result, this research bridged the gap between prioritising retention strategies and developing new retention strategies that will help non-profit organisations reduce employee attrition. For example, most top management understands the importance of work-life balance, just like in the UAE case study but refuses to implement it accordingly. If employees burn out from stress, their motivation and production level will drop (Anthony-Mcmann et al., 2017).

6.3.1.4. Contribution to Leadership in the non-profit Organisations

This study contributed to the effect of outstanding Leadership in regard to employee attrition. Organisations management needs to operate in a way that helps integrate employee engagement to guarantee or try to give employees job satisfaction opportunities (Rihal, 2017). This research helped discover various leadership issues in the NPOs. For example, during the interview session with the top management, it was discovered that some of the factors they mentioned that they utilise to encourage employee retention are theoretical and not practical because the middle and low-level employees argued otherwise. An example is the UK and UAE case study top management stating that they know if their employees are happy or not because they maintain an open-door policy. Still, the middle and low-level employees said they do not feel heard and would like the organisations to have a structured system for measuring job satisfaction and lodging complaints anonymously. The leader's ways of doing things in these organisations need to change by prioritising their employees' welfare and not just assuming they are comfortable. This research helps bridge the gap in leadership methods of operation.

6.3.1.5. Contribution to Information Technology in the non-profit Organisations

This research contributed to the positive effect of Information technology in the non-profit sector. Since the late sixties, information technologies have been in modern existence since Arpanet was introduced and funded by the United States defense department, and ever since, it's been unstoppable (Deb, 2014). Very few studies have been carried out on the effect Information technology can have on NPOs. This research helps outline various Information technologies benefits in the NPOs and their effect on employee attrition. NPO organisations should embrace information technology implementations more. For example, during the Coronavirus pandemic, various non-profit organisations have to shut down. At the same time, some insisted their employees come to work every other day for tasks that employees would have achieved remotely, but they couldn't due to lack of IT infrastructure. For example, the UAE organisation compelled their employees to come to work every other day during the pandemic, which was not safe. In contrast, the UK organisation shut down most of their services, including those that would have been feasible remotely. This research helped unravel the importance of IT and how it helps bridge the gap of limited research on IT in NPOs and its positive effect on employee Retention.

6.3.1.6. Contribution to the process of retention strategies in the non-profit Organisations

This research contributed to the process of retention strategies. Many studies stated that it is essential that organisations start their retention process from the recruitment stage, which is essential (Cloutier et al., 2015). This research bridged the gap by suggesting further follow-up steps to encourage employee retention in the non-profit organisation, starting from the recruitment stage, which helps with job fit up to the disengagement/retirement stage.

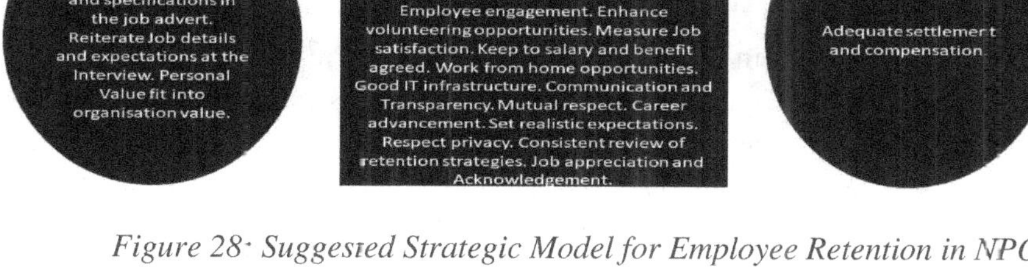

Figure 28: Suggested Strategic Model for Employee Retention in NPOs

6.3.2. Research Contribution to Practice

Below are some of the practical issues this research addressed and contributed to this research

6.3.2.1. Reduction of Workload on Employees

Research has shown that if employees are stressed and burnout due to too much workload, productivity and quality of service will be affected (Che et al., 2017). Therefore, non-profit management can adopt the idea of hiring more volunteers, especially remotely. That way, it would be easier for anyone to contribute to their services regardless of location, thus reducing the workload for the on-site employees. This study confirms that one of the major issues causing employee attrition in the NPOs is too much workload. During the 2020/2021 pandemic, most organisations appreciated the opportunity of working remotely, which has become a norm for some organisations (Koehne et al., 2012). Unfortunately, most non-profit organisations do not invest in information technology infrastructure and human resources, which is a benchmark for remote working (Given et al., 2013). For example, when this researcher was volunteering with a UK non-profit organisation as an IT tutor, all the required resources were made available on-site. A year later, this researcher had to relocate but would love to have carried on with her tutoring role, but there are no relevant resources, infrastructure, and structure to continue remotely; hence, the organisation has to employ and train a new employee.

6.3.2.2. Establishing Retention Policies

Policies are structured procedures that need to be adhered to achieve consistency (Ryner and Lewis, 2020). For organisations to achieve success and maintain competitive power in their industry of operation, it is essential to have some structured policies in place. Based on these research findings, most organisations, especially the NPOs, have various strategies they follow regarding retaining their employee's long term. Still, there are no structured policies for retention. This research contributed to encouraging NPOs to have structured policies in place for employee retention. These policies should be reviewed from time to time and built upon; that way, NPOs will achieve consistency, and everyone in the organisation will understand the role they need to play in encouraging retention. In addition, a good retention policy or practice would encourage employees to stay loyal to their employer long-term (Patro, 2014).

6.3.2.3. Establishing Accurate Task Load and Work-Life Balance

Studies have shown that even though NPO employees earn less than their FPO counterparts, they are happier and well-integrated with their work due to the fulfilling feelings they get at their job (Zulu et al., 2017). All NPOs want to make a difference in their community and society at large, but it should not be to the detriment of the employees working in such organisations; thus, the working environment should always be conducive (Renard and Snelgar, 2017).

This research established the fact that NPOs are committed to their missions; however, because they want to make different impacts within a short period, they overwork their employees. This issue was more accessible for the UAE chosen organisation because the country does not have a compulsory structure for working hours, unlike in the UK, where working hours have a standard (Haider et al., 2016). This research also contributed to knowledge in encouraging employers to maintain an excellent work-life balance regardless of the working hours rule guiding the country of operation because regardless of country, all employees are still human.

6.3.2.4. Establishing Strong Relationships with Employees

Employers will be able to motivate their employees easily if a strong relationship exists because that would also mean that issues can be discussed and resolved quickly (Gregory, 2011). In organisations where transparency is missing, and employees do not feel heard. Such employees have a high probability of quitting their jobs due to being neglected (Cloutier et al., 2015). This research unraveled that because an organisation maintains an open-door policy does not necessarily mean they have a strong relationship with their employees. If there is no cordiality, some employees will find it challenging to open-up. This research contributes these employers should prioritise establishing solid relationships with their employees from the first day of resumption.

6.3.2.5. Valuable Recruitment Strategies for Non-profit Organisations

The discovery from this study will help NPOs take advantage of the power they have over the FPOs, which is the power of unburdening their employees without spending too much. Even though people all over the world need money to survive, they feel more fulfilled if they know they are making a difference in their societies. As a result, NPOs can tap into this stream of opportunities by letting people work for them and make an impact remotely. One of the contributions of this research is to encourage NPO employers to invest in creating remote opportunities and attracting more volunteers.

6.3.3. Model Developed

This research utilised various factors to unravel the cause of employee attrition in non-profit Organisations, and strategies NPOs can adopt to encourage employee retention. This research developed a theoretical framework model that comprises various employee attrition factors and retention strategies for closing the gap of limited study on employee attrition in the non-profit sector. This model is a product of the detailed interviews carried out and self-completed questionnaires designed, which were analysed after considering various proposed models from various multidisciplinary fields. The model developed makes it easier for this research to carry out a cross and within-case analysis. From the analysed results, this research uncovered various factors leading to employee attrition in the non-profit organisation and multiple strategies that will enhance employee retention in NPOs. Other researchers can use this model for further study to help reduce employee attrition in organisations.

6.3.4. Comparative Study

Researchers like Russell and Weaver, 2011; Sharma et al.,2011; Senel, 2017 etc., have used comparative analysis to arrive at unique and detailed research results in their various research fields. This research utilised a comparative analysis of literature and case studies to arrive at unique and more precise research results. This researcher accumulated this comparative study data from two non-profit organisations from two different countries and continents. Research data was collated using semi-structured interviews and self-completed questionnaires from both organisations, and results were analysed using NVivo, supported by statistical analysis of the surveys. The comparative study showed the differences and similarities between the UAE and UK non-profit organisations.

6.4. Recommendations

The primary purpose of this study is to identify key factors leading to employee attrition in non-profit organisations and recommend effective strategies that will help enhance employee retention in the non-profit organisation. Identifying and implementing these strategies will aid the decrease in employee attrition. This research is mostly relevant for non-profit organisations interested in reducing employee attrition in their organisation. Various NPOs can use this research, considering that the study was carried out in two organisations from two different continents. The results from this research offered the following recommendations: For non-profits organisations to retain their employees long-term, NPOs should consider the following strategies.

Implement a clear and structured retention policy in the organisation's policies $_{(1)}$. All departments in an organisation should be enlightened about how to encourage employee retention and not just the Human resources department $_{(2)}$. Non-profits organisations should practice positive organisational culture that will make all employees feel prioritized $_{(3)}$. Employees' comfort and satisfaction should be a priority for all organisations $_{(4)}$. Work-life balance is one of the reasons employees quit their jobs, NPO's should ensure that their employees are not overworked and have a stable work-life balance $_{(5)}$. Organisations should select the right set of people for a leadership role because organisational leadership styles will have a lot of impact on employee retention $_{(6)}$. Information technology should be integrated into non-profits as one of the major necessities for business due to its numerous advantages $_{(7)}$. Organisations should have a structured step for employee's retention plan starting from the recruitment process $_{(8)}$. NPOs should integrate remote working opportunities for their employees, especially for volunteers; that way, people will be able to contribute to the organisational goal from various locations $_{(9)}$. Implementing and reviewing retention strategies should be consistent. Other strategies should be in place if a strategy did not work $_{(10)}$. Employees should be given a clear direction of their tasks and Job specification $_{(11)}$. Employee engagement should always be encouraged $_{(12)}$. Organisation leaders should maintain a strong relationship with their employees $_{(13)}$. Being in a country with no working hour policies does not mean that employees should be overworked $_{(14)}$. Adequate means of communication and transparency should be adopted $_{(15)}$. Organisations should always carry their employees along on organisational changes $_{(16)}$. Performance Appraisal should not be biased, and employees should receive more positive feedback than criticism $_{(17)}$. Mutual respect should be practised in the workplace $_{(18)}$. Employees should know their organisation trust them $_{(19)}$. Understaffing should be avoided $_{(20)}$. Organisation Training and Development schemes should always be upgraded $_{(21)}$. A good Job satisfaction measurement should be in place $_{(22)}$. Employers should avoid setting unrealistic expectations $_{(23)}$. Organisations should give employees concurrent opportunities to air out their problems, especially anonymously (24). Structured employee career advancement should be integrated (25). Employees privacy should be respected. For example, there shouldn't be a camera in the changing room (26). There should be salary or bonus upgrades if responsibilities increases (27). Employees should be given the opportunity of adequate training for adds-on roles (28). Employees should not be made to feel underappreciated (29). A job well done should always be acknowledged (30).

Non-profit organisations in countries with limited work-life balance and other beneficial policies should integrate theirs into their organisation to boost employee retention.

6.5. Research Limitation

Every research has a limitation because it will help unravel ideas for further studies on what a researcher could not achieve and how a researcher drew a study conclusion (Ross and Zaidi 2019). Like every research, this study also has its limitation, which creates opportunities for further studies.

The number of case studies used is one of the main limitations of this research. This research only considered two non-profit case studies due to time constraints, one in the UAE and the other in the UK. At the earlier stage of this research, interviews were conducted with the Top management of the two chosen organisations. The researcher chose these two organisations out of the majority considered because they are more than happy to share enough information with the researcher regarding employee attrition and retention challenges in their organisations. At the beginning of the research, this researcher wanted to consider just one NPO but decided to add another NPO for a comparative analysis to get more insight into the subject area, but further studies can consider more than two organisations in various countries. For the survey used for this research, only 80 self-completed questionnaires were completed in both organisations, even though this percentage helped achieve saturation point due to the high turnout rate from each organisation's department. Only 20 interviews were conducted, ten from each organisation, due to time constraints. The top management respondents are extremely busy people; thus, a lot of time was channelled into getting their audience.

Another limitation of this research is the country selection. Only two countries were considered for this research: UAE and UK, whereby the researcher selected one organisation from each country.

This research is based on the Qualitative research method but supported by statistical elements from the survey carried out. This research used qualitative research (semi-structured interviews) to get top and middle-level management views on employee attrition and retention. Furthermore, the survey was considered to get the opinions of every other level of employees in the case studies to achieve the validity of information shared by the top management to help understand if employees from different levels shared the same ideology on retention. The data collected was analysed using the NVivo data analysis tool.

6.5.1. Suggestions for Further studies

This study has highlighted various areas in which other researchers can carry out further research. One of the suggested areas for future studies is to consider other countries or choose more than one organisation in each country if time permits to get detailed information about the root cause of employee attrition in non-profit organisations. Different organisations and countries operate with different cultural beliefs, and further research in this area can broaden the understanding of various organisational cultures. Further studies can also look into more factors causing employee attrition in a non-profit organisation and other business sectors at large. Future studies can consider interviewing more than 20 participants or mainly focusing on a quantitative approach. Another suggestion for further studies is to attempt a comparative analysis between profit-driven and non-profit organisations regarding employee attrition and retention because this research focuses on non-profit organisations. Future research may consider other research methods in collecting and analysing data from non-profit organisations.

6.6.Conclusion

Non-profit organisations face employee attrition and are not always buoyant enough to persuade their employees in staying as profit-based organisations do. This researcher undertakes this research to identify the factors behind employee attrition and the best way to retain employees in non-profit organisations. In this study, interviews and survey was carried out in non-profit organisations to identify these attrition factors in other to be able to recommend feasible retention strategies that will help keep employees' long term in the non-profit organisations. The employee attrition rate was higher in the UAE organisation when compared to the UK organisation, mostly due to the lack of work-life balance and other identified factors. Based on the research results, this study recommended necessary retention strategies to help enhance employee retention and bridge the gap of limited research on employee attrition and retention in non-profit organizations.

References

Abraham, S. (2012). Job satisfaction as an antecedent to employee engagement. SIES Journal of Management, 8(2).

Abstein, A., and Spieth, P. (2014). Exploring HRM meta-features that foster employees' innovative work behaviour in times of increasing work-life conflict. Creativity and innovation management, 23(2), 211-225.

Adams, K. M. (2012). Ethnographic methods. In Handbook of research methods in tourism. Edward Elgar Publishing.

Adi, A. N. (2012). Driving performance and retention to employee engagement: A case study in the University of Brawijaya. Journal of Basic and Applied Scientific Research, 2(1), 338-350.

Aguenza, B. B., and Som, A. P. M. (2012). Motivational factors of employee retention and engagement in organizations. International journal of advances in management and economics, 1(6), 88-95.

Aguenza, B.B. and Som, A.P.M., 2018. Motivational factors of employee retention and engagement in organizations. IJAME.

Ahammad, M.F., Tarba, S.Y., Liu, Y. and Glaister, K.W., 2016. Knowledge transfer and cross-border acquisition performance: The impact of cultural distance and employee retention. International Business Review, 25(1), pp.66-75.

Ahmad, R., Etp, Y., and Bujan, S. (2013). Relationship between Types of Benefit (leave, loan and retirement plan) and Employees' Retention. International Journal of Education Research, 1(8).

Ahmed, R., Ahmad, N. and Channar, Z., 2016. Relationship between Training and Development and Performance of Business Schools Faculty.

Aikin, S. F., and Talisse, R. B. (2017). Pragmatism, Pluralism, and the Nature of Philosophy. Routledge.

Akingbola, K., 2006. Strategy and HRM in nonprofit organizations: evidence from Canada. The International Journal of Human Resource Management, 17(10), pp.1707-1725.

Akingbola, K., 2013. A model of strategic nonprofit human resource management. Voluntas: International Journal of Voluntary and Nonprofit Organizations, 24(1), pp.214-240.

Akkermans, J., Brenninkmeijer, V., Schaufeli, W.B. and Blonk, R.W., 2015. It's all about CareerSKILLS: Effectiveness of a career development intervention for young employees. Human Resource Management, 54(4), pp.533-551.

Al Mamun, C. A., and Hasan, M. N. (2017). Factors affecting employee turnover and sound retention strategies in business organization: a conceptual view. Problems and Perspectives in Management, 15(1), 63-71.

AlBattat, A.R., Som, A.P.M. and Helalat, A.S., 2014. Higher dissatisfaction higher turnover in the hospitality industry. International Journal of Academic Research in Business and Social Sciences, 4(2), pp.45-52.

Albrecht, S.L., Bakker, A.B., Gruman, J.A., Macey, W.H. and Saks, A.M., 2015. Employee engagement, human resource management practices and competitive advantage: An integrated approach. Journal of Organizational Effectiveness: People and Performance, 2(1), pp.7-35.

Alduayj, S. S., and Rajpoot, K. (2018, November). Predicting employee attrition using machine learning. In 2018 International Conference on Innovations in Information Technology (IIT) (pp. 93-98). IEEE.

Alfandi, A. M., and Alkahsawneh, M. S. (2014). The Role of the Incentives and Reward System in Enhancing Employee's Performance" A Case of Jordanian Travel and Tourism Institutions". International Journal of Academic Research in Business and Social Sciences, 4(4), 326.

Alharahsheh, H., and Pius, A. (2020). A review of key paradigms: Positivism VS interpretivism. Global Academic Journal of Humanities and Social Sciences, 2(3), 39-43.

Alhassan, R. K., Nketiah-Amponsah, E., Spieker, N., Arhinful, D. K., and de Wit, T. F. R. (2016). Assessing the impact of community engagement interventions on health worker motivation and experiences with clients in primary health facilities in Ghana: a randomized cluster trial. PloS one, 11(7).

Alias, N. E., Noor, N., and Hassan, R. (2014). Examining the mediating effect of employee engagement on the relationship between talent management practices and employee retention in the Information and Technology (IT) organizations in Malaysia. Journal of Human Resources Management and Labor Studies, 2(2), 227-242.

Allen, D. G., and Shanock, L. R. (2013). Perceived organizational support and embeddedness as key mechanisms connecting socialization tactics to commitment and turnover among new employees. Journal of Organizational Behavior, 34(3), 350-369.

Allen, D.G., Bryant, P.C. and Vardaman, J.M., 2010. Retaining talent: Replacing misconceptions with evidence-based strategies. Academy of management Perspectives, 24(2), pp.48-64.

Allmark, P., and Machaczek, K. (2018). Realism and Pragmatism in a mixed methods study. Journal of advanced nursing, 74(6), 1301-1309.

Alnaqbi, W. (2011). The relationship between human resource practices and employee retention in public organisations: an exploratory study conducted in the United Arab Emirates.

Alnıaçık, E., Alnıaçık, Ü., Erat, S., and Akçin, K. (2014). Attracting talented employees to the company: Do we need different employer branding strategies in different cultures? rocedia-Social and Behavioral Sciences, 150, 336-344.

Altaf, M., Mokhtar, S. S. M., and Ghani, N. H. A. (2017). Employee critical psychological states as determinants of employee brand equity in banking: A multi-group analysis. Banks and Bank Systems, 12(3), 61-73.

Al-Zawahreh, A. and Al-Madi, F., 2012. The utility of equity theory in enhancing organizational effectiveness. European journal of economics, finance and administrative sciences, 46(3), pp.159-169.

Amankwaa, A. and Anku-Tsede, O., 2015. Linking transformational leadership to employee turnover: The moderating role of alternative job opportunity. International Journal of Business Administration, 6(4), p.19.

Ampoty, J., 2014. An investigation into the effects of career development on employee retention at Anglogold Ashanti Limited, Obuasi Mine (Doctoral dissertation).

Anderson, B. B., and Dees, J. G. (2017). Sector-bending: Blurring the lines between non-profit and for-profit. In search of the non-profit sector (pp. 65-86). Routledge.

Anguzu, P. K., and Basheka, B. (2017). Employee commitment and organisational performance in nile breweries limited uganda.

Anheier, H. K. (2014). Non-profit organizations: Theory, management, policy. Routledge.

Anis, A., Nasir, A., and Safwan, N. (2011). Employee retention relationship to training and development: A compensation perspective. African journal of business management, 5(7), 2679-2685.

Anitha, J. (2016). Role of Organisational Culture and Employee Commitment in Employee Retention. ASBM Journal of Management, 9(1).

Anthony-McMann, P. E., Ellinger, A. D., Astakhova, M., and Halbesleben, J. R. (2017). Exploring different operationalizations of employee engagement and their relationships with workplace stress and burnout. Human Resource Development Quarterly, 28(2), 163-195.

ANZAZI, N., 2017. The Impact of High Staff Turnover On Productivity: A Case Of Telkom Kenya Limited (Doctoral Dissertation, Mua).

Araten-Bergman, T., 2016. Managers' hiring intentions and the actual hiring of qualified workers with disabilities. The International Journal of Human Resource Management, 27(14), pp.1510-1530.

Armstrong, M. A. (2010). Handbook of Human Resource Management Practice. London.

Armstrong, M., 2016. Armstrong's handbook of management and leadership for HR: Developing effective people skills for better leadership and management. Kogan Page Publishers.

Arokiasamy, A.R.A., 2013. A qualitative study on causes and effects of employee turnover in the private sector in Malaysia. Middle-East Journal of Scientific Research, 16(11), pp.1532-1541.

Arora, R. (2012). A research study of factors influencing talent retention in BPO industry. Journal of Strategic Human Resource Management, 1(2), 54.

Aruna, M., and Anitha, J. (2015). Employee retention enablers: Generation Y employees. SCMS Journal of Indian Management, 12(3), 94.

Ary, D., Jacobs, L.C., Irvine, C.K.S. and Walker, D., 2018. Introduction to research in education. Cengage Learning.

Åteg, M. and Hedlund, A., 2011. Researching attractive work: Analyzing a model of attractive work using theories on applicant attraction, retention and commitment. Arbetsliv i omvandling, (2), pp.1-39.

Awan, A.G. and Anjam, K.U., 2014. EMPLOYEES TURNOVER RATE IN OIL REFINERIES-A CASE STUDY OF PAK ARAB REFINERY LTD (PARCO). Global Journal of Human Resource Management, 2(3), pp.73-86.

Aydogdu, S. and Asikgil, B., 2011. An empirical study of the relationship among job satisfaction, organizational commitment and turnover intention. International review of management and marketing, 1(3), pp.43-53.

Aziri, B., 2011. JOB SATISFACTION: A LITERATURE REVIEW. Management Research and Practice, 3(4).

Bacha, N., 2016. Antecedents and Consequences of Employee Attrition: A Review of Literature.

Bailey, T., Belfield, C., Jenkins, D. and Kopko, E., 2016. Matching talents to careers: From self-directed to guided pathways. Matching students to opportunity: Expanding college choice, access, and quality, pp.79-98.

Balakrishnan, C., Masthan, D. and Chandra, V., 2013. Employee retention through employee engagement-A study at an Indian International Airport. International Journal of Business and Management Invention, 2(8), pp.9-16.

Balakrishnan, L. (2014). A Study on Retention Strategy's followed by Education Institutions in Retaining Qualified Employees. SIES Journal of Management, 10(1).

Balkin, R. S., and Sheperis, C. J. (2011). Evaluating and reporting statistical power in counseling research. Journal of Counseling and Development, 89(3), 268-272.

Bambacas, M. and Kulik, T.C., 2013. Job embeddedness in China: How HR practices impact turnover intentions. The International Journal of Human Resource Management, 24(10), pp.1933-1952.

Ban, C. (2019). Beyond Social Science Naturalism: The Case for Ecumenical Interpretivism. Critical Review, 31(3-4), 454-461.

Ban, C., Drahnak-Faller, A. and Towers, M., 2003. Human resource challenges in human service and community development organizations: Recruitment and retention

Bang, H., Ross, S. and Reio Jr, T.G., 2012. From motivation to organizational commitment of volunteers in non-profit sport organizations: The role of job satisfaction. Journal of Management Development, 32(1), pp.96-112.

Basias, N., and Pollalis, Y. (2018). Quantitative and qualitative research in business and technology: Justifying a suitable research methodology. Review of Integrative Business and Economics Research, 7, 91-105.

Bazeley, P., and Jackson, K. (Eds.). (2013). Qualitative data analysis with NVivo.

Beins, B. C. (2017). Research method: A tool for life. Cambridge University Press.

Belout, A. and Gauvreau, C., 2004. Factors influencing project success: the impact of human resource management. International journal of project management, 22(1), pp.1-11.

Bhat, I. A., and Bharel, S. K. (2018). Driving performance and retention through employee engagement. ZENITH International Journal of Multidisciplinary Research, 8(1), 10-20.

Bhattacharya, Y. (2015). Employee engagement as a predictor of seafarer retention: A study among Indian officers. The Asian Journal of Shipping and Logistics, 31(2), 295-318.

Bibi, P., Ahmad, A., and Majid, A. H. A. (2018). The impact of training and development and supervisor support on employee's retention in academic institutions: The moderating role of work environment. Gadjah Mada International Journal of Business, 20(1), 113.

Big society capital. (2015). UK social investment market.

Bisht, S., Chaubey, D. S., and Thapliyal, S. P. (2016). Analytical Study of Psychological Contract and its Impact on Employees Retention. Pacific Business Review International, 8(11).

Blau, P. (1964). Power and exchange in social life.

Borzaga, C. and Tortia, E., 2006. Worker motivations, job satisfaction, and loyalty in public and non-profit social services. Non-profit and voluntary sector quarterly, 35(2), pp.225-248.

Boxall, P. and Purcell, J., 2011. Strategy and human resource management. Macmillan International Higher Education.

Branham, L., 2012. The 7 hidden reasons employees leave: How to recognize the subtle signs and act before it's too late. Amacom.

Brannen, J., 2017. Mixing methods: Qualitative and quantitative research. Routledge.

Braun, V., and Clarke, V. (2021). To saturate or not to saturate? Questioning data saturation as a useful concept for thematic analysis and sample-size rationales. Qualitative research in sport, exercise and health, 13(2), 201-216.

Bray, J. W., Kelly, E. L., Hammer, L. B., Almeida, D. M., Dearing, J. W., King, R. B., and Buxton, O. M. (2013). An integrative, multilevel, and transdisciplinary research approach to challenges of work, family, and health. Methods Report (RTI Press), 1.

Brierley, J. A. (2017). The role of a pragmatist paradigm when adopting mixed methods in behavioural accounting research. International Journal of Behavioural Accounting and Finance, 6(2), 140-154.

Brown, W.A. and Yoshioka, C.F., 2003. Mission attachment and satisfaction as factors in employee retention. Non-profit management and leadership, 14(1), pp.5-18.

Brunetto, Y., Shriberg, A., Farr-Wharton, R., Shacklock, K., Newman, S., and Dienger, J. (2013). The importance of supervisor–nurse relationships, teamwork, wellbeing, affective commitment and retention of North American nurses. Journal of Nursing Management, 21(6), 827-837.

Bryman, A., 2016. Social research methods. Oxford university press.

Buchanan, D., and Bryman, A. (Eds.). (2009). The Sage handbook of organizational research methods. Sage Publications Ltd.

Buckles, J. R. (2011). The Federalization of Fiduciary Obedience Norms in Tax Laws Governing Charities: An Introduction to State Law Concepts and an Analysis of Their Implications for Federal Tax Law. Est. Plan. and Cmty. Prop. LJ, 4, 197.

Butler, R., and Wilson, D. C. (2015). Managing voluntary and non-profit organizations: Strategy and structure. Routledge.

Byrd, M. Y. (2014). Exploring the relationship between the organizational culture and diversity in the workforce. In Diversity in the workforce (pp. 75-88). Routledge.

Cappelli, P. H. (2015). Skill gaps, skill shortages, and skill mismatches: Evidence and arguments for the United States. ILR Review, 68(2), 251-290.

Cardy, R. L., and Lengnick-Hall, M. L. (2011). Will they stay or will they go? Exploring a customer-oriented approach to employee retention. Journal of Business and Psychology, 26(2), 213-217.

Carter, D., and Baghurst, T. (2014). The influence of servant leadership on restaurant employee engagement. Journal of Business Ethics, 124(3), 453-464.

Cascio, W. F. (2014). Leveraging employer branding, performance management and human resource development to enhance employee retention.

Castleberry, A., and Nolen, A. (2018). Thematic analysis of qualitative research data: Is it as easy as it sounds? Currents in Pharmacy Teaching and Learning, 10(6), 807-815.

Cattermole, G. (2019). Developing the employee lifecycle to keep top talent. Strategic HR Review.

Chan, S. C. (2010). Does workplace fun matter? Developing a useable typology of workplace fun in a qualitative study. International Journal of Hospitality Management, 29(4), 720-728.

Chan, S.H. and Kuok, O.M., 2011. A study of human resources recruitment, selection, and retention issues in the hospitality and tourism industry in Macau. Journal of Human Resources in Hospitality and Tourism, 10(4), pp.421-441.

Chandio, J. A., Jhatial, A. A., and Mallah, R. (2013). Modelling the Relationship of Unclear Career Development with Job Dissatisfaction, Job Stress and Employees' turnover Intention: Structural Equation Modelling Approach. International Research Journal of Arts and Humanities (Irjah), 41(41).

Chang, C.C., Chiu, C.M. and Chen, C.A., 2010. The effect of TQM practices on employee satisfaction and loyalty in government. Total Quality Management, 21(12), pp.1299-1314.

Charity Register Data. (2016). England and Wales Charity organisations.

Che, X. X., Zhou, Z. E., Kessler, S. R., and Spector, P. E. (2017). Stressors beget stressors: The effect of passive leadership on employee health through workload and work–family conflict. Work and Stress, 31(4), 338-354.

CHEGE, A. W. (2016). The influence of employee benefits on retention at Safaricom limited (Doctoral dissertation, University of Nairobi, Nairobi, Kenya).

Chen, F. (2019). Employment Duration and Attrition of Federal and State Inspectors General in the United States (Doctoral dissertation, City University of New York).

Chen, H. M., and Hsieh, Y. H. (2006). Key trends of the total reward system in the 21st century. Compensation and Benefits Review, 38(6), 64-70.

Chen, M. (2014, January). The effect of training on employee retention. In 2014 International Conference on Global Economy, Commerce and Service Science (GECSS-14). Atlantis Press.

Chenhall, R. H. (2005). Integrative strategic performance measurement systems, strategic alignment of manufacturing, learning and strategic outcomes: an exploratory study. Accounting, organisations and society, 30(5), 395-422.

Chiang, C. F., and Jang, S. S. (2008). An expectancy theory model for hotel employee motivation. International Journal of Hospitality Management, 27(2), 313-322.

Chiboiwa, M.W., Samuel, M.O. and Chipunza, C., 2010. An examination of employee retention strategy in a private organisation in Zimbabwe. African journal of business management, 4(10), pp.2103-2109.

Chimote, N.K. and Srivastava, V.N., 2013. Work-life balance benefits: From the perspective of organizations and employees. IUP Journal of Management Research, 12(1), p 62.

Chitsaz-Isfahani, A., and Boustani, H. R. (2014). Effects of talent management on employee's retention: The mediate effect of organizational trust. International Journal of Academic Research in Economics and Management Sciences, 3(5), 114.

Choudhary, S. (2016). A study on retention management: how to keep your top talent. International Journal of Advanced Research in Management and Social Sciences, 5(3), 17-31.

Christensen Hughes, J. and Rog, E., 2008. Talent management: A strategy for improving employee recruitment, retention and engagement within hospitality organizations. International Journal of Contemporary Hospitality Management, 20(7), pp.743-757.

Cloutier, O., Felusiak, L., Hill, C. and Pemberton-Jones, E.J., 2015. The Importance of Developing Strategies for Employee Retention. Journal of Leadership, Accountability and Ethics, 12(2).

Coetzee, M., and Stoltz, E. (2015). Employees' satisfaction with retention factors: Exploring the role of career adaptability. Journal of Vocational Behavior, 89, 83-91.

Community life survey data. (2016). Charitable Organisations.

Corry, M., Porter, S., and McKenna, H. (2019). The redundancy of positivism as a paradigm for nursing research. Nursing Philosophy, 20(1), p.e 12230.

Cotton, J. L., and Tuttle, J. M. (1986). Employee turnover: A meta-analysis and review with implications for research. Academy of management Review, 11(1), 55-70.

Craig, M. (2015, July). Cost effectiveness of retaining top internal talent in contrast to recruiting top talent. In Competition Forum (Vol. 13, No. 2, p. 203). American Society for Competitiveness.

Crain's Chicago Business article. (2015). Attrition rate in The United States of America.

Cropanzano, R., and Mitchell, M. S. (2005). Social exchange theory: An interdisciplinary review. Journal of management, 31(6), 874-900.

Crossman, Ashley. (2021, February 16). Positivism in the Study of Sociology. Retrieved from https://www.thoughtco.com/positivism-sociology-3026456

Dabale, W. P., Jagero, N., and Nyauchi, M. (2014). The relationship between training and employee performance: the case of Mutare City council, Zimbabwe. International Journal of Human Resource Studies, 4(4), 61.

Dabirian, A., Kietzmann, J., and Diba, H. (2017). A great place to work! Understanding crowdsourced employer branding. Business horizons, 60(2), 197-205.

Dart, R. (2004). The legitimacy of social enterprise. Nonprofit management and leadership, 14(4), 411-424.

Das, B.L. and Baruah, M., 2013. Employee retention: A review of literature. Journal of Business and Management, 14(2), pp.8-16.

Davis, T.L., 2013. A Qualitative Study of the Effects of Employee Retention on the Organization. Insights to a Changing World Journal, 2013(2).

Dawley, D., Houghton, J.D. and Bucklew, N.S., 2010. Perceived organizational support and turnover intention: The mediating effects of personal sacrifice and job fit. The Journal of Social Psychology, 150(3), pp.238-257.

De Cieri, H., Holmes, B., Abbott, J., and Pettit, T. (2005). Achievements and challenges for work/life balance strategies in Australian organizations. The International Journal of Human Resource Management, 16(1), 90-103.

De Meulenaere, K., Boone, C. and Buyl, T., 2016. Unraveling the impact of workforce age diversity on labor productivity: The moderating role of firm size and job security. Journal of organizational behavior, 37(2), pp.193-212.

Deb, S. (2014). Information technology, its impact on society and its future. Advances in Computing, 4(1), 25-29.

Dechawatanapaisal, D. (2018). Employee retention: the effects of internal branding and brand attitudes in sales organizations. Personnel Review.

Deci, E. L., and Ryan, R. M. (2014). Autonomy and need satisfaction in close relationships: Relationships motivation theory. In Human motivation and interpersonal relationships (pp. 53-73). Springer, Dordrecht.

Deery, M. and Jago, L., 2015. Revisiting talent management, work-life balance and retention strategies. International Journal of Contemporary Hospitality Management, 27(3), pp.453-472.

Deery, M., and Jago, L. (2015). Revisiting talent management, work-life balance and retention strategies. International Journal of Contemporary Hospitality Management, 27(3), 453-472.

Dei Mensah, R. E. B. E. C. C. A. (2014). Effects of human resource management practices on retention of employees in the banking industry in Accra, Ghana.

Deloitte Resource (2004). Talent Management Model, The Develop-Deploy-Connect (DDC).

Demirtas, O., and Akdogan, A. A. (2015). The effect of ethical leadership behavior on ethical climate, turnover intention, and affective commitment. Journal of Business Ethics, 130(1), 59-67.

Dey, S. (2009). Employee retention--A key to organizational growth. GMJ, 3(1), 4549.

Dhar, R. L. (2015). Service quality and the training of employees: The mediating role of organizational commitment. Tourism Management, 46, 419-430.

DiMaggio, P.J. and Anheier, H.K., 1990. The sociology of nonprofit organizations and sectors. Annual review of sociology, 16(1), pp.137-159.

Direnzo, M.S. and Greenhaus, J.H., 2011. Job search and voluntary turnover in a boundaryless world: A control theory perspective. Academy of Management Review, 36(3), pp.567-589.

Direnzo, M.S., Greenhaus, J.H. and Weer, C.H., 2015. Relationship between protean career orientation and work–life balance: A resource perspective. Journal of Organizational Behavior, 36(4), pp.538-560.

Drucker, P., 2012. Managing the non-profit organization. Routledge.

Eaton, Tim V., and Michael D. Akers. "Whistleblowing and good governance." The CPA Journal (2007).

Ebrary. 2020. McClelland's Need Theory. [online] Available at: <https://ebrary.net/2840/management/mcclellands_need_theory> [Accessed 3 June 2020].

Edwards, A. W., and Cavalli-Sforza, L. L. (1965). A method for cluster analysis. Biometrics, 362-375.

Edwards, J. R., Davey, J., and Armstrong, K. (2013). Returning to the roots of culture: A review and re-conceptualisation of safety culture. Safety science, 55, 70-80.

Emerson, R. M. (1976). Social exchange theory. Annual review of sociology, 2(1), 335-362.

Emmel, N., Greenhalgh, J., Manzano, A., Monaghan, M., and Dalkin, S. (Eds.). (2018). Doing realist research. Sage.

Etikan, I., Musa, S.A. and Alkassim, R.S., 2016. Comparison of convenience sampling and purposive sampling. American Journal of Theoretical and Applied Statistics, 5(1), pp.1-4.

Feeley, T.H., Moon, S.I., Kozey, R.S. and Slowe, A.S., 2010. An erosion model of employee turnover based on network centrality. Journal of Applied Communication Research, 38(2), pp.167-188.

Fernandez, D. (2011). Employee retention and transformational leadership: A phenomenological study (Doctoral dissertation, University of Phoenix).

Festing, M. and Schäfer, L., 2014. Generational challenges to talent management: A framework for talent retention based on the psychological-contract perspective. Journal of World Business, 49(2), pp.262-271.

Fey, C.F., Björkman, I. and Pavlovskaya, A., 2000. The effect of human resource management practices on firm performance in Russia. International Journal of Human Resource Management, 11(1), pp.1-18.

Fischer, R. L., Wilsker, A., and Young, D. R. (2011). Exploring the revenue mix of nonprofit organizations: Does it relate to publicness? Nonprofit and Voluntary Sector Quarterly, 40(4), 662-681.

Fitzgerald, S., and Schutte, N. S. (2010). Increasing transformational leadership through enhancing self-efficacy. Journal of Management Development.

Fletcher, A. J. (2017). Applying critical realism in qualitative research: methodology meets method. International journal of social research methodology, 20(2), 181-194.

Flostrand, A. (2017). Finding the future: Crowdsourcing versus the Delphi technique. Business Horizons, 60(2), 229-236.

Foday, A. (2014). Perceived relationship between career development and employee retention at deloitte Kenya. Unpublished MBA Thesis. University of Nairobi, Kenya.

Friedman, B. A., and Schnorr, L. M. Latent Employee Turnover and Prevention—When Job Creation Catches Up with Economic Recovery: An Employee Retention Model and Case Study. (2015) Business Research Consortium of Western New York, 89.

Froehlich, D., Segers, M. and Van den Bossche, P., 2014. Informal workplace learning in Austrian banks: The influence of learning approach, leadership style, and organizational learning culture on managers' learning outcomes. Human resource development quarterly, 25(1), pp.29-57.

Fusch, P., Fusch, G. E., and Ness, L. R. (2018). Denzin's paradigm shift: Revisiting triangulation in qualitative research. Journal of Social Change, 10(1), 2.

Gao, Y. (2017). Business leaders' personal values, organisational culture and market orientation. Journal of Strategic Marketing, 25(1), 49-64.

Garavan, T. N., Carbery, R., and Rock, A. (2012). Mapping talent development: definition, scope and architecture. European journal of training and development.

Gardner, T.M., Wright, P.M. and Moynihan, L.M., 2011. The impact of motivation, empowerment, and skill-enhancing practices on aggregate voluntary turnover: The mediating effect of collective affective commitment. Personnel psychology, 64(2), pp.315-350.

Gavin, H. (2008). Thematic analysis. Understanding research methods and statistics in psychology, 273-282.

Gberevbie, D. E. (2008). Employee retention strategies and organizational performance. An International Journal of Psychology in Africa, 16(2), 131-152.

Gelens, J., Dries, N., Hofmans, J. and Pepermans, R., 2015. Affective commitment of employees designated as talent: signalling perceived organisational support. European Journal of International Management, 9(1), pp.9-27.

Gentles, S.J. and Vilches, S.L., 2017. Calling for a Shared Understanding of Sampling Terminology in Qualitative Research: Proposed Clarifications Derived from Critical Analysis of a Methods Overview by McCrae and Purssell. International Journal of Qualitative Methods, 16(1), p.1609406917725678.

George, C., 2015. Retaining professional workers: what makes them stay?. Employee Relations, 37(1), pp.102-121.

Ghafoor, A., Qureshi, T. M., Khan, M. A., and Hijazi, S. T. (2011). Transformational leadership, employee engagement and performance: Mediating effect of psychological ownership. African journal of business management, 5(17), 7391.

Ghosh, P., Satyawadi, R., Prasad Joshi, J. and Shadman, M., 2013. Who stays with you? Factors predicting employees' intention to stay. International Journal of Organizational Analysis, 21(3), pp.288-312.

Gialuisi, O. and Coetzer, A., 2013. An exploratory investigation into voluntary employee turnover and retention in small businesses. Small Enterprise Research, 20(1), pp.55-68.

Gilbert, S., Horsman, P., and Kelloway, E. K. (2016). The motivation for transformational leadership scale. Leadership and Organization Development Journal.

Given, L. M., Forcier, E., and Rathi, D. (2013). Social media and community knowledge: An ideal partnership for non-profit organizations. Proceedings of the American Society for Information Science and Technology, 50(1), 1-11.

Glaser, B.G. and Strauss, A.L., 2017. Discovery of grounded theory: Strategies for qualitative research. Routledge.

Goswami, B. K., and Jha, S. (2012). Attrition issues and retention challenges of employees. International Journal of Scientific and Engineering Research, 3(4), 1-6.

Goulet, L.R. and Frank, M.L., 2002. Organizational commitment across three sectors: Public, non-profit, and for-profit. Public Personnel Management, 31(2), pp.201-210.

Govaerts, N., Kyndt, E., Dochy, F. and Baert, H., 2011. Influence of learning and working climate on the retention of talented employees. Journal of Workplace Learning, 23(1), pp.35-55.

Grafton, J., Lillis, A. M., and Widener, S. K. (2010). The role of performance measurement and evaluation in building organisational capabilities and performance. Accounting, Organisations and Society, 35(7), 689-706.

Greasley, K., Bryman, A., Dainty, A., Price, A., Soetanto, R. and King, N., 2005. Employee perceptions of empowerment. Employee relations, 27(4), pp.354-368.

Gregory, K. (2011). The importance of employee satisfaction. The Journal of the Division of Business and Information Management, 5, 29-37.

Griffeth RW, Hom PW, Gaertner S (2000). A meta-analysis of antecedents and correlates of employee turnover: update, moderator tests, and research implications for the next millennium. J. Manage., 26(3): 463-488.

Grobler, P. A., and De Bruyn, A. J. (2012). Flexible Work Practices (FWP)-an effective instrument in the retention of talent: a survey of selected JSE-listed companies, South African Journal of Business Management, 42 (4) December 2011: pp. 63-78:: errata. South African Journal of Business Management, 43(1), 93.

Guerra, G. F., and Noll, M. (2021). Scientific Methodology in Integrated High Schools: A Case Study. International Journal of Instruction, 14(2).

Gunawan, J. (2015). Ensuring trustworthiness in qualitative research. Belitung Nursing Journal, 1(1), 10-11.

Hafiza, N.S., Shah, S.S., Jamsheed, H. and Zaman, K., 2011. Relationship between rewards and employee's motivation in the non-profit organizations of Pakistan. Business Intelligence Journal, 4(2), pp.327-334.

Haider, M., Rasli, A., Akhtar, S., Yusoff, R. B. M., Malik, O. M., Aamir, A., nd Tariq, F. (2015). The impact of human resource practices on employee retention in the telecom sector. International Journal of Economics and Financial Issues, 5(1S).

Haider, S. H., Fatima, M., Asad, M., and Ala'A, Z. A. A. (2016). A study on the issues of employment contracts and practices of employment contracts in UAE. Paradigms, 10(1), 58.

Haines III, V.Y., Jalette, P. and Larose, K., 2010. The influence of human resource management practices on employee voluntary turnover rates in the Canadian non-governmental sector. ILR Review, 63(2), pp.228-246.

Hallam, P. R., Chou, P. N., Hite, J. M., and Hite, S. J. (2012). Two contrasting models for mentoring as they affect retention of beginning teachers. NASSP Bulletin, 96(3), 243-278.

Hammack, D. C. (2001). Introduction: Growth, transformation, and quiet revolution in the non-profit sector over two centuries.

Hammer, C. S. (2011). The importance of participant demographics. American Journal of Speech-Language Pathology, 20(4), 261.

Hancock, J.I., Allen, D.G., Bosco, F.A., McDaniel, K.R. and Pierce, C.A., 2013. Meta-analytic review of employee turnover as a predictor of firm performance. Journal of Management, 39(3), pp.573-603.

Harhara, A. S., Singh, S. K., and Hussain, M. (2015). Correlates of employee turnover intentions in oil and gas industry in the UAE. International journal of organizational analysis, 23(3), 493-504.

Harp, G. J. (2010). Positivist republic: Auguste Comte and the reconstruction of American liberalism, 1865-1920. Penn State Press.

Harper, D. (2011). Choosing a qualitative research method. Qualitative research methods in mental health and psychotherapy, 83-98.

Hartmann, E., Feisel, E., and Schober, H. (2010). Talent management of western MNCs in China: Balancing global integration and local responsiveness. Journal of world business, 45(2), 169-178.

Hassan, S. (2013). Does fair treatment in the workplace matter? An assessment of organizational fairness and employee outcomes in government. The American Review of Public Administration, 43(5), 539-557.

Hausknecht, J.P. and Trevor, C.O., 2011. Collective turnover at the group, unit, and organizational levels: Evidence, issues, and implications. Journal of management, 37(1), pp.352-388.

Heimerl, F., Lohmann, S., Lange, S., and Ertl, T. (2014, January). Word cloud explorer: Text analytics based on word clouds. In 2014 47th Hawaii International Conference on System Sciences (pp. 1833-1842). IEEE.

Held, P., Klassen, B. J., Hall, J. M., Friese, T. R., Bertsch-Gout, M. M., Zalta, A. K., and Pollack, M. H. (2019). "I knew it was wrong the moment I got the order": A narrative thematic analysis of moral injury in combat veterans. Psychological trauma: theory, research, practice, and policy, 11(4), 396.

Herman, H.M., Huang, X. and Lam, W., 2013. Why does transformational leadership matter for employee turnover? A multi-foci social exchange perspective. The Leadership Quarterly, 24(5), pp.763-776.

Hezarvand, E. M. (2013). An Investigation of Job Satisfaction Organizational Commitment and Turnover Intention in Iranian Insurance Industry (Doctoral dissertation, Universiti Teknologi Malaysia).

Hoat, L. (2008). Moving the mountain: Renovating medical education in a changing Vietnam.

Holtom, B. C., and Burch, T. C. (2016). A model of turnover-based disruption in customer services. Human Resource Management Review, 26(1), 25-36.

Hom, P. W., and Xiao, Z. (2011). Embedding social networks: How guanxi ties reinforce Chinese employees' retention. Organizational Behavior and Human Decision Processes, 116(2), 188-202.

Hom, P. W., Lee, T. W., Shaw, J. D., and Hausknecht, J. P. (2017). One hundred years of employee turnover theory and research. Journal of Applied Psychology, 102(3), 530.

Homans, G. C. (1958). Social behavior as exchange. American journal of sociology, 63(6), 597-606.

Hong, E.N.C., Hao, L.Z., Kumar, R., Ramendran, C. and Kadiresan, V., 2012. An effectiveness of human resource management practices on employee retention in institute of higher learning: A regression analysis. International journal of business research and management, 3(2), pp.60-79.

Hopkins, W.G., 2017. Estimating Sample Size for Magnitude-Based Inferences. Sport science, 21.

Hossain, S.M., Roy, M.K. and Das, P.K., 2017. Factors Affecting Employee's Turnover Intention in Banking Sector of Bangladesh: An Empirical Analysis. ASA University Review, 11(2).

Hughes, J. C., and Rog, E. (2008). Talent management: A strategy for improving employee recruitment, retention and engagement within hospitality organizations. International Journal of Contemporary Hospitality Management, 20(7), 743-757.

Huhtala, M., and Feldt, T. (2016). The path from ethical organisational culture to employee commitment: Mediating roles of value congruence and work engagement. Scandinavian Journal of Work and Organizational Psychology, 1.

Humanities and Social Sciences, 2(13), 1-12.

Hussain, T., and Rehman, S. S. (2013). Do human resource management practices inspire employees' retention. Research Journal of Applied Sciences, Engineering and Technology, 6(19), 3625-3633.

Hutto, P. N. (2017). The relationship between student retention in community college courses and faculty employment status. Community College Journal of Research and Practice, 41(1), 4-17.

IBRAHIM, M. H. (2019). Interpersonal Relationship and Employee Retention. Ilorin Journal of Administration and Development, 5(2), 95-102.

Ibrahim, M., and Al Falasi, S. (2014). Employee loyalty and engagement in UAE public sector. Employee Relations.

Idris, A. (2014). Flexible working as an employee retention strategy in developing countries. Journal of Management Research, 14(2), 71-86.

Iqbal, A., 2010. Employee turnover: Causes, consequences and retention strategies in the Saudi organizations. The Business Review, Cambridge, 16(2), pp.275-281.

Iriana, R., Buttle, F., and Ang, L. (2013). Does organisational culture influence CRM's financial outcomes? Journal of Marketing Management, 29(3-4), 467-493.

Islam, N., Mavengere, N., Ahlfors, U. R., Ruohonen, M., Serenko, A., and Palvia, P. (2018). A Stress-Strain-Outcome Model of Job Satisfaction: The Moderating Role of Professional Self-efficacy.

Jackson, K., and Bazeley, P. (2019). Qualitative data analysis with NVivo. Sage.

James, L., and Mathew, L. (2012). Employee retention strategies: IT industry. SCMS Journal of Indian Management, 9(3), 79.

Jehanzeb, K. and Bashir, N.A., 2013. Training and development program and its benefits to employee and organization: A conceptual study. European Journal of business and management, 5(2).

Jiang, K., Liu, D., McKay, P.F., Lee, T.W. and Mitchell, T.R., 2012. When and how is job embeddedness predictive of turnover? A meta-analytic investigation. Journal of Applied Psychology, 97(5), p.1077.

Johara, F., Yahya, S., and Tehseen, S. (2018). Employee retention, market orientation, and organizational performance–An empirical study. International Academic Journal of Business Management, 5(3), 176-187.

Judge, T. A., Zhang, S. C., and Glerum, D. R. (2020). Job satisfaction. Essentials of Job Attitudes and Other Workplace Psychological Constructs, 207-241.

Kabungaidze, T., Mahlatshana, N. and Ngirande, H., 2013. The impact of job satisfaction and some demographic variables on employee turnover intentions. International Journal of Business Administration, 4(1), p.53.

Kaliyadan, F., and Kulkarni, V. (2019). Types of variables, descriptive statistics, and sample size. Indian dermatology online journal, 10(1), 82.

Kaplan, R. S., Robert, N. P. D. K. S., Kaplan, R. S., and Norton, D. P. (2001). The strategy-focused organisation: How balanced scorecard companies thrive in the new business environment. Harvard Business Press.

Kar, S., and Misra, K. C. (2013). Nexus between work life balance practices and employee retention-The mediating effect of a supportive culture. Asian social science, 9(11), 63.

Karatepe, O.M., 2012. The effects of coworker and perceived organizational support on hotel employee outcomes: The moderating role of job embeddedness. Journal of Hospitality and Tourism Research, 36(4), pp.495-516.

Karatepe, O.M., 2013. High-performance work practices and hotel employee performance: The mediation of work engagement. International Journal of Hospitality Management, 32, pp.132-140.

Karatepe, O.M., 2013. High-performance work practices work social support and their effects on job embeddedness and turnover intentions. International Journal of Contemporary Hospitality Management, 25(6), pp.903-921.

Karl, K. A., and Peluchette, J. V. (2006). Does workplace fun buffer the impact of emotional exhaustion on job dissatisfaction? A study of health care workers. Journal of Behavioural and Applied Management, 7(2), 128-142.

Kassambara, A. (2017). Practical guide to cluster analysis in R: Unsupervised machine learning (Vol. 1). Sthda.

Kaur, R. (2017). Employee retention models and factors affecting employee's retention in IT companies. International Journal of Business Administration and Management, 7(1), 61-174.

Kaur, R. (2017). Employee retention models and factors affecting employee's retention in IT companies. International Journal of Business Administration and Management, 7(1), 61-174.

Kawar, T. I. (2012). Cross-cultural differences in management. International Journal of Business and Social Science, 3(6).

Kazi, G.M., Aziz, S. and Zadeh, Z.F., 2012. The contribution of organizational variables and its impact on job turnover and job satisfaction of employees. Interdisciplinary Journal of Contemporary Research in Business, 3(10), pp.1067-1073.

Kelchtermans, G. (2017). 'Should I stay, or should I go?': unpacking teacher attrition/retention as an educational issue. Teachers and Teaching, 23(8), 961-977.

Kellner, A., Townsend, K., and Wilkinson, A. (2017). 'The mission or the margin? 'A high-performance work system in a non-profit organisation. The International Journal of Human Resource Management, 28(14), 1938-1959.

Khan, M. A., and Ahmad, N. S. A. (2011). Modelling link between internal service quality in human resources management and employee's retention: A case of Pakistani privatized and public sector banks. African Journal of Business Management, 5(3), 949.

Khan, M.A., 2014. Organizational Cynicism and Employee Turnover Intention: Evidence from Banking Sector in Pakistan. Pakistan Journal of Commerce and Social Sciences, 8(1).

Khan, M.A., Safwan, N. and Ahmad, A., 2011. Modelling link between internal service quality in human resources management and employee's retention: A case of Pakistani privatized and public sector banks. African Journal of Business Management, 5(3), pp.949-959.

Khan, S. N. (2014). Qualitative research method: Grounded theory. International Journal of Business and Management, 9(11), 224-233.

Khoele, A., and Daya, P. (2014). Investigating the turnover of middle and senior managers in the pharmaceutical industry in South Africa. SA Journal of Human Resource Management, 12(1), 1-10.

Kibui, A. W., Gachunga, H., and Namusonge, G. S. (2014). Role of talent management on employee's retention in Kenya: A survey of state corporations in Kenya: Empirical review. International journal of Science and Research, 3(2), 414-424.

Kiger, M. E., and Varpio, L. (2020). Thematic analysis of qualitative data: AMEE Guide No. 131. Medical teacher, 42(8), 846-854.

Kim, K. and Jogaratnam, G., 2010. Effects of individual and organizational factors on job satisfaction and intent to stay in the hotel and restaurant industry. Journal of Human Resources in Hospitality and Tourism, 9(3), pp.318-339.

King, N., and Brooks, J. (2018). Thematic analysis in organisational research. The Sage handbook of qualitative business and management research methods: Methods and challenges.

Klijn, M. and Tomic, W., 2010. A review of creativity within organizations from a psychological perspective. Journal of Management Development, 29(4), pp.322-343.

Knesek, G. (2015). Creating a feedback-rich workplace environment: Lessons learned over a 35+ year career in human resources. The Psychologist-Manager Journal, 18(3-4), 109.

Knight, R. L. (2014). Organisational culture change readiness and retention: a human services perspective (Doctoral dissertation, Queensland University of Technology).

Koehne, B., Shih, P. C., and Olson, J. S. (2012, February). Remote and alone: coping with being the remote member on the team. In Proceedings of the ACM 2012 conference on Computer Supported Cooperative Work (pp. 1257-1266).

Kooij, D.T. and Boon, C., 2018. Perceptions of HR practices, person–organisation fit, and affective commitment: The moderating role of career stage. Human Resource Management Journal, 28(1), pp.61-75.

Korstjens, I., and Moser, A. (2018). Series: Practical guidance to qualitative research. Part 4: Trustworthiness and publishing. European Journal of General Practice, 24(1), 120-124.

Kossek, E. E., Petty, R. J., Bodner, T. E., Perrigino, M. B., Hammer, L. B., Yragui, N. L., and Michel, J. S. (2018). Lasting Impression: Transformational Leadership and Family Supportive Supervision as Resources for Well-Being and Performance. Occupational Health Science, 2(1), 1-24.

Kossivi, B., Xu, M., and Kalgora, B. (2016). Study on determining factors of employee retention. Open Journal of Social Sciences, 4(05), 261.

Kuria, S., Alice, O. and Wanderi, P.M., 2012. Assessment of causes of labour turnover in three and five star-rated hotels in Kenya. International journal of business and social science, 3(15).

Kwenin, D. O. (2013). Relationship Between Work Environment. Career Development Opportunities and Employee Retention in Vidavone Ghana Limited. Global Journal of Human Resource Management, 1(4), 1-9.

Kwenin, D.O., Muathe, S. and Nzulwa, R., 2013. The influence of employee rewards, human resource policies and job satisfaction on the retention of employees in Vodafone Ghana Limited. European Journal of Business and Management, 5(12), pp.13-20.

Lai, H. H. (2011). The influence of compensation system design on employee satisfaction. African Journal of Business Management, 5(26), 10718.

Lambert, S. J., Haley-Lock, A., and Henly, J. R. (2012). Schedule flexibility in hourly jobs: Unanticipated consequences and promising directions. Community, Work and Family, 15(3), 293-315.

Lashley, C., 1999. Employee empowerment in services: a framework for analysis. Personnel Review, 28(3), pp.169-191.

Latham, C. L., Ringl, K., and Hogan, M. (2011). Professionalization and retention outcomes of a university–service mentoring program partnership. Journal of Professional Nursing, 27(6), 344-353.

Laureani, A. and Antony, J., 2010. Reducing employees' turnover in transactional services: a Lean Six Sigma case study. International Journal of Productivity and Performance Management, 59(7), pp.688-700.

Lawler II, E. E. (1969). 3. Job design and employee motivation. Personnel psychology, 22(4), 426-435.

Lawler III, E. E. (1999). Employee involvement makes a difference. The Journal for Quality and Participation, 22(5), 18.

Lawless, H. T., and Heymann, H. (2010). Descriptive analysis. In Sensory evaluation of food (pp. 227-257). Springer, New York, NY.

Lehmann, H., Razzolini, T., and Zaiceva, A. (2012). Chapter 8 Job Separations and Informality in the Russian Labor Market'. Informal Employment in Emerging and Transition Economies (Research in Labor Economics, Volume 34). Emerald Group Publishing Limited, 257-290.

Leshem, S. and Trafford, V., 2007. Overlooking the conceptual framework. Innovations in education and Teaching International, 44(1), pp.93-105.

Levinson, D.J., 1977. The mid-life transition: A period in adult psychosocial development. Psychiatry, 40(2), pp.99-112.

Li, J.J., Lee, T.W., Mitchell, T.R., Hom, P.W. and Griffeth, R.W., 2016. The effects of proximal withdrawal states on job attitudes, job searching, intent to leave, and employee turnover. Journal of Applied Psychology, 101(10), p.1436.

Lichtenthaler, U. (2011). Open innovation: Past research, current debates, and future directions. Academy of management perspectives, 25(1), 75-93.

Lin, H.C., Lee, Y.D. and Tai, C., 2012. A study on the relationship between human resource management strategies and core competencies. International Journal of Organizational Innovation (Online), 4(3), p.153.

Liu, B., Liu, J. and Hu, J., 2010. Person-organization fit, job satisfaction, and turnover intention: An empirical study in the Chinese public sector. Social Behavior and Personality: an international journal, 38(5), pp.615-625.

Liu, G., Eng, T. Y., and Takeda, S. (2015). An investigation of marketing capabilities and social enterprise performance in the UK and Japan. Entrepreneurship Theory and Practice, 39(2), 267-298.

Lohman, C., Fortuin, L., and Wouters, M. (2004). Designing a performance measurement system: A case study. European journal of operational research, 156(2), 267-286.

Lohmann, S., Heimerl, F., Bopp, F., Burch, M., and Ertl, T. (2015, July). Concentri cloud: Word cloud visualization for multiple text documents. In 2015 19th International Conference on Information Visualisation (pp. 114-120). IEEE.

Long, C. S., Ajagbe, A. M., Nor, K. M. and Suleiman, E. S. (2012). The approaches to increase employees' loyalty: A review on employees' turnover models. Australian Journal of Basic and Applied Sciences, 6(10), 282-291.

Low, C.H., Bordia, P. and Bordia, S., 2016. What do employees want and why? An exploration of employees' preferred psychological contract elements across career stages. Human Relations, 69(7), pp.1457-1481.

Lu, L., Lu, A.C.C., Gursoy, D. and Neale, N.R., 2016. Work engagement, job satisfaction, and turnover intentions: A comparison between supervisors and line-level employees. International Journal of Contemporary Hospitality Management, 28(4), pp.737-761.

Lumley, E.J., Coetzee, M., Tladinyane, R. and Ferreira, N., 2011. Exploring the job satisfaction and organisational commitment of employees in the information technology environment. Southern African Business Review, 15(1).

Lyons, S.T., Ng, E.S. and Schweitzer, L., 2014. Changing demographics and the shifting nature of careers: Implications for research and human resource development. Human Resource Development Review, 13(2), pp.181-206.

MacKusick, C. I., and Minick, P. (2010). Why are nurses leaving? Findings from an initial qualitative study on nursing attrition. Medsurg Nursing, 19(6).

Maguire, M., and Delahunt, B. (2017). Doing a thematic analysis: A practical, step-by-step guide for learning and teaching scholars. All Ireland Journal of Higher Education, 9(3).

Mahal, P.K., 2012. HR practices as determinants of organizational commitment and employee retention. IUP Journal of Management Research, 11(4), p.37.

Maheshwari, V., Gunesh, P., Lodorfos, G., and Konstantopoulou, A. (2017). Exploring HR practitioners' perspective on employer branding and its role in organisational attractiveness and talent management. International Journal of Organizational Analysis.

Major, A.M., 2016. Strategies to reduce voluntary employee turnover in small business.

Maldonado, S., Flores, Á., Verbraken, T., Baesens, B., and Weber, R. (2015). Profit-based feature selection using support vector machines–General framework and an application for customer retention. Applied Soft Computing, 35, 740-748.

Mallol, C. M., Holtom, B. C., and Lee, T. W. (2007). Job embeddedness in a culturally diverse environment. Journal of Business and Psychology, 22(1), 35-44.

Maloney, J. C. (2018). What it is Like to Perceive: Direct Realism and the Phenomenal Character of Perception. Oxford University Press.

Maphanga, C. H. (2014). The Relationship between manager supoort, work-life balance and talent retention in a South African utility organisation (Doctoral dissertation, University of Pretoria).

Mayes, B.T., Finney, T.G., Johnson, T.W., Shen, J. and Yi, L., 2017. The effect of human resource practices on perceived organizational support in the People's Republic of China. The International Journal of Human Resource Management, 28(9), pp.1261-1290.

Mbah, S.E. and Ikemefuna, C.O., 2012. Job satisfaction and employees' turnover intentions in total Nigeria PLC in Lagos State. International Journal of Humanities and Social Science, 2(14), pp.275-287.

McClelland, D. A. V. I. D. (2005). Achievement motivation theory. Organizational behavior: Essential theories of motivation and leadership, 46-60.

McClelland, D. C. (1987). Human motivation. CUP Archive.

McDonald, K.S. and Hite, L.M., 2005. Reviving the relevance of career development in human resource development. Human Resource Development Review, 4(4), pp.418-439.

McDonnell, A., 2008. Outward foreign direct investment and human capital development: a small country perspective. Journal of European Industrial Training, 32(6), pp.452-471.

McKinney, J. B. (2015). Effective financial management in public and nonprofit agencies. ABC-CLIO.

McLeod, S. (2007). Maslow's hierarchy of needs. Simply psychology, 1, 1-8.

McMillan, E. J. (2008). Model policies and procedures for not-for-profit organisations. John Wiley and Sons.

McPhail, G., and Lourie, M. (2017). Getting real: is realism a blind spot in research methodology? New Zealand Journal of Educational Studies, 52(2), 285-299.

Medina, E., 2012. Job satisfaction and employee turnover intention: What does organizational culture have to do with it? Columbia university, pp.1-44.

Mehta, M., Kurbetti, A. and Dhankhar, R., 2014. Review Paper–Study on Employee Retention and Commitment. International journal of advance research in computer science and management studies, 154(5).

Memon, M.A., Salleh, R., Baharom, M.N.R. and Harun, H., 2014. Person-Organization Fit and Turnover Intention: The Mediating Role of Employee Engagement. Global Business and Management Research, 6(3).

Mendes, F., and Stander, M. W. (2011). Positive organisation: The role of leader behaviour in work engagement and retention. SA Journal of Industrial Psychology, 37(1), 1-13.

Menon, S., 2001. Employee empowerment: An integrative psychological approach. Applied psychology, 50(1), pp.153-180.

Mettl.com (2020). Motivation Inventory Test | Online Motivation Inventory Assessment for Hiring, L and D and Recruitment -Mettl. [online] Available at: <https://mettl.com/en/test/psychometric-test-new-motivation-inventory/> [Accessed 24 May 2020].

MICHAEL, B., PRINCE, A. F., and CHACKO, A. (2016). IMPACT OF COMPENSATION PACKAGE ON EMPLOYEE RETENTION. CLEAR International Journal of Research in Commerce and Management, 7(10).

Miller, P. G., Strang, J., and Miller, P. M. (Eds.). (2010). Addiction research methods. John Wiley and Sons.

Miner, J. B. (2015). Expectancy theories: Victor Vroom, and Lyman Porter and Edward Lawler. In Organizational Behaviour 1 (pp. 110-129). Routledge.

Mishra, P. S. (2007). Increasing rate of attrition in BPO. Management and Labour Studies, 32(1), 7-21.

Mohajan, H. K. (2018). Qualitative research methodology in social sciences and related subjects. Journal of Economic Development, Environment and People, 7(1), 23-48.

Mohan, M.D., Muthaly, S. and Annakis, J., 2015. Talent Culture's Role in Talent Development among academics: Insights from Malaysian government linked Universities. Journal of Contemporary Issues in Business and Government, The, 21(1), p.46.

Mohr, D.C., Young, G.J. and Burgess, Jr, J.F., 2012. Employee turnover and operational performance: The moderating effect of group-oriented organisational culture. Human Resource Management Journal, 22(2), pp.216-233.

Moore, L. L., Grabsch, D. K., and Rotter, C. (2010). Using achievement motivation theory to explain student participation in a residential leadership learning community. Journal of leadership education, 9(2), 22-34.

Mowday, R.T., Porter, L.W. and Steers, R.M., 2013. Employee—organization linkages: The psychology of commitment, absenteeism, and turnover. Academic press.

Moynihan, D. P., and Pandey, S. K. (2008). The ties that bind: Social networks, person-organization value fit, and turnover intention. Journal of public administration research and theory, 18(2), 205-227.

Msengeti, D. M., and Obwogi, J. (2015). Effects of pay and work environment on employee retention: A study of Hotel industry in Mombasa County.

Muogbo, U. S. (2013). The impact of employee motivation on organisational performance (a study of some selected firms in anambra state nigeria). The international journal of engineering and science, 2(7), 70-80.

Mwanje, S.M., 2010. Career development and staff motivation in the banking industry: a case study of bank of Uganda (Doctoral dissertation, Makerere University).

Nadler, J. T., and Kufahl, K. M. (2014). Marital status, gender, and sexual orientation: Implications for employment hiring decisions. Psychology of Sexual Orientation and Gender Diversity, 1(3), 270.

Nagabhaskar, M. (2014). Motivational factors of employee retention and engagement in organizations. International Journal of Development Research, 4(2), 221-224.

National council of voluntary organisations (NCVO). 2016. Non-profit Organisation activities.

Nawab, S. and Bhatti, K.K., 2011. Influence of employee compensation on organizational commitment and job satisfaction: A case study of educational sector of Pakistan. International Journal of Business and Social Science, 2(8).

Nelsey, L., and Brownie, S. (2012). Effective leadership, teamwork and mentoring–Essential elements in promoting generational cohesion in the nursing workforce and retaining nurses. Collegian, 19(4), 197-202.

Newman, A., Thanacoody, R. and Hui, W., 2011. The effects of perceived organizational support, perceived supervisor support and intra-organizational network resources on turnover intentions: A study of Chinese employees in multinational enterprises. Personnel Review, 41(1), pp.56-72.

Newman, A., Thanacoody, R. and Hui, W., 2011. The impact of employee perceptions of training on organizational commitment and turnover intentions: a study of multinationals in the Chinese service sector. The International Journal of Human Resource Management, 22(8), pp.1765-1787.

Nica, E., 2016. Employee voluntary turnover as a negative indicator of organizational effectiveness. Psychosociological Issues in Human Resource Management, 4(2), p.220.

Nicholson, L. M., Schwirian, P. M., Klein, E. G., Skybo, T., Murray-Johnson, L., Eneli, I., and Groner, J. A. (2011). Recruitment and retention strategies in longitudinal clinical studies with low-income populations. Contemporary clinical trials, 32(3), 353-362.

Noble, C., Sly, C., Collier, L., Armit, L., Hilder, J., and Molloy, E. (2019). Enhancing feedback literacy in the workplace: A learner-centred approach. In Augmenting health and social care students' clinical learning experiences (pp. 283-306). Springer, Cham.

Nowell, L. S., Norris, J. M., White, D. E., and Moules, N. J. (2017). Thematic analysis: Striving to meet the trustworthiness criteria. International journal of qualitative methods, 16(1), 1609406917733847.

Nwokocha, I., and Iheriohanma, E. B. J. (2012). Emerging trends in employee retention strategies in a globalizing economy: Nigeria in focus.

Ogbeibu, S., Senadjki, A., and Gaskin, J. (2018). The moderating effect of benevolence on the impact of organisational culture on employee creativity. Journal of Business Research, 90, 334-346.

Oladapo, V. (2014). The impact of talent management on retention. Journal of business studies quarterly, 5(3), 19.

Olckers, C., and Du Plessis, Y. (2012). Psychological ownership: A managerial construct for talent retention and organisational effectiveness.

Omerzel, D. G., Biloslavo, R., Trnavčevič, A., and Trnavčevič, A. (2011). Knowledge management and organisational culture in higher education institutions. Journal for East European Management Studies, 111-139.

Omonijo, D.O., Oludayo, O.O., Uche, O.O.C., Eche, G.A. and Ohunakin, F., 2015. Intentional turnover of the administrative staff in a private faith-based higher institution, southwest Nigeria. Mediterranean Journal of Social Sciences, 6(2 (S) 1), pp.424-434.

Ongori, H. (2007). A review of the literature on employee turnover.

Osibanjo, A. O., Adeniji, A. A., Falola, H. O., and Heirsmac, P. T. (2014). Compensation packages: a strategic tool for employees' performance and retention. Leonardo Journal of Sciences, (25), 65-84.

Osman, S., Mohammad, S., Abu, M.S., Mokhtar, M., Ahmad, J., Ismail, N. and Jambari, H., 2018. Inductive, Deductive and Abductive Approaches in Generating New Ideas: A Modified Grounded Theory Study. Advanced Science Letters, 24(4), pp.2378-2381.

Palistha Maharjan, "Expectancy Theory of Motivation," in Businesstopia, January 9, 2018, https://www.businesstopia.net/human-resource/expectancy-theory-motivation.

Parijat, P., and Bagga, S. (2014). Victor Vroom's expectancy theory of motivation–An evaluation. International Research Journal of Business and Management, 7(9), 1-8.

Park, Y. S., Konge, L., and Artino, A. R. (2020). The positivism paradigm of research. Academic Medicine, 95(5), 690-694.

Part Streets People article UK. (2015.) Turnover rate in the United Kingdom.

Patro, C. S. (2014). A study on the impact of employee retention policies on organisation productivity in private sector. International Journal of Asian Business and Information Management (IJABIM), 5(3), 48-63.

Perryer, C., Jordan, C., Firns, I. and Travaglione, A., 2010. Predicting turnover intentions: The interactive effects of organizational commitment and perceived organizational support. Management Research Review, 33(9), pp.911-923.

Pham, L. T. M. (2018). Qualitative approach to research a review of advantages and disadvantages of three paradigms: Positivism, interpretivism and critical inquiry. University of Adelaide.

Prayson, R. A., and Rowe, J. J. (2017). Effective feedback in the workplace. Critical Values, 10(3), 24-27.

Presbitero, A., Roxas, B., and Chadee, D. (2016). Looking beyond HRM practices in enhancing employee retention in BPOs: focus on employee–organisation value fit. The International Journal of Human Resource Management, 27(6), 635-652.

Prugsamatz, R., 2010. Factors that influence organization learning sustainability in non-profit organizations. The learning organization, 17(3), pp.243-267.

Rahman, S., Ali, N., Jennings, L., Seraji, M., Mannan, I., Shah, R., Al-Mahmud, A., Bari, S., Hossain, D., Das, M., Baqui, A., El Arifeen, S. and Winch, P., (2010). Factors affecting recruitment and retention of community health workers in a newborn care intervention in Bangladesh. Human Resources for Health, 8(1).

Raja, D. V. A. J., and Kumar, R. A. R. (2015). A Study To Reduce Employee Attrition In It Industries. International Journal of Marketing and Human Resource Management, 6(3), 01-14.

Ramachandran, S. D., Chong, S. C., and Ismail, H. (2011). Organisational culture. International Journal of Educational Management.

Ramachandran, S., and Krishnan, V. R. (2009). Effect of transformational leadership on followers' affective and normative commitment: culture as moderator.

Ramdhani, A., Ramdhani, M. A., and Ainissyifa, H. (2017). Conceptual Framework of Corporate Culture Influenced on Employees Commitment to Organization. International Business Management, 11(3), 826-830.

Rayner, C., and Lewis, D. (2020). Managing workplace bullying: The role of policies. In Bullying and harassment in the workplace (pp. 497-519). CRC Press.

Reimers, J.E., Farmer, C.L. and Klein-Gardner, S.S., 2015. An introduction to the standards for preparation and professional development for teachers of engineering. Journal of Pre-College Engineering Education Research (J-PEER), 5(1), p.5.

Reitz, O. E., and Anderson, M. A. (2011). An overview of job embeddedness. Journal of Professional Nursing, 27(5), 320-327.

Reitz, O. E., Anderson, M. A., and Hill, P. D. (2010). Job embeddedness and nurse retention. Nursing administration quarterly, 34(3), 190-200.

Renard, M., and Snelgar, R. J. (2016). The engagement and retention of non-profit employees in Belgium and South Africa. SA Journal of Human Resource Management, 14(1), 1-12.

Ridder, H.G. and McCandless, A., 2010. Influences on the architecture of human resource management in nonprofit organizations: An analytical framework. Nonprofit and Voluntary Sector Quarterly, 39(1), pp.124-141.

Rihal, C. S. (2017). The importance of leadership to organizational success. NEJM Catalyst, 3(6).

Rissanen, A., 2017. An investigation into voluntary employee turnover and retention factors in sport organizations.

Roberts, P., and Analytics, T. (2015). The CFO and CHRO guide to employee attrition. Workforce Solutions Review, 6(1), 8-10.

Robinson, R. N., Kralj, A., Solnet, D. J., Goh, E., and Callan, V. (2014). Thinking job embeddedness not turnover: Towards a better understanding of frontline hotel worker retention. International Journal of Hospitality Management, 36, 101-109.

Rodriguez, J., and Walters, K. (2017). The importance of training and development in employee performance and evaluation. Worldwide Journal of Multidisciplinary Research and Development, 3(10), 206-212.

Rodriguez, J.K. and Scurry, T., 2014. Career capital development of self-initiated expatriates in Qatar: cosmopolitan globetrotters, experts and outsiders. The International Journal of Human Resource Management, 25(7), pp.1046-1067.

Roslan, N., Arshad, R., and Pauzi, N. F. M. (2017). Accountability and governance reporting by non-profit organisations. In SHS Web of Conferences (Vol. 36, p. 00041). EDP Sciences.

Ross, P. T., and Zaidi, N. L. B. (2019). Limited by our limitations. Perspectives on medical education, 8(4), 261-264.

Rousseau, V. and Aubé, C., 2010. Social support at work and affective commitment to the organization: The moderating effect of job resource adequacy and ambient conditions. The Journal of Social Psychology, 150(4), pp.321-340.

Russell, C. B., and Weaver, G. C. (2011). A comparative study of traditional, inquiry-based, and research-based laboratory curricula: impacts on understanding of the nature of science. Chemistry Education Research and Practice, 12(1), 57-67.

Ryan, G., 2018. Introduction to positivism, interpretivism and critical theory. Nurse researcher, 25(4), pp.14-20.

Sageer, A., Rafat, S. and Agarwal, P., 2012. Identification of variables affecting employee satisfaction and their impact on the organization. IOSR Journal of business and management, 5(1), pp.32-39.

Sahay, A. (2016). Peeling Saunder's Research Onion. Research Gate, Art, 1-5.

Şahin, F., 2011. Affective commitment as a mediator of the relationship between psychological climate and turnover intention. World Applied Sciences Journal, 14(4), pp.523-530.

Sahoo, K.K., Sahoo, C.K. and Tripathy, S.K., 2017. Outcomes of Training and Development Measures in Public Sector Banks of India: An Overview. Productivity, 57(4), p.401.

Saini, M. (2020). Simplified research methods: with exercises and examples.

Saleem, M., and Affandi, H. (2014). HR Practices and Employees Retention: An empirical analysis of Pharmaceutical sector of Pakistan. IOSR Journal of Business and Management, 16(6), 111-116.

Salleh, I. S., Ali, N. S. M., Yusof, K. M., and Jamaluddin, H. (2017). Analysing qualitative data systematically using thematic analysis for deodoriser troubleshooting in palm oil refining. Chemical Engineering Transactions, 56, 1315-1320.

Sandhya, K. and Kumar, D.P., 2011. Employee retention by motivation. Indian Journal of science and technology, 4(12), pp.1778-1782.

Sandhya, K., and Kumar, D. P. (2011). Employee retention by motivation. Indian Journal of science and technology, 4(12), 1778-1782.

Sangeetha, K. (2010). Effective Recruitment: A Framework. IUP Journal of Business Strategy, 7.

Sanjeev, M. A., and Surya, A. V. (2016). Two factor theory of motivation and satisfaction: an empirical verification. Annals of Data Science, 3(2), 155-173.

Saunders, M., Lewis, P., and Thornhill, A. (2009). Research methods for business students. Pearson education.

Schabracq, M. J. (2003). What an organisation can do about its employees' well-being and health: An overview. The handbook of work and health psychology, 585.

Scharp, K. M., and Sanders, M. L. (2019). What is a theme? Teaching thematic analysis in qualitative communication research methods. Communication Teacher, 33(2), 117-121.

Schwartz, D. B., Spencer, T., Wilson, B., and Wood, K. (2011). Transformational leadership: implications for nursing leaders in facilities seeking magnet designation. AORN journal, 93(6), 737-748.

Scott, D., McMullen, T., and Royal, M. (2012). Retention of key talent and the role of rewards. WorldatWork Journal, 21(4), 58-70.

Sears, L. E., Shi, Y., Coberley, C. R., and Pope, J. E. (2013). Overall well-being as a predictor of health care, productivity, and retention outcomes in a large employer. Population health management, 16(6), 397-405.

Senarathna, I., Warren, M., Yeoh, W., and Salzman, S. (2014). The influence of organisation culture on E-commerce adoption. Industrial Management and Data Systems.

Senel, G. (2017). A comparative research on the definition of soft point. International Journal of Computer Applications, 163(2), 1-5.

Serbin, K. M. (2013). Promoting a Health Work Environment: Addressing Harassment and the "Charged" Workplace. Professional case management, 18(4), 199-201.

Sessa, V. I., and Bowling, N. A. (Eds.). (2020). Essentials of Job Attitudes and Other Workplace Psychological Constructs. Routledge.

Shahid, A., and Azhar, S. M. (2013). Gaining employee commitment: Linking to organizational effectiveness. Journal of management research, 5(1), 250.

Shahin, N. (2014). Role of employee retention practices in Indian industry-A study of select MNCs in Jamshedpur. International Journal of Engineering and Management Research (IJEMR), 4(4), 206-213.

Sharma, J. P., Bajpai, N., and Holani, U. (2011). Organizational citizenship behavior in public and private sector and its impact on job satisfaction: A comparative study in Indian perspective. International Journal of Business and Management, 6(1), 67.

Shen, J. and Jiuhua Zhu, C., 2011. Effects of socially responsible human resource management on employee organizational commitment. The International Journal of Human Resource Management, 22(15), pp.3020-3035.

Shim, M., 2010. Factors influencing child welfare employee's turnover: Focusing on organizational culture and climate. Children and Youth Services Review, 32(6), pp.847-856.

Shipp, A.J., Furst-Holloway, S., Harris, T.B. and Rosen, B., 2014. Gone today but here tomorrow: Extending the unfolding model of turnover to consider boomerang employees. Personnel Psychology, 67(2), pp.421-462.

Silva, N.D., Hutcheson, J. and Wahl, G.D., 2010. Organizational strategy and employee outcomes: A person–organization fit perspective. The Journal of psychology, 144(2), pp.145-161.

Simpson, B. (2017). Pragmatism: a philosophy of practice. The SAGE handbook of qualitative business and management research methods: History and traditions, 54-68.

Singh, A. K. (2011). HRD practices and managerial effectiveness: role of organisation culture. Indian Journal of Industrial Relations, 138-148.

Singh, J. K., and Jain, M. (2013). A STUDY OF EMPLOYEES'JOB SATISFACTION AND ITS IMPACT ON THEIR PERFORMANCE. Journal of Indian Research (ISSN: 2321-4155), 1(4).

Singh, P. and Loncar, N., 2010. Pay satisfaction, job satisfaction and turnover intent. Relations industrielles/industrial relations, 65(3), pp.470-490.

Singh, S. K., Burgess, T. F., Heap, J., and Al Mehrzi, N. (2016). Competing through employee engagement: a proposed framework. International Journal of Productivity and Performance Management.

Slattery, J. P., and Rajan Selvarajan, T. T. (2005). Antecedents to temporary employee's turnover intention. Journal of Leadership and Organizational Studies, 12(1), 53-66.

Slideteam.net. 2020. David Zinger's Employee Engagement Model. [online] Available at: <https://www.slideteam.net/human-resources-performance-management-metrics-powerpoint-presentation-slides.html> [Accessed 3 June 2020].

Sofijanova, E., and Zabijakin-Chatleska, V. (2013). Employee involvement and organisational performance: Evidence from the manufacturing sector in Republic of Macedonia.

Sorensen, T. J., and McKim, A. J. (2014). Perceived Work-Life Balance Ability, Job Satisfaction, and Professional Commitment among Agriculture Teachers. Journal of Agricultural Education, 55(4), 116-132.

Starks, G. L. (2007). The effect of person–job fit on the retention of top college graduates in federal agencies. Review of Public Personnel Administration, 27(1), 59-70.

Steffen, B., Rüthing, O. and Huth, M., 2018. Inductive Approach: Potential, Limitations, and Pragmatics. In Mathematical Foundations of Advanced Informatics (pp. 209-218). Springer, Cham.

Steingold, F. S. (2017). The Employer's Legal Handbook: How to Manage Your Employees and Workplace. Nolo.

Steward, G. L., and Brown, K. G. (2009). Human Resource Management. Linking Strategy to Practice.

Sundaray, B.K., 2011. Employee engagement: A driver of organizational effectiveness. European Journal of Business and Management, 3(8), pp.53-59.

Sundler, A. J., Lindberg, E., Nilsson, C., and Palmér, L. (2019). Qualitative thematic analysis based on descriptive phenomenology. Nursing Open, 6(3), 733-739.

Suppiah, V., and Sandhu, M. S. (2011). Organisational culture's influence on tacit knowledge-sharing behaviour. Journal of knowledge management.

Sushil, S. (2013). Motivation and retention: HR strategies in achieving quality of work life. Global Journal of Management and Business Studies, 3(7), 763-768.

Sutherland, M. and Jordaan, W., 2004. Factors affecting the retention of knowledge workers. SA Journal of Human Resource Management, 2(2), pp.55-64.

Tanwar, K., and Prasad, A. (2016). Exploring the relationship between employer branding and employee retention. Global Business Review, 17(3_suppl), 186S-206S.

Taslim, M. (2011). Organisation Culture And Employee Motivation: An Empirical Study On Impact Of Organisation Culture On Employee Extrinsic and

Intrinsic Motivation At SBI. International Journal of Management Prudence, 3(1), 84.

Tatlah, I. A., Anwar, M., and Amin, M. (2017). Effect of Human Resource Practices on Employees' Retention in a Private University of Pakistan. Journal of Educational Research, 20(1), 100.

Taylor, J., and Westover, J. H. (2011). Job satisfaction in the public service: The effects of public service motivation, workplace attributes and work relations. Public Management Review, 13(5), 731-751.

Terera, S. R., and Ngirande, H. (2014). The impact of rewards on job satisfaction and employee retention. Mediterranean Journal of Social Sciences, 5(1), 481.

Terry, G., Hayfield, N., Clarke, V., and Braun, V. (2017). Thematic analysis. The Sage handbook of qualitative research in psychology, 17-37.

Tews, M. J., Michel, J. W., and Stafford, K. (2013). Does fun pay? The impact of workplace fun on employee turnover and performance. Cornell Hospitality Quarterly, 54(4), 370-382.

The process of conducting a trustworthy Thematic analysis (King and Brookes, 2018)

The UAE Philanthropy Law report. (2016). Non-profit organisation guidelines.

The World Bank Data Report. (2017). UAE and United Kingdom Overall data

Thomas, A., and Letchmiah, L. (2017). Retention of high-potential employees in a development finance company. SA Journal of Human Resource Management, 15(1), 1-9.

Thomas, G. F., Zolin, R., and Hartman, J. L. (2009). The central role of communication in developing trust and its effect on employee involvement. The Journal of Business Communication (1973), 46(3), 287-310.

Thompson, C. B. (2009). Descriptive data analysis. Air medical journal, 28(2), 56-59.

Thompson, N. W. (2011). Managing the millennials: Employee retention strategies for Generation Y.

Thrush, A., (2012). Leadership in Higher Education. International Journal of Human

Thwala, W. D., Ajagbe, A. M., Enegbuma, W. I., and Bilau, A. A. (2012). Sudanese small and medium sized construction firms: An empirical survey of job turnover. Journal of Basic and Applied Scientific Research, 2(8), 7414-7420.

Tillott, S., Walsh, K., and Moxham, L. (2013). Encouraging engagement at work to improve retention. Nursing Management, 19(10).

Tirtha, R., 2017, March. Role of Human Resource Management in Local Self Government: Towards Effective Rural Development in West Bengal, India. In Proceedings of International HR Conference (Vol. 2, No. 1).

Tracey, J.B. and Hinkin, T.R., 2006. The cost of employee turnover: When the devil is in the details. Cornell University, School of Hotel Administration, The Center for Hospitality Research.

Tran, D., Davis, A., McGillis Hall, L., and Jaglal, S. B. (2012). Comparing recruitment and retention strategies for rehabilitation professionals among hospital and home care employers. Physiotherapy Canada, 64(1), 31-41.

Tuan, L. T. (2011). Organisational culture and trust as organisational factors for corporate governance. International Journal of Management and Enterprise Development, 11(2-4), 142-162.

Tumwesigye, G., 2010. The relationship between perceived organisational support and turnover intentions in a developing country: The mediating role of organisational commitment African Journal of Business Management, 4(6), pp.942-952.

Turner, S.F., Cardinal, L.B. and Burton, R.M., 2017. Research design for mixed methods: A triangulation-based framework and roadmap. Organizational Research Methods, 20(2), pp.243-267.

UN Office for the Coordination of Humanitarian affairs. (2014). UAE Charitable Data

Vaismoradi, M., and Snelgrove, S. (2019, September). Theme in qualitative content analysis and thematic analysis. In Forum Qualitative Sozialforschung/Forum: Qualitative Social Research (Vol. 20, No. 3).

Vaismoradi, M., Turunen, H., and Bondas, T. (2013). Content analysis and thematic analysis: Implications for conducting a qualitative descriptive study. Nursing and health sciences, 15(3), 398-405.

Van Dijk, D., and Kluger, A. N. (2011). Task type as a moderator of positive/negative feedback effects on motivation and performance: A regulatory focus perspective. Journal of Organizational Behavior, 32(8), 1084-1105.

Van Dyk, J., Coetzee, M., and Takawira, N. (2013). Satisfaction with retention factors as predictors of the job embeddedness of medical and information technology services staff. Southern African Business Review, 17(1), 57-75.

Varnum, M. E., Grossmann, I., Kitayama, S., and Nisbett, R. E. (2010). The origin of cultural differences in cognition: The social orientation hypothesis. Current directions in psychological science, 19(1), 9-13.

Vasquez, D. (2014). Employee retention for economic stabilization: A qualitative phenomenological study in the hospitality sector. International Journal of Management, Economics and Social Sciences, 3(1), 1-17.

Vinokur-Kaplan, D., Jayaratne, S. and Chess, W.A., 1994. Job satisfaction and retention of social workers in public agencies, non-profit agencies, and private practice: The impact of workplace conditions and motivators. Administration in Social Work, 18(3), pp.93-121.

Voon, M.L., Lo, M.C., Ngui, K.S. and Ayob, N.B., 2011. The influence of leadership styles on employees' job satisfaction in public sector organizations in Malaysia. International Journal of Business, Management and Social Sciences, 2(1), pp.24-32.

Vroom, V., Porter, L., and Lawler, E. (2005). Expectancy theories. Organizational behavior, 1, 94-113.

Waldman, J.D., Kelly, F., Arora, S. and Smith, H.L., 2010. The shocking cost of turnover in health care. Health Care Management Review, 35(3), pp.206-211.

Wambugu, L. (2014). Effects of Organizational Culture on Employee Performance (Case Study of Wartsila-Kipevu Ii Power Plant). European Journal of Business and Management, 6(32).

Wanjiku, N. A. (2014). Effect of organisation culture on employee performance in non govermental organizations.

Waterman, S., and He, Y. (2011). Effects of mentoring programs on new teacher retention: A literature review. Mentoring and Tutoring: Partnership in Learning, 19(2), 139-156.

Watson, M.R. and Abzug, R., 2005. Finding the ones you want, keeping the ones you find. Handbook of Nonprofit Leadership and Management, Jossey-Bass, San Francisco, CA, pp.623-660.

WeiBo, Z., Kaur, S. and Zhi, T., 2010. A critical review of employee turnover model (1938-2009) and development in perspective of performance. African Journal of Business Management, 4(19), pp.4146-4158.

Westover, J. H., Westover, A. R., and Westover, L. A. (2010). Enhancing long-term worker productivity and performance: The connection of key work domains to job satisfaction and organizational commitment. International Journal of Productivity and Performance Management.

Wheeler, A. R., Richey, R. G., Tokkman, M., and Sablynski, C. J. (2006). Retaining employees for service competency: The role of corporate brand identity. Journal of Brand Management, 14(1), 96-113.

Whitaker, B. G., and Levy, P. (2012). Linking feedback quality and goal orientation to feedback seeking and job performance. Human Performance, 25(2), 159-178.

Whittaker, A. (2011). Social defences and organisational culture in a local authority child protection setting: challenges for the Munro Review?. Journal of Social Work Practice, 25(4), 481-495.

Wierzchoń, S. T., and Kłopotek, M. A. (2018). Modern algorithms of cluster analysis. Springer.

Wong, C. A., and Laschinger, H. K. S. (2015). The influence of frontline manager job strain on burnout, commitment and turnover intention: A cross-sectional study. International journal of nursing studies, 52(12), 1824-1833.

Wong, S. S., Firestone, J. B., Lamb, R. L., and Luft, J. A. (2015). Perceived Support and Retention of First Year Secondary Science Teachers. In Newly Hired Teachers of Science (pp. 31-42). Sense Publishers, Rotterdam.

Wong, W. P., Tseng, M. L., and Tan, K. H. (2014). A business process management capabilities perspective on organisation performance. Total Quality Management and Business Excellence, 25(5-6), 602-617.

Wood, S., Van Veldhoven, M., Croon, M. and de Menezes, L.M., 2012. Enriched job design, high involvement management and organizational performance: The mediating roles of job satisfaction and well-being. Human relations, 65(4), pp.419-445.

Woon, W., Tan, C.L. and Nasurdin, A.M., 2017. Linking Organizational Climate, Psychological Ownership, and Intention to Stay: A Proposed Model. Global Business and Management Research, 9.

Word, J., and Park, S. M. (2015). The new public service? Empirical research on job choice motivation in the nonprofit sector. Personnel Review.

Wright, S., Marston, G., and McDonald, C. (2011). The role of non-profit organisations in the mixed economy of welfare-to-work in the UK and Australia. Social Policy and Administration, 45(3), 299-318.

Yamamoto, H. (2011). The relationship between employee benefit management and employee retention. The International Journal of Human Resource Management, 22(17), 3550-3564.

Yang, J.T., Wan, C.S. and Fu, Y.J., 2012. Qualitative examination of employee turnover and retention strategies in international tourist hotels in Taiwan. International Journal of Hospitality Management, 31(3), pp.837-848.

Yeşil, S., and Kaya, A. (2012). The role of organizational culture on innovation capability: An empirical study. International Journal of Information Technology and Business Management, 6(1), 11-25.

Yi, Y., Nataraajan, R. and Gong, T., 2011. Customer participation and citizenship behavioral influences on employee performance, satisfaction, commitment, and turnover intention. Journal of Business Research, 64(1), pp.87-95.

Yoerger, M., Crowe, J., and Allen, J. A. (2015). Participate or else!: The effect of participation in decision-making in meetings on employee engagement. Consulting Psychology Journal: Practice and Research, 67(1), 65.

Yoo, J., and Arnold, T. J. (2016). Frontline employee customer-oriented attitude in the presence of job demands and resources: The influence upon deep and surface acting. Journal of Service Research, 19(1), 102-117.

Young, D. R. (2013). If not for profit, for what? (1983 Print Edition) Lexington Books.

Young, J. A., Stone, J., Aliaga, O., and Shuck, B. (2013). Job Embeddedness Theory: Can It Help Explain Employee Retention among Extension Agents?

Zaniboni, S., Truxillo, D. M., and Fraccaroli, F. (2013). Differential effects of task variety and skill variety on burnout and turnover intentions for older and younger workers. European Journal of Work and Organizational Psychology, 22(3), 306-317.

Zeghal, D. and Maaloul, A., 2010. Analysing value added as an indicator of intellectual capital and its consequences on company performance. Journal of Intellectual capital, 11(1), pp.39-60.

Zhang, I. X. (2007). Economic consequences of the Sarbanes–Oxley Act of 2002. Journal of accounting and economics, 44(1-2), 74-115.

Zheng, C. and Lamond, D., 2010. Organisational determinants of employee turnover for multinational companies in Asia. Asia Pacific journal of management, 27(3), pp.423-443.

Zheng, W. B., Kaur, S., and Wei, J. (2009, September). Empirical contrasting of talents retention between samples of China and Malaysia. In 2009 International Conference on Management Science and Engineering (pp. 1069-1074). IEEE.

Zietlow, J., Hankin, J. A., Seidner, A., and O'Brien, T. (2018). Financial management for non-profit organisations: policies and practices. John Wiley and Sons.

Zin, S. M., Ahmad, N., Ngah, N. E. B., Ismail, R. B., Ibrahim, N. B., and Abdullah, I. H. T. B. (2012). Motivation model for employee retention: Applicability to HRM practices in Malaysian SME sector. Canadian Social Science, 8(5), 8-12.

Zopiatis, A., Constanti, P., and Theocharous, A. L. (2014). Job involvement, commitment, satisfaction and turnover: Evidence from hotel employees in Cyprus. Tourism Management, 41, 129-140

Zulu, K., Chetty, N., and Karodia, A. M. (2017). The Impact of Staff Turnover on Organisational Performance: A Case of the Three Non-Profit Organisations in Verulam, Republic of South Africa. Oman Chapter of Arabian Journal of Business and Management Review, 34(5310), 1-30.

www.ingramcontent.com/pod-product-compliance
Lightning Source LLC
LaVergne TN
LVHW052307200926
848481LV00002B/488